The FREEDOM LETTER

The

FREEDOM LETTER

By

ALAN F. JOHNSON

*A contemporary analysis of Paul's Roman letter
that changed the course of Christianity*

MOODY PRESS
CHICAGO

Printed in the United States of America

To
Rea, Jan, Kris, Lynn, and Lisa—
without whose loving companionship
this book
would have been finished
five years ago

FREEDOM

"Public freedom at last depends on spiritual freedom, and spiritual freedom is not in human nature but in its redemption."

P. T. FORSYTH

Contents

THE BOOK OF ROMANS IN ONE SENTENCE

"What is man? Man is God's creature; Yes, but man is God's image, and through the misuse of his God-bestowed freedom, man is God's shame and man is God's problem; But by that incredible strategy of the cross, God makes it possible for man to become the Creator's child; And man may become the Creator's co-laborer, and man, finite man, may become the friend of an infinite and all-holy God; And ultimately man may be, if he will have it so, God's glory."

VERNON C. GROUNDS

Preface

EVERY BOOK must be read in view of its intended purpose if the author's efforts are to be found helpful. This book is not the book of Romans. At best it is a brief attempt to explain and comment on some of Paul's main themes in the letter. As such, it must not be used as a substitute for Paul's own letter which is far more important than anything we could say about it. You must read and reread the book of Romans itself as you use this commentary. Every reader should have open before him the actual letter of Paul and first read each paragraph section of Romans and then consult the suggested explanation.

These notes are human, fallible, and subject to revision. The aim is not sermonic or devotional but a fresh interpretation of the ageless letter in the light of our contemporary age and its needs.

Though the main body of the book has the college student and the concerned layman in mind, the more important exegetical and theological problems are briefly addressed. Thus there are two books in one.

It has been an inexpressible experience of joy and learning for me to have spent these many hours poring over the rich truths found in Paul's letter to the Romans. This epistle has changed my life. What I have learned of God and myself from the book has definitely affected the whole quality of my life. If even some small spark of this enthusiasm and joy can reach across these pages to the reader, I shall be deeply grateful.

Introduction

IMPORTANCE OF ROMANS

SINCE THE CONTENT of the book of Romans is weighty and without much practical personal application until chapter 12, I would like at the outset to stress the great significance of the book lest discouragement over mastering its content turn you away too soon from its inspiring pages.[1]

A few quotations will help put Romans into perspective. Coleridge said of Romans that it was "the profoundest work in existence." Luther remarked that it was "the chief part of the New Testament and the perfect Gospel." "If a man understands it," Calvin stated, "he has a sure road open for him to the understanding of the whole Scripture." Godet referred to it as the "Cathedral of Christian Faith." More recently the notable Princeton scholar, Bruce Metzger, has called Romans the "Constitution of Universal Christianity."

Great intellects like Augustine, Luther, Calvin, and Edwards have studied Romans only to discover depths beyond their depths. George Wilson of Scotland, the distinguished poet, biographer, and scientist, received Christian instruction from his friend, Dr. John Cairns, who wrote to him of Romans: "The Gospel tide nowhere forms so many deep, dark pools where the neophyte may drown. . . . You will have something like a glimpse of the divine

---

1. For a thorough discussion of all the introductory questions pertaining to Romans, among the best sources are Donald Guthrie, *New Testament Introduction, Pauline Epistles* (Downers Grove, Ill.: Inter-Varsity, 1961), p. 216ff.; Everett F. Harrison, *Introduction to the New Testament* (Grand Rapids: Eerdmans, 1964), pp. 280ff.; Paul Feine and Johannes Behm, *Introduction to the New Testament*, ed. Werner G. Kümmel, trans. A. J. Matthill, Jr. (Nashville: Abingdon, 1966), pp. 216ff.

depth and richness of that despised old textbook, the New Testament."[2]

It may be because Romans is the greatest treatise on God that has ever been written that the letter has figured prominently in every significant evangelical renaissance in history.[3] Such was the case with Saint Augustine, Luther, and John Wesley. While not a full return to evangelical faith, the more recent work of Karl Barth on Romans (*Romerbrief*, 1919) broke the stranglehold of liberal theology on the scholarly world and brought some significant return to a biblical theology.

A book which has been so used by God in days past might also in our day play a role in the awakening of God's people from their slumber. That such a need exists can be abundantly documented. Consider, for example, the timely words of Dr. John A. MacKay, president of Princeton Seminary for twenty-three years:

> It seems increasingly clear that the chief need of contemporary Christianity and of society in general in this confused and revolutionary time is an evangelical renaissance. By that I mean a rediscovery of the Evangel, the Gospel, in its full dimension of light and power, together with the elevation of the Gospel to the status that belongs to the Gospel in the thought, life, and activity of all persons and organizations that bear the name "Christian."[4]

Or consider the timely words of C. Rene Padilla of Buenos Aires, Argentina, who, in reviewing three recent books on missions in *Christianity Today*, suggests that the important questions they raise can all be reduced to one: "What is the Gospel?"[5]

With this important historical precedent in mind, we can well afford to apply ourselves to the careful study of Paul's letter, expecting that God may in some small measure kindle anew our love and devotion to Him and perhaps enable us to be a part of a new evangelical renaissance in our day.

2. Cited by A. Skevington Wood, *Life by the Spirit* (Grand Rapids: Zondervan, 1963), p. 8.

3. Leon Morris, "The Theme of Romans" in *Apostolic History and the Gospel,* ed. Ward Gasque and Ralph Martin (Grand Rapids: Eerdmans, 1970), p. 263.

4. John A. MacKay, "Toward an Evangelical Renaissance," *Christianity Today* 16, no. 9 (February 4, 1972): 6-8.

5. C. Rene Padilla, "What Is the Gospel?" *Christianity Today* 17 (July 20, 1973):1106.

AUTHOR, DATE, AND PLACE OF WRITING

So conclusive is the argument for Pauline authorship of this epistle that no serious scholar doubts that it comes from the noted apostle to the Gentiles. Not only in the great theme of the grace of God, but in the evidence that the person who wrote the letter was without doubt a Jew who was thoroughly familiar with Pharisaical Judaism (Ac 23:6), as well as one who was burdened to minister to the Gentiles (Ac 13:47; Gal 2:2, 8; see Ro 11:13), we have further support for the letter's authorship by Paul.

Romans was most probably written in Corinth during Paul's last visit, which lasted about three months, in the spring of A.D. 57 or 58 (Ac 20:1-3).[6] This date depends upon internal references to the apostles' circumstances as they relate to information in the book of Acts. A key factor in the actual year date involves Proconsul Gallio who heard charges against Paul at Corinth on Paul's second missionary journey (Ac 18:12-18). According to an inscription found at Delphi, Gallio was installed as proconsul at Corinth about A.D. 52. Calculating from this date until Paul finally left Corinth for the last time would involve another five years (Ac 20:1-3).

Recognizing the early date of the book of Romans as probably occurring before any of the written gospels adds importance to its portrait of Christianity.

OCCASION AND PURPOSE

Paul apparently had finished his work in the east and after depositing the collection for the poor saints in Jerusalem, he plans to visit Rome on his way to Spain (15:22-28). The apostle therefore wants to introduce himself and give a sample of his message to the saints in Rome before he arrives in hopes that the important Roman church might be an aid to his missionary endeavors in the far west. But does this account for the lengthy and intricate explanation of his gospel message which the letter contains? Why not send a brief note through Phoebe (16:1) and indicate that he would give a full verbal statement of his message when he arrived in Rome?

One explanation of the long, weighty letter might be that he

6. Guthrie, p. 25.

expected trouble in Jerusalem which could prevent him from
ever reaching Rome. The treatise, then, would provide a final
memorial to his ministry and a basis for the Roman church to
evangelize the west in his absence,[7] More certain is the fact that
there is a strong emphasis in the letter on the Christian view of
salvation versus the Jewish concept and the integrity of his gospel
over against alleged charges of moral permissiveness. Paul must
expect to find in Rome such objections to the gospel, as he customarily preaches it.[8] In any event, Romans provides us, as well
as the ancient Italians, an introduction to some of the main cur-
rents in Paul's theological thoughts.

The Roman Church

There is considerable speculation both as to the origin of the
church in Rome and its constituency. Nothing is known with certainty, but some general directions may be suggested. Concerning the Roman Catholic view of Peter founding the church, there
is no historical evidence. Furthermore, Peter was still in Jerusalem at the time of the Jerusalem Council (Ac 15, c. A.D. 50), yet
it is almost certain that Christians were gathering in church homes
in Rome before this time (1:7).[9] It is difficult to imagine Paul
writing to the church at Rome as he did, if Peter indeed had
founded it, or why he should omit reference to Peter anywhere
in the letter if the fisherman was the apostle in residence in Rome.

A further suggestion explains the origin of the church as arising from Roman Jews who were present in Jerusalem on the day
of Pentecost and, having been converted, returned to establish
the church (Ac 2:10). However, there is no evidence that any
Roman Jews were in fact among the converted at Pentecost. Furthermore, the word "dwelling" in Acts 2:5 (KJV) could also refer
to permanent residents *living* in Jerusalem.

Another view, which likewise has no certainty, is that the
church was founded by various converts of Paul who had heard

7. Harrison, p. 286.
8. Feine and Behm, pp. 221-22; Guthrie, p. 27.
9. Acts 18:2-3 implies that Aquila and Priscilla (Prisca in Ro 16:3,
NASB), who came to Corinth from Rome, were already Christians which
would further confirm the earlier existence of the church in Rome before
A.D. 49.

his preaching in other parts of the world and were converted and then traveled to Rome for various reasons. Paul certainly knew by name a large number of people at Rome (Ro 16:3-15)—which might support this view. On the other hand, if this is the correct explanation, it is difficult to see why Paul was so anxious to go to Rome to preach the gospel to those who had already heard him before.

Concerning the constituency of the church in Rome, it seems quite evident from the internal references that it consisted mainly of Gentiles with some Jewish intermixture (1:5-8; 1:12-14; 6:19; 11:13; 11:28-31; 15:17; 15:15). It is estimated that the Roman church must have grown to considerable size during Paul's time.[10] This growth may account for the multiple meeting places referred to in the letter (16:5, 14, 15, 16). The frequency of the names mentioned in chapter 16 in the catacombs and other early Roman inscriptions is well documented by C. H. Dodd in his *Epistle to the Romans*.[11]

THEME AND CHIEF CHARACTERISTICS

The theme of Romans can be stated in different ways. Some prefer to call it "salvation as the revelation of God's righteousness"; others, "the righteousness of God by faith"; or "justification by grace through faith"; and "God saving men in Christ." It is all but universally agreed that the theme of Romans finds brief statement in the words of Romans 1:16-17: "For I am not ashamed of the gospel, for it is the power of God for salvation to every one who believes, to the Jew first and also to the Greek. For in it the righteousness of God is revealed from faith to faith; as it is written, 'But the righteous man shall live by faith.'"

This theme of salvation as the righteous act of God accomplished in Jesus Christ's death and resurrection and proclaimed in the gospel message is set forth meticulously in Paul's exposition. He first shows the desperate need of all men before God for this salvation. Gentiles are seen as notoriously given over to idolatry and various perversions which prove their rebellion against the Creator (1:18-32), while Jews are no better off for

10. Guthrie, p. 24.
11. C. H. Dodd, *Epistle to the Romans* (Naperville, Ill.: Allenson, 1932).

their religious heritage because they have perverted God's grace
into self-righteousness (2:1–3:20). Only God's mighty act of grace
and love accomplished in Jesus Christ's death and resurrection
and received freely on the basis of faith can effect the pardon and
reconciliation of men who are under God's condemnation (3:21–
4:25).

Next, Paul unfolds the truth that this new standing before God
also brings into existence a new being realized in the Christian
experience of joy and certainty (5:1-21), and in the progressive
defeat of the rule of sin in one's life through the power of the indwelling Spirit of Christ (6:1–8:39). After treating the historical
problem of Israel's rejection of the Messiah and His gospel, and
Gentile apathy and ignorance (9–11), he turns to general exhortations concerning specific areas of Christian living—personal, societal, political, and fraternal (12:1–15:13).

Among the chief characteristics of the letter are its long introduction, the unusual number of personal greetings at the close
of the letter, more extensive use of the Old Testament in quotations (about 57 times) than all his other letters combined, and
the rich theological emphasis, especially on God Himself. The
most common words in the letter are "God" (153 times), "law"
(72 times), "Christ" (65 times), "sin" (48 times), "Lord" (43
times), and "faith" (40 times).

INTEGRITY OF THE LETTER

The chief critical questions relate to the nature of chapter 16
and the different textual traditions at points in the letter. The
benediction ("the grace of our Lord Jesus Christ be with you") is
placed in chapter 16 either at the end of verse 20 (most witnesses), or at verse 24 (some), or after verse 27 (some). The
position of the doxology (16:25-27) constitutes the greatest textual
problem. We can only summarize the facts and state our conclusion in brief. More interested students should consult lengthier
treatments.[12]

Though the doxology appears in many manuscripts after 14:23,
and in one early witness after 15:33, and in several texts both

12. Guthrie, pp. 28-41; Harrison, pp. 288-92; John Murray, *The Epistle
to the Romans,* 2 vols. (Grand Rapids: Eerdmans, 1959), 2:262-68.

after 14:23 and at 16:25, the weight of early evidence favors placing it at 16: 25-27.[13] Certainly the doxology is Pauline and relates in content to the epistle of Romans. No serious attention should be given to theories such as the Ephesian destination of chapter 16, or that the original letter ended at 14:23 or 15:33. The theory that traces the varied history of the textual tradition of chapters 15 and 16 to the influence of the early heretic, Marcion, is probably least open to dispute.[14]

---

13. Murray, p. 268. Since most of the lectionary texts support the placing of the doxology at 14:23, it may be that the majority of manuscripts were influenced by this tradition.

14. Guthrie, p. 41.

Outline of Romans

18

PART 1

The Opening of the Letter

1

The Opening

(1:1-17)

ANCIENT GREEK LETTERS in the first century, unlike ours, customarily began with the names of sender and recipient, and a short greeting involving thanksgiving to God. Paul expands the usual address in an unusually long and highly significant form to express a brief statement of his Christian faith and his ministry (vv. 1-7) and to relate his genuine concern for those in Rome (vv. 8-17). Paul has not yet visited Rome. It is this fact that explains the length of the introduction—he is jealous to inform the church at Rome of his earnest desire and determination to go there. Since most of the key ideas occurring throughout the remainder of the letter are found in this introduction, we can profitably pay close attention to it in attempting to understand Paul's thought.

The following overall view of the introduction may be helpful to refer back to as the details are discussed.

Greeting   ┌─ Author (1)
   (1-7) ───────┼─ Gospel (2-6)
                  └─ Recipients (7)

Paul and the Romans   ┌─ Proof of his interest in those at Rome (8-10)
   (8-17) ───────────┼─ Reasons for his interest (11-15)
                        └─ The theme of his letter (16-17)

THE APOSTLE'S GREETING

(1:1-7)

In verses 1-7 Paul identifies and describes himself, relates his calling, gives the essential essence of the gospel, and greets the Roman Christians. Paul, the author, describes himself in verse 1 in a three-fold manner. He is first of all a "bond-servant of Christ Jesus." This term occurs as a frequent identification of the followers of Christ in the New Testament (Gal 1:10; Ja 1:1; 2 Pe 1:1; Jude 1). In Greek usage the word "bond-servant"— *doulos*— denotes a slave and would not be used of a Greek citizen's relationship to his ruler or divine king. While it is possible that Paul could be thinking of serving Jesus Christ as an actual slave in the Greek or Roman sense, it is more likely that he had the Semitic idea of a slave in mind. The Hebrew kings could be served, and the highest of his ministers might be regarded as his slaves (1 Sa 8:11-14). Distinguished members and citizens of the theocratic kingdom of Israel were also called the servants of God (2 Sa 7: 19, Amos 3:7). Paul, then appears as an outstanding member and chief minister or slave of God in His new divine program.

Second, he refers to himself as (divinely) "called *as* an apostle." Again, Paul's idea probably goes back to the Rabbinic Jewish usage of "apostle" (Gk. *apostolos;* Heb. *shluh*) as a term to denote one who is legally authorized to act as the representative or proxy of another and who carries the full authority of the one who commissions him.[1] Thus Paul claims direct divine authority as a validly commissioned representative of Jesus Christ Himself (Gal 1:11-12). One should not, then, hesitate in accepting the teaching of Paul as having anything less than the very authority of Christ Himself.

Third, Paul declares himself to be "set apart for the gospel of God." He may have the calling of the prophets of old in mind (Jer 1:5) as he relates his peculiar experience of having God mark him out as a special missionary to the Gentiles (Ac 13:1-2; Gal 1:15). He was set apart "for the gospel of God," that is, in order to proclaim it. Paul's word for gospel, *euaggelion*, should be

---

1. G. Kittel and G. Friedrich, eds., *Theological Dictionary of the New Testament* (Grand Rapids: Eerdmans, 1964), 1:415. (This reference is hereafter referred to as TDNT).

translated "good news" (i.e., something good has happened) to bring out its full sense. It is this gospel or message of God's salvation which burdens Paul's heart throughout the whole letter (1:1, 9, 15, 16).

In verses 2-6 Paul digresses briefly from his greeting to dwell upon the essential subject of the good news, "Jesus Christ our Lord" (v. 4). For his Jewish readers he is especially eager to state that this gospel has historical continuity with God's revelations to Israel in the promises given through the prophets in the Old Testament (Ro 3:21, 31; 4:6; Lk 24:25-27, 44-47; 1 Pe 1:10-12). "Scripture" designates the officially recognized body of temple writings that were considered divinely originated (inspired) and thus authoritative for teaching and conduct (2 Ti 3:15-16). "Holy" (only used here of Scripture) further emphasizes its source as distinctively *divine* revelation (3:2; 9:17; 15:4).

Paul now proceeds to identify the substance of his gospel as that which pertains to God's Son, Jesus Christ, who as true man and true God in one mysterious being bestows upon him whatever grace and authority he possesses (vv. 3-5). Here in two lines of antithetical parallelism (vv. 3-4), one finds a brief statement of the unique person of Jesus of Nazareth.

First, in respect to his real humanity ("according to the flesh"), Jesus was born a Jew (descended from Abraham) in the family line of David (Mt 1:6; Lk 3:31; Ac 2:30; Rev 5:5). While Paul does not dwell upon the actual historical facts of Jesus' life on earth, it is evident that he nevertheless considers that real historical life (as the gospels relate) to be of the utmost importance to the validity of the gospel he preaches.

Yet something else must be said about Jesus, not contradictory to His true humanity but complementary. "According to the flesh" in verse 3 stands in antithesis to "according to the Spirit" in verse 4. While the expression, "Spirit of holiness," may be a reference to the Holy Spirit, many commentators feel it is more appropriate to understand this expression as a reference to Christ's divine personality which would, because of the parallelism, form a complement to the previous expression about His human nature.

The church has always taught that though the life Jesus lived on earth was wholly human, the personality revealed was God, the

Son of the Father. It must be stressed that without this truth of the dual character of Jesus not only is our concept of God affected but the gospel becomes pointless.[2]

The word "declared" in the Greek (*horizō*) is related to our English word "horizon" which is the clear boundary between the sky and the earth. In God's powerful deed of raising Jesus from the dead there lies irrefutable evidence to clearly mark out or distinguish this human life as the divine Son of God and hence rightfully and solely our *Lord*.

It is from this person that Paul claims to have received grace (gifts of enablement) and apostleship (commission as an ambassador) for the purpose of everywhere securing men to put their trust wholly in Christ and be obedient to Him. His mission for the sake of Christ's name (i.e., for Christ Himself) brings him into contact with those at Rome who are Jesus Christ's called ones like Paul himself.

Finally, in verse 7 he finishes the address by referring to the recipients in their earthly status as Romans and in their relation to God as loved by Him (for Christ's sake) and called to a life of separation unto God as saints. They are not "called to be saints," not "called because saints" but "saints (holy) because called" (Augustine). "The holiness is not primarily that of individual moral character, but that of consecration to God's service." Sainthood is "therefore ascribed to all Christians, who are, however, bound by this very consecration to personal holiness of life."[3] As "saints" they are to be separated from the world's values and consecrated wholly for God's use. "Grace" was customarily used in Greek letter addresses, while "peace" (Heb. *shalom*) was and still is the common greeting among Semitic peoples (Num 6:24-26). Paul enriched these standard terms with added Christian significance.

Having now introduced his letter, himself, and his gospel (vv. 1-7), he will go on to explain further his interest in the Romans and the full meaning of God's good news.

---

2. Donald Baillie, *God Was in Christ* (New York: Scribner, 1948), pp. 144ff. contains a worthwhile discussion of how the trinitarian concept of God among Christians uniquely advances a concept of God as a God of grace.
3. E. H. Gifford, "Romans," in *The Bible Commentary: New Testament* (New York: Scribners, 1881), 3:57.

PAUL AND THE ROMANS

(1:8-15)

In verses 8-17 Paul briefly relates his own genuine personal concern for those in Rome, giving proof of his feelings in his thankfulness for their faith (v. 8), in his unceasing remembrance of them in prayer (v. 9), in his unrelieved desire to visit them and labor among them in preaching the gospel which he briefly summarizes (vv. 10-17).

Paul's thanksgiving to God (v. 8) reveals not only his own large heart of love, since many of those addressed were probably not his own converts, but also the virility of their witness to Christ in the non-Christian communities. "Your faith" would not mean "the Christian faith which you hold in common with all other Christians" but rather "the Christian faith *as* you hold it."[4] Their zeal for Christ and their love for one another was so manifested that others announced everywhere that something had happened to the Romans (1 Th 1:6-8).[5] This confirms Jesus' words that a city built on a mountain cannot be hid (Mt 5:14).

In his prayer and earnest desire to visit them he offers another proof of his sincere concern for their welfare (vv. 9-15). Note the expression, "serve in my spirit" (v. 9). His service consisted not merely in outward activity but more significantly in the service of worship to God in his inner man that issued forth in the outward labor of preaching the gospel of His Son. "If perhaps now at last by the will of God" (v. 10) reflects the delicate, beautiful, and important relationship between praying expectantly to God for a specific matter and at the same time recognizing a submission to the will of God that what we earnestly desire may not be His will, at least at the present. Paul desires that by his com-

4. C. K. Barrett, *The Epistle to the Romans* (New York: Harper & Row, 1957), p. 24.
5. This testimony becomes more meaningful when it is remembered that according to the Roman historian Suetonius, the emperor Claudius had forced the Jews out of Rome in A.D. 49 (Ac 18:2) because of "trouble instigated under the influence of Chrestus" (*Lives of the Twelve Caesars* [New York: Random House, Mod. Lib., n.d.], chap. 25). "Chrestus" is probably a mispelling for Christus (Christ), and the disturbances were probably caused by the agitation and rivalry between Christians and Jews in the synagogues of Rome as Christ was preached as Messiah and Lord (C. K. Barrett, ed., *The New Testament Background: Selected Documents* [New York: Macmillan, 1957], p. 14).

ing and ministry the Holy Spirit would so use him that the Romans would receive the benefit of the presence and power of God (v. 11), yet not themselves only but—in a beautiful touch of humility—that Paul himself also might be mutually strengthened in the practice of his faith by his interaction with them in this service (v. 12; 1 Co 12:7).

It may be asked why Paul, if he was so eager to come to Rome, had not come before this? He answers by further assuring them of his love by explaining that he had repeatedly attempted to come, but in each former case he had been prevented (Ro 15:22-23). Paul was the author of his purposes but not of his circumstances (v. 13). He did not have a constant, unending series of successes!

Another reason for his burden to preach especially to the Romans relates to the universal character of the gospel message (vv. 14-15). Because of Paul's calling he is morally obligated to minister the gospel to all men without respect to their culture or social status. "Greeks . . . barbarians . . . wise . . . foolish" (v. 14) refers to those inhabitants of the regularly recognized Greek city-states (Greeks, "wise") and those outside these areas (barbarians, "foolish") such as the Gauls, Scythians, Celts, and Spaniards who were considered by the Greeks as uncultured in that they were unable to speak Greek clearly (1 Co 14:11). Thus, because the relation in which men stand to Christ and His gospel is deeper and more essential than all national, racial, and personal distinctions, Paul, the Jew, stands eager and willing (if God permits) to preach to those also in Rome, the capital of the whole world. How many of us today are ready to go (not wait for them to come) to Washington, D. C., to the senators of our country as well as to the hippies of Haight-Ashbury or Greenwich Village?

But what really is the gospel? What would Paul preach in Rome? Why should he go to such trouble?

THE THEME OF HIS LETTER
(1:16-17)

Initially, his first response to these questions lies in his statement in verses 16-17, and yet the whole rest of the letter does not exhaust the answers.

In the mention of Rome (v. 15), Paul no doubt is excited as he contemplates the capital and theater of the world where he would ultimately come face-to-face with the mighty power concentrated in that stronghold of heathenism and the multitudes of peoples gathered there from every nation of the Mediterranean world. He responds, "I am not ashamed of the gospel," even though for its sake he had been despitefully treated in other great cities such as Athens, Ephesus, and even in Corinth from which he now writes.

His confidence in spite of these hindrances lies in the true greatness of the reality discovered in the message he proclaims. For the gospel itself is nothing less than the power of God. This expression "power [Gk. *dynamis*] of God" should not be overlooked. In Paul's usage the power of God is often associated with the wisdom of God in contrast to man's wisdom (1 Co 1:24; 2:4; 2 Co 6:7). It is a resurrection life power (2 Co 13:4), always associated with God's action toward us in Jesus Christ resulting in salvation (1 Co 1:18) and actually manifested in some manner in contrast to mere words or ideas (1 Co 2:4). Beyond this how can the decisive activity of God in the human life be analyzed? For Paul no other expression could convey the reality of his own experience and that of others. In the gospel resided the living revelation of God Himself flowing forth to save men.

"Salvation" (Gk. *sōtēria*) probably conveys the thought of the widest possible inclusion of all God's benefits in Christ to believers. While not a frequent word of Paul, it certainly is central to his thoughts.[6] In this epistle alone, salvation includes forgiveness of sin and acceptance before God (chaps. 1-4), as well as deliverance from the future wrath of God (5:9), the present new life in the Spirit of God (chaps. 6-8), and the future resurrection of the body (8:11).

Elsewhere in the New Testament Peter teaches that the salvation from sin and darkness to peace and fellowship with God which began in the ministry, death, and resurrection of Jesus will be completed in the future in those who believe. That future

6. The noun occurs only eighteen times in Paul's letters, including five times in Romans (1:16; 10:1, 10; 11:11; 13:11). The verb form "to save" occurs more frequently (twenty-nine times) including eight times in Romans (5:9, 10; 8:24; 9:27; 10:9, 13; 11:14, 26).

salvation is now presently at work in Christians through the power
of the gospel (1 Pe 1:3-5). To this Paul also agrees (Ro 13:11).

The divine power in the gospel is not dependent upon any
human wisdom or virtue or condition such as works done in
obedience to any law or ceremony, however sacred. Paul declares
that the saving power of God is effective alone by faith "to every
one who believes." Faith can only be that response to the gospel
of God's saving power that is characterized by obedient trust in
the God who has decisively acted in Jesus Christ's death and
resurrection to provide for us what we could never do for ourselves (v. 5). It is this attitude of turning away from all self-
effort and human devices and casting ourselves totally upon the
God and Father of Jesus Christ that effects the mighty working of
God's power resulting in our salvation. Salvation is something
freely given rather than earned. God gives this grace without
regard to merit or national origin, without regard even to special
religious distinction. Why, then, "to the Jew first"? Historically
they were the first to hear from Jesus' own lips this new thing God
would do through Him (Heb 2:3), and second, because unto
them were committed the covenants (Ac 3:26; Ro 3:2; 9:4).

The substance of Paul's gospel is spelled out more fully in
verse 17. It consists in the manifestation of "the righteousness of
God." It might be helpful to show the parallelism between verse
16 and verse 17 in the following manner:

VERSE 16	VERSE 17
gospel	in it (gospel)
power . . . for salvation	righteousness (life and salvation)
of God	of God
everyone who believes	faith to faith . . . the righteous man shall live by faith

In the gospel the "righteousness (*dikaiosunē*) of God" finds expression. But what is the righteousness of God? By the righteousness of God Paul might have meant that quality or attribute of
God whereby he reveals himself to be right or righteous and man
sinful. But this could hardly be "good news." Or it could mean
the righteousness which God requires of me. But again how is this
good news to me? Better, as Luther saw, the righteousness of God

is that righteousness of God by which we are made righteous (justified). In the Old Testament the righteousness of God can be seen almost as a synonym for salvation in the same way Paul parallels the two in verses 16 and 17 (see also Is 46:13; 51:5; Ps 24:5; 31:1; 98:1, 2; 143:11).[7] So the righteousness of God is that righteousness which he imparts or gives in order to make men righteous (Augustine).

The term primarily refers to the way in which God relates himself historically to man in his dilemma. Gifford remarks that this righteousness has "God as its author, and man as its recipient, who by it becomes righteous; its effect is salvation, and its condition faith: it is embodied first in the person of Christ '*who* is made unto us wisdom from God, *and righteousness*' (I Cor. i.30), and it is bestowed on us because of Christ's redeeming work, wherein He 'was made sin for us, *that we might be made the righteousness of God in him*' (2 Cor. v.21)."[8]

God's righteousness is revealed "from faith to faith" (v. 17). Though a difficult expression with many interpretations, it seems best to relate this to the parallel in verse 16, "every one who believes," and to understand the phrase to emphasize that salvation (God's righteousness) is solely (utterly) by faith.[9] Paul's quotation of Habakkuk 2:4 stresses that the Old Testament taught that this righteousness came (solely) by faith and the man who has it (the just) also lives by faith (Gal 3:11; Heb 10:38).[10]

7. For a full discussion of this point and how Paul's concept of justification should be related to the Hebrew concept of righteousness rather than (as usually) the Greek concept, see Norman M. Snaith, *The Distinctive Ideas of the Old Testament* (New York: Schocken, 1964), chaps. 4 and 8 especially. The NEB translation, "God's way of righting wrong" completely obscures Paul's thought.

8. Gifford, p. 61.

9. Grammatical parallels to this construction seem to have this effect, e.g., Ro 6:19, "Lawlessness, resulting in further lawlessness" (utter lawlessness); 2 Co 2:16, "death to death" (utter death).

10. The NASB ("The righteous man shall live by faith") is preferable to the RSV translation ("He who through faith is righteous shall live"). The emphasis is not on the *life* of the faith-righteous man but on *how* he lives, i.e., *by faith*. This rendering of the passage (NASB) emphasizes again the idea of "faith all the time" (Barrett, *Epistle to the Romans*, p. 31) and seems to be the meaning of the Habakkuk passage in the Hebrew text, the Targum (Aramaic translation), the LXX, as well as the Qumran commentary on Hab and Gal 3:11. John Murray (1:33) following J. B. Lightfoot adopts this sense. See also L. C. Allen, "The Old Testament in Romans 1-8," *Vox Evangelica* 3 (1964).

These two verses contain a rich sampling of Paul's chief words: gospel, power of God, salvation, faith, Jew and Gentile, and righteousness of God. They have each been touched on briefly in this section, but it will be necessary to return again and again to them in this book as Paul does in his. The scope of the gospel is universal. It is God's saving power for all men at all times. At the same time the gospel shows forth and interprets God's righteousness. It is this theme that Paul develops in Romans. God's righteousness is available for those who will appropriate it by obedient trust in Jesus Christ.

PART 2

The Doctrinal Foundation
of Christianity

In this lengthy section (1:18—11:36) Paul argues out the main kernel of his gospel. He first asserts that all men—regardless of race, nationality, personal distinctions, or religious heritage—are under God's judgment and stand morally guilty before the Judge of the universe (1:18—3:20). Paul then turns to the provision of the gift of God's righteousness in the sacrificial death of Jesus, the manner in which this provision is secured by faith, and the resulting new life with its abundance (3:21—5:21). He then proceeds to answer two major questions raised by his gospel: What is the relationship between God's grace and man's freedom? (6:1—8:39); and, What about God's faithfulness in light of the Jew's unbelief? (9:1—11:36).

2

Mankind's Condition: Under the Judgment of God

(1:18—3:20)

PAUL CANNOT ADEQUATELY DECLARE the significance of the manifestation of the righteousness of God (3:21-22) until he has first painted the canvas with the actual human situation in God's sight. Over against God's righteousness stands the unrighteousness of man (1:18-32), as well as the righteousness of man's own making (2:1—3:8). Paul's burden is to show that all men have true moral guilt in the presence of a holy God. Paul will first charge that the Gentiles or persons who do not have God's written Word are without excuse before a revealed Creator to whom they are responsible (1:18-32). Second, he turns toward the other major segment of humanity, those who have the written law of God, and accuses them of not keeping this law (2:1—3:8). He finds that both groups, in effect all men, are equally under God's judgment and without hope in themselves (3:9-20).

MAN WITHOUT THE KNOWLEDGE OF THE BIBLE

(1:18-32)

In only three places in the New Testament do we find material relating to how the gospel was preached to strictly non-Bible-oriented audiences. The first was in Lystra (Ac 14:15-17) where Paul preached to the pagan (though cultured) Lycaonians, but the message is brief and interrupted. Second, in Athens (Ac 17:16-32), Paul again confronts non-Jewish pagan philosophers (Stoics and Epicureans) with the message about Jesus. The third

instance comes also from Paul and is found in Romans 1:18-32
and portions of chapter 2. Our generation has rightfully been
characterized as the post-Christian age.[1] Out of many past years
of biblical emphasis and knowledge our present western culture
reflects the beginning of the emergence of a society largely made
up of men without the knowledge of Bible. While some, holding
to a nonrational optimism, have entitled our days as the "Age of
Aquarius," others more realistically describe our condition as
"The Twilight of Western Thought."[2] This fact alone makes the
content and approach of this section (1:18-32, 2:1-16) of great
importance in understanding how to relate the gospel to our
generation.

REVELATION OF GOD'S WRATH (1:18)

Having just spoken of the revelation of God's righteousness (v.
17), Paul turns to the revelation of God's wrath (v. 18). Someone
might say, "Why do I need salvation?" Paul answers: "Because
you are under the wrath of God." "But why am I under His
wrath?" "Because you suppress the truth."

Before commenting on these questions and answers, it might be
helpful to clear up the problem of the relationship between this
section (v. 18) and the previous (vv. 16, 17). Some see Paul
taking a long digression which continues until he resumes the
thought about the gospel in 3:21. This is a mistake for two reasons. First, it ignores the ordinary sense of the Greek particle "for"
(*gar*) which begins verse 18 and intimately binds the thought of
this verse to verse 17. Second, the word "revealed" (and tense)
Paul uses for the wrath of God (v. 18) is identical to the word
(and tense) he uses in reference to the righteousness of God
(v. 17). While the thought is complicated, it seems to run along
these lines: just as the future salvation of believers is now in the
present being revealed in the gospel of Jesus Christ and appropri-

1. Dorothy L. Sayers, *Christian Letters to a Post-Christian World* (Grand
Rapids: Eerdmans, 1969); Francis A. Schaeffer, *The God Who Is There*
(Downers Grove, Ill.: Inter-Varsity, 1968); *Escape from Reason* (Downers
Grove, Ill.: Inter-Varsity, 1968); *Death in the City* (Downers Grove, Ill.:
Inter-Varsity, 1969); and Os Guiness, *The Dust of Death* (Downers Grove,
Ill.: Inter-Varsity, 1972).
2. See book of similar title by the Dutch philosopher, Hermann Dooye-
weerd, *In the Twilight of Western Thought* (Philadelphia: Presb. & Ref.,
1960).

ated by faith, so the future wrath of God (2:5) is now in the present revealed in the human scene and experienced by those who turn away from the truth of God.

Whatever else, it seems clear from this connection that the true preaching of the gospel can only occur with the concurrent preaching of the real wrath of God upon men. This seems to be a truth which is lacking among many of our generation of gospel preachers.[3] Wrath is God's dynamic and personal (though never malicious) reaction against sin (3:5; 9:22), and it has cosmic significance in that it is "from heaven."

But why is God's wrath directed toward me? Because men in their "ungodliness and unrighteousness" suppress the truth.[4] Paul's word for "suppress" ("hold" in the KJV) is important but unfortunately ambiguous in the Greek (*katechō*). It may mean, and often does, to "hold to" something such as spiritual values (1 Th 5:21). In this case Paul would be saying that men in spite of their unrighteousness still "hold to" a certain basic truth about their existence.[5] On the other hand, since he is developing the thought of men's refusal to acknowledge the truth of God implicit in the creation (vv. 19-20), we prefer the alternate idea in the word. Men "hold back" or "resist" (Lk 4:42; 2 Th 2:6, 7) the truth of God as Creator so that the truth does not find expression in their lives (v. 21).[6]

REVELATION OF THE KNOWLEDGE OF GOD (1:19-20)

But how can God direct His wrath toward me for suppressing

3. "There is no real preaching of the Christian gospel except in light of the fact that man is under the wrath of God" (Schaeffer, *Death in the City*, p. 93). It also seems evident that the true wrath of God is only seen against the background of the norm in the gospel—the righteousness of God in Jesus Christ.

4. The terms "ungodliness" and "unrighteousness" are best understood as an emphatic expression of one and the same thing (Anders Nygren, *Commentary on Romans* [Philadelphia: Fortress, 1949], p. 101). The single expression "in unrighteousness" of the latter phrase seems to confirm this. Man's moral condition of unrighteousness is never separated from religious corruption and is seen by Paul as a result of man's religious apostasy.

5. Schaeffer, *Death in the City*, p. 102, explains Paul's thought thus, "They . . . hold some of the truth about themselves and about the universe . . . but they refuse to carry these truths to their reasonable conclusions."

6. Perhaps even "to hold imprisoned" (TDNT, 2:829).

the truth of His Creatorship when I have never even heard of the God of the Bible or the gospel? The answer is that all men know certain truths about God (v. 19). How? "For" (reason number 1) God has continually in past history, as long as there has been a universe, (and in the present) revealed Himself among men through the created order of existence. This knowledge of God, though limited, is nevertheless real and clear ("clearly seen"), even though men's suppression of it has to them dimmed or extinguished it.

Calvin's remark is striking: "In saying that *God manifested it,* he means that the purpose for which man is created is to be the spectator of the fabric of the world; the purpose for which eyes have been given him is that by gazing on so fair an image he may be led on to its Author."[7] What is manifested to them and thus known to all men everywhere is God's "eternal power and divine nature" (v. 20)—that is, that God is God and not man. Man perceives in the created existence not only his own finiteness, but because of God's revelation to him he knows his creatureliness. He knows that he is not the autonomous (independent) center of his life and world, but that God as Creator and Lord stands infinitely above him as the Source and Goal of his created life.[8] Therefore Paul can say of men: "So that they are without excuse."[9]

Man, then, may be justly visited with the wrath of God because, though he may not have heard about God in the Bible or in the gospel, he has suppressed this rudimentary truth of creatureliness which God continually makes available to him in (or, by) "what has been made."[10] God does not reap (wrath) where He has not sown (knowledge).

7. John Calvin, *Epistle of Paul to the Romans,* trans. Ross MacKensie (Grand Rapids: Eerdmans, 1961), p. 31.
8. These verses do not argue for the Thomistic natural theology or natural religion. Paul does not have in mind deductive (Aristotelian) logical arguments which can prove God's existence, but as vv. 21-23 show, he is referring to an actual continuous revelation of God to all men that they possess (which could not be true of logical systems leading to belief in God) but have abandoned. The traditional logical arguments for God's existence do not prove God exists but simply show that once God is assumed, then the world can be logically and adequately explained.
9. The "so that" indicates not merely result but purpose.
10. Or "in His works" not only in the beginning but throughout the whole history of mankind God has made Himself known in His works (Nygren, p. 104).

REJECTION OF THE KNOWLEDGE OF GOD (1:21-23)

In these verses (21-23) Paul gives a second reason ("for" in v. 21) why God justly visits His wrath on men. Not only do men have the possibility of knowing God through creation and history and fail to do so; Paul indicates the root of the matter is that men actually possessed a knowledge of God ("knew God"), but failed in a proper acknowledgement: "They did not honor Him as God, or give thanks [to Him]" (v. 21). Instead they became senseless and practiced disobedience (idolatry) and rebellion. Man's failure was not so much that he failed to recognize God, but that he would not acknowledge God as *Lord* and live in grateful obedience—in fact (in Paul's view) to "believe," is to have "faith." Rather, man chose to be his own Lord ("professing themselves to be wise"). By throwing off his obligations to God, he thought to rise above creatureliness. Instead the new gods of man's own making which he exchanged for the Creator, while for a time his servants, eventually became his masters and brought him to a more debased and lower state than before. In the end men "worshipped and served the creature" (vv. 23, 25).

Five steps downward have been noted in this whole process, beginning significantly with the attitude of the heart of rebellion against Lordship, in that they honored Him not, neither were thankful, futile in their speculations, professing to be wise, exchanged the glory of God (vv. 21-23): (1) practical indifference to God truth, (2) worthless speculation about God, (3) death of the God idea, (4) pride of human reason, and (5) fetishism (devotion to occult objects). This whole description should be understood as a sort of philosophy of heathenism's development in any given setting and not as an historical account of a specific religious apostasy.

Here it may be appropriate to ask a few questions about false religions and idolatry. It has been popular since the resurgence in recent days of comparative religious studies to think of the world religions as preparatory to Christianity. In them, we are told, God is revealed to man in an incomplete fashion, whereas in Christianity the full revelation of God is seen. But Paul saw no divine revelation in the heathen religions. It is not God who is revealed in the non-Christian religions of the world but the cor-

ruption of man; not God's truth but man's falsehood.[11] While
there is a general revelation of God given in all the world, this
revelation is suppressed and opposed by sinful man. Actually the
religions of the world, which display a good bit of commonality,
find their commonality not in some true knowledge of God but in
a common reaction to the revelation of God which comes to them
continually in the things which are made. Nonbiblical religions
are a reaction, an answer, a resistance to, and a defense against
God's revelation. Disobedience, not obedience, is the explanation
of the commonality. However, this fact does not exclude the possibility that some individuals within these systems may have responded to this true revelation of God (2:14-15). So the very
presence of false religion in the world is evidence of the continual
revelation of God that leaves all men inexcusably guilty before
Him.[12]

Is there idolatry in the Western world today? Idolatry begins
in the mind when we pervert or exchange our idea of God into
something other than what He really is.[13] Luther said, "Whatever your heart clings to and relies on is your god." Science,
reason, progress, secularism, pleasure, and mysticism have become
for many the new gods of the Western world.[14] To such men
today comes the gospel with its call to radical conversion in the
midst of the modern pantheon of gods.

RESULTS OF THE REJECTION OF THE KNOWLEDGE OF GOD (1:24-32)

In these final verses of the chapter, Paul shows how the wrath
of God works its way out in the concrete human situation of men
who have abandoned God as Lord. Let it be repeated that this
does not mean that there will be no final wrath of God in the
future (2:5), but even now in history God makes His wrath opera-

11. Nygren, p. 108.
12. See G. C. Berkouwer, *General Revelation* (Grand Rapids: Eerdmans,
1952), chap. 7, "Revelation and Knowledge," for a full discussion of this
thesis; also Dooyeweerd, "What is Man?" *In the Twilight of Western
Thought;* William M. Ramsay, "The Pauline Philosophy of History" in *The
Cities of St. Paul* (Grand Rapids: Baker, 1960).
13. A. W. Tozer, *The Knowledge of the Holy* (New York: Harper & Row,
1961), p. 11.
14. Note also the rapid increase today of occultism, oriental mysticism,
and drugs, which may be a transitional stage on the road to a full-blown
reversion to idolatry.

tive. Paul indicates this by three times repeating the same dire expression, "God gave them over" (vv. 24, 26, 28). Not that God makes men sin but He abandons them to their own passions as a form of his wrath. This is an awesome truth. In modern societies moral permissiveness, especially in its sexual perversion and inversion, can be seen as God's acts of wrath upon men who have turned away from the truth and have suppressed the acknowledgement of God as God. The point is that man is really a significant being in a significant history. When he chooses to abandon God and make himself lord, he is abandoned by God to his own lusts. Since man is not only an individual but a social creature, when he chooses to leave God, he also affects his fellow men in society as well as his descendants.

Today's culture everywhere reflects the loneliness, despair, fragmentation, and loss of personal identity that results from the sense in man of the loss of God. To many, God is dead, but so is man.[15] Our culture is increasingly characterized by relativism which teaches that all values are personal shifting opinions, there is no objective truth or right. Nowhere has the tendency to try to relativize absolutes become more evident than in the erosion of conscience in the moral realm.[16] One characteristic of our day is nihilism, the determined effort to destroy everything, to break down every institution, every system of thought, every abiding norm. Nihilism begins with the abandonment of God. Without God there are no abiding truths, lasting principles, or norms, and man is cast upon a sea of speculation and skepticism and attempted self-salvation.

So Paul continues with, "God gave them over in the lusts of their hearts to impurity that their bodies might be dishonored among them" (v. 24). In their freedom from God's absolutes they turned to perversion and even inversion of the created order. In the end their humanism (man-centeredness) resulted in dehumanization of each other. To "dishonor" their bodies must refer

15. Some materials on this are the books of Francis A. Schaeffer already cited; Kenneth Hamilton, *In Search of Contemporary Man* (Grand Rapids: Eerdmans, 1967); C. Stephen Evans, *Despair: A Moment or a Way of Life?* (Downers Grove, Ill.: Inter-Varsity, 1971); John W. Sanderson, Jr. *Encounter in the Non-Christian Era* (Grand Rapids: Zondervan, 1970).

16. By "moral realm" we mean the whole spectrum of human values including, but not limited to, sexual values.

not to the normal sexual relations of married couples (which in the Bible is always beautiful) but as Paul will show (vv. 26-27) to perverted sex and inverted relations of homosexuality. This fate came to those who "exchanged the truth of God [see v. 21] for a [Gk. "the"] lie [that *man* is absolute]" (v. 25).

Having inverted the creature-Creator relationship, God visits them with the hideous results of creature-creature inversion. In the rest of the chapter nothing new is added to this point until verse 32, but a number of illustrations are given of how God's abandonment of men to their own desires works in the personal and social realms.

In verse 26 Paul again repeats the pathetic sounding, "God gave them over," that connects the moral degradation to their apostasy from God, and goes on to speak first of the perversion of the created order (natural) by women. While homosexuality is clearly in Paul's mind in verse 27, some feel that the female counterpart (lesbianism) is not expressly described in verse 26. Yet the "in the same way" of verse 27 seems to indicate that he is describing in verse 26 the same kind of sin in the female as he goes on to condemn in men.

Homosexuality (v. 27) among men is further evidence of the inversion of the created order ("abandoned the natural function of the woman") which results in "indecent acts." They are now receiving that "due penalty of their error" (of worshiping the creation, v. 25). What due penalty? Perhaps Paul refers to the gnawing unsatisfied lust itself, together with the dreadful physical and moral consequences of debauchery. This sin, it must be borne in mind, is not worse than other sins or one that removes us from the human race or the grace of God. Those caught up in homosexual sins need compassion as any other sinner, but it must be pointed out that homosexuality is wrong, and the increase of this practice in today's society (as in Paul's) is further evidence of mankind's apostasy from the truth of God.[17]

Paul adds in verse 28 the reason for this debauchery: "Just as they did not see fit to acknowledge God any longer, God gave

17. *Time* magazine reports that there are no less than four million homosexuals in the United States ("Gay People," *Time* 96 [July 13, 1970]:2). See Klaus Blockmühl, "Homosexuality in Biblical Perspective," *Christianity Today* 17 (February 16, 1973):488-94.

them over to a depraved mind." Something of the Greek play on words is lost in the English. It goes like this: "As they found God worthless to their knowledge . . . God gave them over to a worthless (depraved) mind." Having first chosen in their unrighteousness to suppress God's truth as it was revealed to them, men were given over by God to a form of thinking that practices "things which are not proper" or things which are not fitting in God's moral order (obscenities). How we live quite often determines how we think. When one has lived awhile in a particular sinful manner, his mind begins to justify and rationalize his actions.

There follows in verses 29-31 a listing of various sins that illustrate Paul's point. They almost defy classification or groupings. Among them are personal sins, social sins, sins of pride, greed, injustice, perversions. It is a picture of utmost degeneracy. A meditation on these shows at once how complete a disorientation of the life results when the creature is alienated from the Creator.

There is a species of ant that lives in some parts of Africa: it lives in subterranean tunnels many feet in the earth, where the young are sheltered and the queen is housed. The workers go on foraging trips to distant places, returning to the nest with that on which the colony feeds. It is said that if, while they are away, their queen is molested, the workers, far away, become nervous and uncoordinated. If she is killed, they become frantic, rush around aimlessly, and eventually die in the field. It is thought that the workers in the normal situation are constantly oriented to the queen by some radarlike device; if she is killed, all orientation ceases and frenzy ensues, a frenzy that ends in death. Can we find a better parable of man in his alienation?

Paul concludes in verse 32 with, "Although they know the ordinance [sentence] of God, that those who practice such things are worthy of [eternal] death, they not only do the same [occasionally, in a more restricted way], but also give hearty approval [Gk. *syneudokeō*, "agree with" or "applaud"] to those who practice [habitually] them."[18] To do these things against one's sense of right is culpable, but to be in moral agreement with others who practice these obscenities (even if one does not do them) shows

18. The Greek word here translated "practice" is *prassō*, meaning "habitually practice." It is much stronger than the word "commit" (KJV).

that the sympathies lie there and render them inexcusable. That these men who are without the Bible "know the ordinance of God" seems to anticipate the argument from conscience in 2:14-15.

In summation of Paul's argument dealing with the man without the knowledge of the Bible (1:18-32), it may be said that (1) the visible revelation of God's wrath upon the pagan world can be seen most clearly in their moral perversions and inversions (individual and social) of the created order; (2) these perversions are the direct result of their exchanging the worship of the Creator for the creation; (3) they are under the judgment of God and inexcusable because God has made the rudimentary knowledge of Himself continuously available to all men, yet this knowledge has been willfully suppressed.

So, why do men without the Bible's knowledge need the salvation offered in the gospel? Because they are under the wrath (judgment) of God. Why are they under the wrath of God? Because they have individually suppressed God's Lordship in their lives, and they have inherited a perverted religious tradition.

What evidence is there from the human situation that God's wrath is already being manifested? Paul finds the proof in the moral degradation of the lives of those who have been abandoned to follow their own whimsical lusts.

Paul has not yet brought all men under this judgment. He must now consider the case of those who possess the knowledge of God in the Bible.

MAN WITH THE KNOWLEDGE OF THE BIBLE
(2:1–3:8)

While Paul no doubt has both the proud Jew and the proud cultured Gentile (Greek and Roman) in mind in 2:1-16, he does not specifically mention the Jew until verse 17. His burden consists in showing that those who have not sunk to the depths of depravity that some in the pagan world have, because they have the light of God's will in the Bible, are nevertheless under the same judgment of God. Not the possession of the knowledge of the truth but the practice of the spirit of the truth shows who has really acknowledged the Creator. The idea that God shows no partiality (2:11) means that the proud Jew is brought to judgment on the same basis as the Gentile, as Paul will illustrate in more detail (vv. 12-16).

Turning directly to the Jew in verse 17, he accuses them of false pride in both their religious knowledge (vv. 17-25) and in their religious rite of circumcision (vv. 25-29). Finally, Paul discusses the main advantages of being a Jew (3:1-4) and answers objections to his position (3:5-8).

PRINCIPLE OF GOD'S JUDGMENT: NO PARTIALITY (2:1-16)

After having just heard the detailed description of the plight of the pagan world, a morally minded person might heartily agree with Paul's condemnation and even at this point offer an amen. But how can "good" people who are not idolators come under Paul's sweeping thesis that all have sinned and that they can only be delivered by the righteousness of God in the gospel?

In our day there are many moralistic people in and out of the churches. We generally think of them as middle- or upper middle-class society, the silent majority. Many of these people still attempt in principle to hold to the basic Christian morality but have abandoned the radical biblical religious root of regeneration. They want the fruit of Christianity without its root, personal relationship to Jesus Christ. What of these, Paul? His answer consists of charging that the critic of others has condemned himself, because the criticism of such sinners (1:18-32) reveals that in the act of criticism he knows what is right and has no excuse for his own violation of God's law (vv. 1-3).

In verse 1, Paul strikes an immediate blow to the conscience of the moralist by asserting, "Therefore [because what was true of those in 1:18-32 is also true of the self-righteous critic] you are without excuse [see also 1:20 for the same word!], every man of you [whether Jew or pagan moralist], who passes judgment. . . you condemn yourself." "Every man of you" (or my good man) alerts us that Paul has in mind here (and throughout the letter) a real objector or heckler.[19]

19. This diatribe style was common to the philosophers and preachers in Paul's day. It is not impossible that some of the arguments in this book were first worked out by Paul in actual confrontation and debate with non-Christians as they interjected remarks and received Paul's replies (3:5-8; 6:1, 15).

The moralist might say, "The wrath of God rests on the Gentiles but not on the Jews." There are two reasons why the moralist is on thin ice with respect to the judgment of God. In the first place he reveals by his criticism of the heathen vices that he knows God's moral requirement. He cannot plead ignorance of God's will. And yet Paul alleges they "practice the same things." Not that these people were necessarily homosexuals or violent or disobedient to parents, but they were sinners (vv. 21-24, stealing, adultery, sacrilege) and broke the same law of God that the pagans violated in grosser fashion. E. J. Carnell has noted, "Self-righteous people make one of two capital mistakes: either they misunderstand the height of God's law or they misunderstand the depth of their own moral conduct."[20]

Second, behind all the sins in 1:29-32 lies the sin of idolatry, which reveals man's ambition to put himself in the place of God and so be his own Lord.[21] But this is precisely what the judge does when he assumes the right to condemn his own fellow creatures and excuse himself (Ja 4:11-12). True, God's judgment rightly falls on the pagan (v. 2), but do you think *you* of all men, *you* who know God's will, can do as they do and yet get away with it ("escape," v. 3)? Anticipating his answer, Paul would say no, "For there is no partiality with God" (v. 11).

Furthermore, since the moralist has escaped the present wrath of God to a large extent because he has not so overtly suppressed the truth as has the man without the Bible, he should not misread God's kindness to him (in not visiting wrath) as if such delay were an indication that God has somehow favored him. The moralist should repent of his sin and wickedness and realize that God judges on the basis of a man's work or deeds and not on the basis of his national or religious heritage (vv. 4-11).

These verses (4-11) touch on the vital matter of the future judgment of God. Is there a literal future hell?[22] Paul, it seems,

20. E. J. Carnell, *Christian Commitment* (Grand Rapids: Eerdmans, 1957), p. 202.
21. C. K. Barrett, *The Epistle to the Romans*, p. 44.
22. If 1:18-32 gives us some indication of the present result of the wrath of God in the loss of man's humanity, then the future withdrawal of all (perhaps not *all;* even in judgment there is mercy) of God's grace and kindness from man can only be dreadfully imagined. "Deprivation," rather than the medieval imagery of burning or physical pain (Dante's *Inferno*),

speaks unhesitatingly in verse 5 of "the day of wrath and revelation of the righteous judgment of God." The moralist wrongly thinks that he will escape God's judgment by taking God's side and condemning the unrighteous person (vv. 1-3). Further, he is also in error in thinking that because of his religious and national heritage, he is excused from judgment and God is now extending special favor ("kindness, forbearance and patience," v. 4) to him.[23]

But all such thinking is wrong, because God's judgment is completely impartial (v. 11). He judges not on the basis of who the person is, but with respect alone to the nature of the deeds he has done (v. 6). The religious moralist (Jew or pagan) must recognize that God's kindness (absence of visible judgment) is extended to him out of grace. Rather than interpret this "forbearance" (Gk. *anochē*, restraint) as a special favor in judgment, God's longsuffering should be viewed as a persuasive force to try to bring men to their knees in "repentance" and faith (v. 4).

The Jew of Paul's day thought that, because he was receiving little wrath now from God, it must be evidence that in the future life he would have unmixed reward. In reality, Paul declares, they were by their "unrepentant heart . . . storing up wrath" (v. 5)[24] against themselves for the future day of judgment. This unexpected inversion by Paul clearly reminds us that a form of supposed sincerity, even before God, can be sincerely misleading because of man's sinfulness and may lead to eternal judgment.

Verses 7-9 have been a source of perplexity to many Christians. In them Paul establishes the truth that God's judgment of all men

may depict more of the biblical concept (see C. S. Lewis, *Problem of Pain* [New York: Macmillan, 1961], pp. 106-116).

23. These ideas can be seen in the Jewish Apocryphal book of the *Wisdom of Solomon* (15:1-4), which Paul evidently knew.

24. The Greek tense (connotative present) can signify action being attempted but not successfully completed (e.g., Jn 13:6); in such cases "tries to" supplies a good auxiliary (F. Blass and A. Debrunner, *A Greek Grammar of the New Testament and Other Early Christian Literature,* ed. and trans. Robert W. Funk [Chicago: U. of Chicago, 1961], par. 319, p. 167). Repentance (Greek, *metanoia*) in the NT does not basically signify sorrow for sin or even remorse but stands for the radical change in thought and will that turns a person away from himself to acknowledge God as Lord and away from disobedience of God's will to obedience. For Paul repentance is divinely worked (2 Co 7:9-11) and includes the action of faith in Jesus Christ (the latter is Paul's more common word).

will be on the basis of their works or deeds. This thought has led many Protestants to feel an uncomfortable tension over what appears to be a contradiction between salvation by faith alone, without works, and Paul's teaching here. In brief, the solution (as well as the tension) lies in understanding the nature of the works to which Paul here makes mention.

First, Paul considers those described as receiving "eternal life" (v. 7). Most of the translations have missed the actual thought of Paul. Paraphrased, the Greek would mean something like this, "To those who with patient endurance in good work (as an outward life style) seek for the glory, honor, and incorruption God alone can give (as the object of their inward motivation), He will render eternal life." Those who by their good works prove they seek the things that alone are God's are contrasted in verse 8 with those who are self-seekers, who are "selfishly ambitious and do not obey the truth."[25] The self-seeker suppresses the truth in unrighteousness (v. 8); and against such the wrath and fury of God are directed (1:18).

The "doing good" in verse 7 (contrast, "does evil," v. 9) refers to the whole Christian life of righteousness through faith in Christ which Paul will develop later. The patient continuance in good works (Eph 2:10) demonstrates that the life's source is faith in God and the gospel. The real issue is whether a man sees his good works as evidence that he is doing a good job for God or whether (as in Paul's view) he sees them as marks not of human achievement but of hope in God.

There can be no question then of God showing any special favoritism (Mt 5:45). Each man faces an impartial Judge who will determine whether the life was lived in pursuit of God's glory or in self-seeking unrighteousness (v. 11).

But Paul, one might interject, you forget that the Jew has had the privilege of God's special revelation in the Bible (law). Doesn't this give him an advantage over the heathen whom God has not so blessed? In verses 12-16 Paul begins to break down yet another prop. The sorest point of all for the Jew was Paul's con-

25. Greek for "selfishly ambitious" is *eritheia* which is derived from a word meaning hireling. The idea, then, is not "contentious" (KJV) but "base self-seeking" since they use their works as evidence of human achievement (see TDNT 2:660).

tention that there is no protection from the wrath of God in the possession of the Bible (law): "For not the hearers [listeners— Sabbath by Sabbath] of the Law are just before God, but the doers of the Law will be justified" (v. 13).[26] It is performance of God's will, not possession (or knowledge) that averts the wrath of God (Ja 1:22). God's revelation (law) does not protect one from judgment. It is rather the instrument for a more severe reckoning with the exceeding sinfulness of sin (7:7). More knowledge brings more responsibility and greater accountability. Thus the law becomes the possessor's accuser—his destruction, not his salvation.

In order to maintain his thesis of the equality before God of both the man without and the man with the Bible, Paul must answer yet another objection. If the law will be my standard of judgment, the religious moralist might object, how can God treat the pagan equally with me when he has no law to judge him? Won't the absence of the law to judge him allow the pagan to escape God's wrath? No, Paul answers, because though the pagan is without the biblical revelation (law of Moses), he is not thereby outside all revelation from God ("law to themselves," v. 14). How does the pagan without the Bible have the knowledge of God's will? More disturbingly, are the heathen lost because they are without the knowledge of the Bible and Christ's gospel? In trying to answer these questions we must be careful to note what Paul does say on this point and what he does not say.

Some feel that Paul is referring to Christian Gentiles in verse 14 when he says, "When Gentiles who do not have the Law do instinctively the things of the Law." He would then be anticipating his argument later on in the epistle about justification without the law for all men (3:21-28). But Paul obviously speaks here about those who have no knowledge *at all* of the law and those who do *instinctively* what the law requires. These factors show he has in mind those who have never heard about God in either the Old Testament or the gospel.

26. Hypothetically at least, this seems to be the point. In Gal 3:21 Paul argues that, if a law could have given life, then surely righteousness would have come to man through the keeping of the Mosaic law, but since all are sinners and transgressors of the intent of the law, God brought righteousness to man in a different manner.

It will help to begin with the matter of the "conscience" whose role Paul describes as "bearing witness" (v. 15). Conscience is not acquired through our environment. Rather, man finds himself already in his earliest years functioning morally as a creature made in the image of God. Dogs or other domesticated animals seem to have a conscience only because of their association with man. Conscience is the man functioning in the native act of deciding right from wrong. It is important to note that this moral voice within does not function legislatively but only judicially. Conscience assumes the presence of a valid norm. It anticipates a complementary something whereby it may then govern itself. As an umpire it does not make the rules but decides in the light of the existing rules. It refuses to be normless. That conscience is innate in every human being is unquestioned; what standard it approves or disapproves is quite a different matter. The content or norm by which the conscience decides the right from the wrong is not innate or at least not entirely innate but is controlled by the creation order, the environment, and local social standards.[27] Conscience, therefore, can be educated or changed by the introduction of new norms.

Scripture refers to a dulled or calloused conscience. Through repeated ignorings of the "no" voice, the moral faculty grows numb (1 Ti 4:2). The familiar experience of repeatedly shutting off the alarm clock in the morning and then going back to sleep illustrates in the physical-psychical realm how the conscience in the moral realm can be ignored until we no longer hear its voice. If we convince ourselves in a relativized society that there are no norms, then the function of conscience will deteriorate.

Paul says that there are three witnesses which agree together that the pagan has a basic knowledge of right and wrong (a norm), even though he does not have the written revelation of

27. This is well-illustrated in the story told by a missionary to northern Brazil. He had observed a very nervous and fidgety native with sweat on his brow enter the village and seem very uneasy even in the presence of his friends. Later, the missionary had learned that this fellow had just killed a man of another tribe. Although in this society it was not considered wrong to kill a member of another tribe, this man was obviously under the pressure of a guilty conscience. While societal norms do set the conscience, there is also the witness of God in the nature of our relations with other human beings that overrides the errant social standard.

God. They are: (1) the outward (phenomenological) or natural ("instinctively," v. 14) establishment of societal laws for controlling behavior; (2) the conscience which judges each man concerning his own actions with reference to the natural norms (v. 15); and (3) alternately accusing or else excusing thoughts we have about the behavior of others which may be publicly debated (v. 15).[28]

The pagan by natural moral instinct sets up certain social standards which include some of the same rules as the laws of God in the Bible, such as the pursuit of lawful vocations, the procreation of offspring, filial and natural affections, the care of the poor and sick, and numerous other natural virtues which are required by the Mosaic law. Paul teaches that since he does this, he is not without a law to judge him. The "things of the Law" (v. 14) which the Gentiles do naturally must mean certain things which the biblical law also requires. We should not take this to mean that the whole Mosaic law or even all the Ten Commandments are written on the hearts of pagans. Paul does not say this. Similarly the expression "work of the Law" (v. 15) is not the law itself but the effect of the law, that is, the setting of the conscience. So in effect he himself (in virtue of being a person) becomes a law (norm) to himself.

In other words, there is something, Paul argues, in the very pattern of created human existence, which should (and sometimes does) lead the Gentiles to an attitude of humble, grateful, dependent creatureliness. There does exist a moral standard among the heathen not identical to, but certainly similar to, certain things in the Bible.[29] This similarity, Paul says, is not simply

28. The construction is very difficult in the Greek. Two possibilities exist here grammatically: (1) the idea of "meanwhile . . . one another" (KJV) (Gk. *metaxy allēlōn*) refers to mutual judgment of each other's behavior and is different though not unrelated to the functioning of conscience; or (2) these words refer to their inward thoughts: "their conflicting thoughts accuse or perhaps excuse them" (RSV). It is difficult to decide, though the KJV idea seems better. See H. P. Liddon, *An Explanatory Analysis of St. Paul's Epistle to the Romans* (Grand Rapids: Zondervan, 1961), pp. 46-49; Nygren, p. 125; William Sanday and Arthur Headlam, *A Critical and Exegetical Commentary on the Epistle to the Romans* (Edinburgh: T. &. T. Clark, 1900), p. 60.

29. C. S. Lewis states, "There have been differences between their moralities [speaking of different civilizations and ages], but these have never amounted to anything like a total difference" (*Mere Christianity* [New York: Macmillan, 1943], p. 5).

coincidental but reflects God's revelation of His will to man in the natural or created order (1:20-21). When the pagan violates this standard, he stands under the judgment of God and should in humble repentance cast himself upon the mercy of the Creator for forgiveness. His sin consists principally in his failure through rebellion to humble himself, nevertheless God will judge him on the basis of the specific violations of his own conscience.[30] Can he be saved? Paul does not answer this question directly. Our answer will depend on whether we believe (1) that the knowledge of God revealed to the pagan is enough for salvation, and (2) that such people do *de facto* respond positively to this revelation of God. A *no* response to either of these would justify Christian missions.

So Paul concludes this section by returning in verse 16 to the thought of verse 13. We connect the words from verse 13, "not the hearers of the Law are just before God, but the doers of the Law will be justified" with those in verse 16, "on the day when . . . God will judge the secrets of men." Yet the reference to "the secrets of men" shows that Paul also includes in this summary verse his thoughts expressed in verses 14-15 that not only men's outward deeds but also their inner motivations, feelings, and thoughts will be the subject matter of God's examination in the future day of judgment. The standards of judgment will be Paul's gospel,[31] that is, the very truths he has been revealing in chapters one and two; and the agent of judgment will be Jesus Christ Himself (Jn 5:27; Ac 17:31).[32]

30. It seems that missionary as well as evangelistic effort among young people in our country should pay closer attention to this point. We may see places where another is violating *our* standards, but our point of contact with him may have to be in an area where he is actually rejecting by his life a standard that he has committed himself to. This is an area where he will feel guilty.

31. Not Paul's gospel in distinction to Jesus' or Peter's or John's gospel, but the gospel which Paul taught as the norm and to which the other apostles were in agreement (see Gal 2:9).

32. While the Christian is never described by Paul or any NT writer as being saved by works but ever by faith alone, yet saving faith is never alone. Salvation involves the life we are saved to as well as the life we are saved from. We are saved to holiness and good works (Eph 2:10). Thus while judgment always proceeds on the basis of works (Rev 20:12), God's salvation is never on the basis of works but always faith. Yet the outworking of this salvation produces a life-style characterized by good works before God, and therefore the principle of God's judgment is maintained even in the case of the believer (1 Co 3:11-13).

PERIL OF THE JEW: PRIDE (2:17–3:8)

Paul now turns directly to the Jew who has the written law of God. He is still dealing with the thought of God's universal judgment on all men and the further principle that it is not the listeners to the law that are right before God but the doers of the law. Paul has already rejected the fallacy that the Jew has a special privilege and advantage before God even when he doesn't respond appropriately (2:14-15). Now he wants to nail this down further and leave no way of escape. It was not that the Jew was wrong in prizing his possession of the law and esteeming its knowledge an advantage. The problem was that he trusted in the mere knowledge and possession of the law and clung merely to its outward observances. But the Jew in Paul's day did not let the law convict him of his sin and lead him into obedient faith that would result in his keeping the real intent of the law. The moralist, thus, reveals his rebellion against God, not by his outward immorality and corruption, but by the hardening of his heart (2:5) and by his refusal to repent of his bankrupt self-righteousness.

In verses 17-20 Paul sets forth the acknowledged advantage on which the Jew prided himself: (1) "bear the name 'Jew'" (a member of the covenant people); (2) "rely upon the Law" (trusted the law for his standing before God); (3) "boast in God" (the true worship of God); (4) "know His will" (the revealed will of God; (5) "approve the things that are essential" (keen sense of moral discernment); (6) "guide to the blind" (in spiritual insight and light for them in darkness); (7) "corrector of the foolish" (unlearned); (8) "a teacher of the immature" (last word in proper parental education). He could do all this confidently because he had the "embodiment of knowledge and of the truth" in the biblical revelation of God (v. 20).

But, Paul argues, it is not in the law one should trust, for sin reigns despite the law. "You therefore who teach another, do you not teach yourself? You who preach that one should not steal, do you steal? You who say that one must not commit adultery, do you commit adultery (see John 8:11)? You who abhor idols, do you rob temples?" (vv. 21-23). The great wrong in the life of this Jew was that while he boasted in the law and boasted of relationship to God, he dishonored God by "breaking the Law" (v.

23) and brought God's reputation to nothing in the eyes of the Gentiles (v. 24).

Why be a Jew at all? Really to be a Jew is to obey God in faith from the heart (v. 29). His outward sign (circumcision) that he possesses of the covenant relationship cannot shield him from the wrath of God. Circumcision was only a visible seal of a true heart relationship to God of love and obedience (Deut 30:6; Ro 4:11). The Jews mistook the seal for the reality. When they evidenced by their breaking of God's law that the reality was not there, God invalidated the sealing significance of the rite (v. 25).

On the other hand, when a person does not have the seal but demonstrates by loving obedience to God and His will that he possesses the inward reality, his uncircumcision by nature will be counted by God as if he were circumcised and in covenant relationship (v. 26). The word Jew means "praise" (Gen 29:35). Paul states that the true Jew is not the one who glories and trusts in the outward appearance of circumcision, or in the listening to the law and legalistically following its precepts. The true Jew is one who in his heart has entered into a relationship with God of humble response (faith) to God's gracious love and election (Deu 10:16). Such a one looks to God for His praise and not to men.

Paul is not actually arguing that Gentiles who fulfill the intent of the law become true Jews (despite much appeal to these verses to the contrary). He is speaking to his fellow countrymen (v. 17) to the effect that the real significance of a Jew lies in his relationship to God and not in his nationality or religious heritage. Although it is true that Paul says, "If therefore the uncircumcised man [Gentile] keep the requirements of the Law, will not his uncircumcision be regarded as circumcision [covenant relationship to God]?" (v. 26), he does not go so far here or elsewhere (on Gal 6:16 see chap. 8, note 14) to call Gentiles true Jews. "Circumcision . . . of the heart" (v. 29) refers to true repentance before God (Jer 4:4); "by the Spirit, not by the letter" either has reference to the Holy Spirit's work or to the inward spiritual relationship to God contrasted with the mere performance of the rite (1:9); "his praise is not from men, but from God" (v. 29) picks up the thought of verse 17 ("name 'Jew'") and excludes all criticism of others based on pride of superiority. Thus the truth is established that it is the spirit of the law which is efficacious, not its mere outward forms and ritual performance.

Is there then any advantage *at all* in being a Jew and having circumcision (3:1)? The answer expected from what Paul has just said might appear to be no! But rather he says, "Great in every respect" (3:2). "First" (Gk. *prōton*) anticipates a list of advantages, but Paul gets sidetracked and gives only the first and no doubt the most important reason: because "they were entrusted with the oracles of God" (3:2). The "oracles" (Gk. *logia*, words or pronouncements) of God refers to the whole Old Testament revelation of God in the Bible, though from verse 3 it may be inferred that the promises of a Messiah are prominent (see also Ac 7:38; Heb 5:12; 1 Pe 4:11). What Paul is saying is that this revealed salvation-history (oracles) was of tremendous advantage to the Jew in that it gave him a special understanding of God, man's condition, the salvation of God, His will, and especially the promises of the coming of the Christ (Lk 24:44).

There now follow three objections to Paul's thesis that the Jews do have an advantage in the Word of God given to them (3:3-8). Perhaps by listing them together with Paul's answers they can be seen more clearly:

Objection Number 1 (implied): "The Jews have disbelieved these (Messianic) promises."
Answer: "What then? If some did not believe" (vv. 3-4).
Objection Number 2: "But if our unrighteousness demonstrates" (v. 5).
Answer: "May it never be! For otherwise how will God judge?" (v. 6).
Objection Number 3: "But if through my lie" (vv. 7-8).
Answer: "Their condemnation is just" (v. 8).

The first objection touches on the problem of the unbelief of Israel in the Messiah which Paul later develops in detail (chaps. 9-11). How is Israel's possession of the oracles of God any advantage if they don't believe them? Perhaps the Words of God aren't really reliable after all. Paul's answer is that the unbelief of "some" (not all) does not nullify the reliability of God's Words.

Nor does such unbelief cancel the great advantage to the nation
of possession the knowledge of God in the Scriptures and of being
a covenant people. Can man's lack of response to God's promises
(unbelief) cancel out His faithfulness (and make Him a liar) to
His own words? (v. 3).

In verse 4 after reacting with abhorrence for such a thought,
Paul adds a further statement about the relationship of God's
faithfulness to man's sin and includes a reference to Psalm 51.
"May it never be![33] Rather, let God be found true, though every
man be found a liar . . . that thou mightest be justified." Even if
all (not just some) were to disbelieve God's Words, it would only
serve to highlight the truth and faithfulness of God. For example,
David declares that his sin, rather than making God unjust for
condemning him, has vindicated God's justice (Ps 51:4). If sin
does not disestablish God's justice, then neither can man's unbelief cancel out God's faithfulness and truthfulness.

This approach of Paul raises further objections concerning how
God can be just in condemning the sinner when his sin really
serves to establish the righteousness of God (v. 5).[34] Paul answers again in abhorrence of the thought and appeals to God's
moral government of the world, "How will God judge the world?"
(v. 6).

Further, it is objected, if God gets glory through sin, why not
go on sinning and bring more glory to God (v. 7)? At this point
Paul dismisses the question with a rather rude slap across the
cheek, "Their condemnation [judgment] is just" (v. 8), that is
all those who object to being judged as sinners. But he will return
to these moral problems again later on in the letter (chaps. 6 and
9-11).

Paul has shown that the man with the knowledge of God in the
Bible stands equally under God's wrath with the pagan. He has
no advantage before God's judgment. Such a man demonstrates

33. The expression in the Greek (*mē genoito*) literally translated means
"perish the thought!" or "may it not be!" However, since in the Greek OT
(LXX) this same expression is used in connection with the name of God
(1 Sa 24:6; 26:11; 1 Ki 21:3), the KJV translation which adds the stronger
idea of God's abhorrence ("God forbid") is to be preferred (John Murray,
The Epistle to the Romans, 1:94, footnote 1).
34. "I am speaking in human terms" means simply that he is adopting the
diatribe method of interjecting objections opposed to his views that he
might further clarify his teaching.

by his judgment of the pagan that he knows what is right, yet by his own life he shows that his relationship to God is all external and formal, not personal and real. The great advantage of possessing the Bible's promises is not invalidated by any amount of unbelief. God's promises remain true regardless of man's rejection.

CONCLUSION: MORAL GUILT OF THE WHOLE WORLD

(3:9-20)

In this final paragraph of the long section dealing with mankind's condition under the judgment of God (1:18–3:20), Paul concludes by bringing both the sinner without the Bible (1:18-32) and the sinner with the Bible (2:1–3:8) together as equally "under sin" (3:9). The Jew (or moralist) is no better off than the pagan. Both are equally guilty before God. Paul appeals to the statements of the Old Testament Scriptures concerning both Jews and Gentiles (vv. 10-18) and concludes that man is universally and totally affected by rebellion against God (vv. 19-20).[35]

THE CHARGE (3:9)

"What then [does this argument amount to]? Are we [Jews] better [off] than they [the pagan Gentiles]? Not at all."[36] It might be inferred from Paul's statements in verse 2 that the Jew was in a better position than the pagan because he had the advantage of the oracles of God. Paul dispels that error and adds that he has already "charged" (Gk. *proaitiaomai*) that both are

---

35. Total depravity must not be understood to mean that all men are as bad or as depraved as they can get; or that men in this condition show no love, kindness, honesty, morality, etc., but that man is infected with rebellion against his Creator, and this rebellion has extended itself in some measure throughout our whole being. If sin were blue in color, I would be some shade of blue all over. Even in my best deeds there is a discoloration of self-centeredness instead of God-centeredness. Charles H. Spurgeon, the great English preacher, once remarked, "He who doubts total depravity had better study himself."

36. This latter sentence has two major interpretive problems in determining Paul's exact thought. The first involves the word "better" (Gr. *proechomai*) which has three possible meanings; the second involves the words "not at all" (Gr. *oy pantōs*) which has two different senses. We have given the sense in the above translation which seems preferable to us as well as to others. See E. H. Gifford, "Romans" in *The Bible Commentary: New Testament*, p. 85; TDNT; RSV. For a full discussion, see Barrett, pp. 66-69.

"under sin." To be under sin means, as Paul has shown in 1:18–2:29, to be under God's wrath and judgment for sin (7:14; Gal 3:22). It may also mean "under the power [dominion] of sin" (NEB, RSV). Paul is saying that all men (no exceptions) are under the dominion of both the moral guilt and the corruption of sin.

THE PROOF (3:10-18)

Paul now turns to six selective passages from the Psalms and the book of Isaiah to demonstrate that the Bible teaches that all men are unrighteous before God and do not acknowledge Him as Lord in their lives. They require little comment.

1. The *character* of men (vv. 10-12). In five negative statements Paul leaves no hope for man having a divine spark of righteousness in him that only needs to be fanned.

2. The *conduct* of men (vv. 13-17). Men betray the inner condition of their heart by their speech ("throat," "tongue," "mouth," see Mt 12:37; Mk 7:20, 21) and by their actions ("feet," "paths," "path of peace"). The heart blazes the way, the mouth and feet follow.

3. The *cause* of their conduct is put last (v. 18): "There is no fear of God before his eyes" (Ps 36:1).

THE CONCLUSION (3:19-20)

The Jew, of course, might think to escape from the force of these quotations from his own Bible by insisting that they refer to pagans and not to the Jewish covenant people. While even a careful study of the context of the quotes shows otherwise, Paul responds somewhat differently by reminding the objector that "whatever the Law says, it speaks to those who are under the Law." This revelation in the Old Testament law (whole OT)[37] which reveals the universal sin of all mankind before God also declares the judgment of God equally upon both Jew and pagan.

The two-fold purpose for which the Old Testament declared this judgment was: (1) that no man, whether Jew or pagan, may

37. The "law" (as in chaps. 2 and 3) refers not only to the Mosaic codes but also to the prophets and Psalms, i.e., the whole OT (F. F. Bruce, *The Epistle of Paul to the Romans* [Grand Rapids: Eerdmans, 1963], p. 99).

plead before God any righteousness of his own: "That every mouth may be closed" (Gk. *phrassō*, shut up), or as Phillips puts it: "that every excuse may die on the lips of him who makes it"; and (2) that the whole human race (world) should "become accountable to God." The law then cannot be used as an excuse or repose. Man must be silent and confess that he is a sinner: "It is the straight-edge of the Law that shows us how crooked we are" (Phillips).

But why did the Old Testament speak in this harsh manner about man? Because God must reveal to him his true condition before Him, the Creator, that he has no righteousness of his own. A man must, then, abandon law works[38] as a means of acceptance before God: "By the works of the Law no flesh will be justified in His sight" (v. 20). The psalmist exclaims, "If Thou, Lord, shouldst mark iniquities, O Lord, who could stand?" (Ps 130:3). Therefore the proper response before God is to invite God to *not* "enter into judgment with Thy servant, for in Thy sight no man living is righteous" (Ps 143:2). The first true function of the law (whether of Moses or the prophets) is to unmask us and show us that we are sinners ("knowledge of sin") and that it is impossible to be accepted before God on the basis of keeping the law. But can we accept this exposure?

According to an old tale, certain clever philosophers approached an emperor offering to weave for him a rare and costly garment which would have the marvelous capacity of making known to him the fools and knaves in his realm. Because of the magical quality of the threads, the garment would be invisible to all but the wise and pure in heart. Delighted, the emperor commissioned the weaving of the royal robes at great cost, only to find, to his dismay, that he obviously was a fool and knave, for he saw nothing on the looms. On the day set for the grand parade, the knavish philosophers collected their royal fee, dressed the emperor in his potbellied nakedness, and skipped out of town as the parade began. The whole populace joined the courtiers in praising the king's garments, none daring to admit that they saw nothing but

---

38. "Works of the law" are not merely good works but carry the added significance of works done in obedience to the law and *regarded as, in themselves,* a means of justification.

the emperor's nudity, lest they be branded as self-admitted fools and knaves. The entire parade of folly collapsed, as the shame of king and people was exposed by a child's honest remark, "The emperor has no clothes!"

None were consciously naked until the boy's truth destroyed their lie, ripping away their fig leaf of common hypocrisy. Thus, everyone's pride was hurt, and everyone's shame exposed. Yet so long as men live under the illusion that they are righteous in themselves and refuse to acknowledge the folly of their sinfulness in the presence of the truth of God's revelation, there can be no appreciation of the gospel that Paul preaches. It is not enough to admit that man (emperor) has no overcoat or that he has no shirt. We must see that whether we have the knowledge of the Bible, or do not know the Bible, in the sight of God we are absolutely naked! It is not merely that we have committed sins (partially unclothed), but we must see ourselves as sinful before God and in rebellion (totally unclothed) completely incapable in ourselves of providing any acceptable clothing (righteousness) in the sight of our Creator.

Man has, in rebelling, suppressed the truth of his creaturehood revealed in the external nature of his existence (vv. 20-23). He has also rebelled against God's law in his inward nature by violating his conscience (2:14-15). Sin, as Paul has explained, is basically a wrong relationship to God; it is active or passive rebellion against His lordship over our lives. This is the Bible's concept of man's sin that leaves him without excuse and under the judgment and wrath of God. Man's predicament renders him hopeless unless God has found some other means of accepting sinful men apart from either law works or religious rites. Will He give man righteousness? How will He do it and still remain just and holy?

3

The Good News: The Righteousness of God by Faith

(3:21—4:25)

THANKFULLY, God's word of judgment is not His only word. "But now" (v. 21), Paul says, something utterly new has entered human history. This is the great turning point of the letter. All that man has been able to accomplish stands justly under God's wrath. But our own need is met by God's intervention in mercy and grace through Jesus Christ. Now *God's* righteousness affecting man's salvation has been revealed as a free gift to the guilty. It is obtained solely on the basis of faith in Jesus Christ apart from any moralistic works (3:21-26). Therefore, all meritorious boasting in works is excluded by the principle of complete trust in Jesus Christ for acceptance before God (3:27-31). This faith method of salvation taught in the good news of the gospel is in fact the very one revealed in the Old Testament and illustrated beautifully and irrefutably by the lives of Abraham and David (4:1-25).

GOD'S PROVISION: THE GIFT OF RIGHTEOUSNESS
(3:21-31)

In the brief span of a few verses, Paul sets forth God's finished plan and how He dealt with the sinful human condition. Since Paul compresses such a tremendous amount of truth into a brief section, we will need to examine and enlarge (from other Pauline passages) upon a number of the key words found here such as redemption, grace, justification, faith, and propitiation. Paul's precise thought is also revealed by his use of about twenty independent prepositions and eight prepositions compounded with other words. These syntactical relationships are difficult to explain in a brief commentary, but one should be aware that there is far more in the text than the word meanings.

In short, Paul teaches that what man could not effect for himself (righteousness) because he is under the wrath of God, God has provided as a free gift through faith in Jesus Christ. The actual historical and public crucifixion of the young Jewish carpenter, Jesus of Nazareth, reveals God's righteousness and provides the basis for this full forgiveness and deliverance from God's wrath of all who put their trust in God's Son (1:16). Paul refers to the death of Jesus in the language of the Old Testament sacrificial system (vv. 24-25). Since God's deliverance comes to us solely by faith, there can be no place for boasting or self-congratulation (vv. 27-30).

THE RIGHTEOUSNESS OF GOD IS NOT BY THE LAW (3:21)

Paul likes to speak paradoxically: "apart from the Law" and yet "being witnessed by the Law and the prophets."[1] It has already been shown by Paul that law-righteousness (legalism) rests upon human achievement and because of man's self-centered nature leads to God's wrath (4:15). So God's righteousness must be manifested in a different way so as to lead to man's justification. On the other hand, the law (OT) itself, if men correctly understand it, points in the same direction (3:31). In the *law* Abraham and David (chap. 4) are illustrations of how God's gift-righteousness came to men of old through faith. Paul has already referred to Habakkuk 2:4 from the prophets (1:17). Paul's rich use of the word *law* (*nomos*) should not be overlooked. Here Paul stresses that the righteousness of God comes not by legalism (law), yet the law (OT) as God's revelation witnesses to the importance of faith.

1. "The law and the prophets" probably refers to the whole OT in a twofold division. Such a division is found in the Qumran *Manual of Discipline,* Zadokite fragments, and other Qumran literature (Laird Harris "What Books Belong in the Canon of Scripture?" in *Can I Trust My Bible?,* ed. H. Vos [Chicago: Moody, 1968], p. 76.).

The "righteousness of God" once again comes before us. Paul has in 1:17 related this term to the gospel and the power of God working salvation to all who believe. The reader is referred for further help to the discussion under justification (3:24). Briefly it may be recalled that "the righteousness of God" refers to God's free gift of salvation through Jesus Christ which issues in both a new standing in future eternity and a changed condition in the present life (5:1-2). The righteousness of (from) God is God Himself going forth in power to effect a radical deliverance for those who trust Him totally.

THE RIGHTEOUSNESS OF GOD IS THE RIGHTEOUSNESS OF FAITH
      (3:22-23)

As in 1:17, Paul again immediately links this saving activity of God with man's faith. An additional element appears here: "through faith in Jesus Christ" (v. 22). The object of our trust is the person of Jesus Christ. Faith has an intelligent and personal content. God's righteousness not only becomes operative in our case through our faith in Christ, but furthermore it makes absolutely no difference who or what we are, "for all those who believe."[2] Just as sin was shown to be universal and God's judgment impartial, so now Paul declares God's gift of righteousness to be available to all indiscriminately.

"There is no distinction" (e.g., between Jew and Gentile, those with the knowledge of the Bible and those without the knowledge of the Bible, moralist and pornographer) "for all have sinned" (v. 23). They have sinned in the sense of Paul's concept of sin in 1:18–3:20, namely, that regardless of the differences among men in respect to the kind and intensity of their offenses against God's law, all without exception are in the category of rebellious sinners ("under sin," 3:9). They have willfully suppressed the outward and inward knowledge of God who claims as Creator to be Lord of their lives. In doing this, they "fall short of the glory of God."

The tenses in the two verbs are important. All "have sinned"

2. "And upon all" is added in some versions but omitted in a number of ancient Greek manuscripts; many manuscripts, however, include the expression, and it seems perfectly suited to the thought of Paul (John Murray, *The Epistle to the Romans*, 1:111, footnote 16), even though the NASB translators omit it.

64 *The Freedom Letter*

(Greek past tense)[3] and "fall short" (present tense). The historical fact of man's continued sinful condition leads to his present falling short or "lack" (Gk. *hystereō,* "in need of") of the "glory of God." God created man in his own image that in dependence upon Him man might reflect the Creator's own personal and moral excellence. Sin breaks man's relationship with God and fractures the full imaging activity of the creature. Jesus Christ, as man, perfectly imaged the invisible God (Heb 1:3). Through Him sinful men are restored to the fully intended image and glory of God (2 Co 3:18; Col 3:10).

THE DIVINE PLAN OF COMMUNICATING THE RIGHTEOUSNESS OF GOD
TO MAN (3:24-26)

How does God actually provide this grace-gift of His saving righteousness? What role does Jesus Christ, and His death, play in this plan? Can even God account a sinful man as being righteous? How is God's gift attained? Some comment on each of the key words in verses 24-25 may help to illuminate the apostle's thoughts on these questions.

1. *Justification* (v. 24). What does Paul mean by being justified? Considerable discussion has revolved around attempted definitions of this concept. It is without doubt the key theme of the whole epistle. The Greek verb translated "justify" (*dikaioō*) has exactly the same stem as the Greek noun for "righteousness" (*dikaiosynē*). To justify someone, then, would logically mean to make someone righteous in the sense of infusing goodness. Although Chrysostom (A.D. 407) and the church likewise followed this view for centuries, it is now generally held to be wrong (an exception being some Roman Catholics). Even from one consideration alone this view is questionable. In the epistles frequent mention is made of

3. The aorist tense of this verb has been unwisely limited by some interpreters to refer to participation in Adam's sin. However, the complexive (constative) aorist may simply view many acts as a whole (F. Blass and A. Debrunner, *A Greek Grammar of the New Testament and Other Early Christian Literature,* par. 332, p. 171). In this case the past tense is simply gathering the whole human race under one canopy of sinfulness. "Sinned" is the Greek word *hamartanō* which literally means in classical Greek "to miss the mark," but in biblical literature refers to rebellion against God or to transgression of His will.

Christians who are not entirely ethically good (righteous), yet are nevertheless justified (e.g., 1 Co 3:3; 6:11).

In its place is offered the rendering to "declare (or treat) as righteous."[4] This idea suggests that God now views the sinner as if he were righteous (good) or had never sinned. While this rendering escapes the difficulty of asserting that in justification men are infused with ethical righteousness, it likewise flounders on linguistic and theological grounds. If God *treated* as ethically righteous those who were not morally righteous, would this not be a sort of legal fiction? Can even God pretend that black is white or that bad is good?

It is far better and more in harmony with Paul's whole teaching to understand justification to mean *to make righteous.*[5] At the same time it is necessary to recognize that "righteous" (in this instance) has no reference to ethical goodness or virtue, but means *right, clear, acquitted* in God's court.[6] Justification, then, is God's activity in behalf of guilty sinners whereby He goes forth in power to *forgive* and *deliver* them in the present time from judgment by His grace, to declare a *new reality* to exist, and to *transform* and *empower* them so that they can act to become what they are in the new reality. It is more than—but certainly includes—the mere forensic (legal acquittal) act of God. God actually works to for-

4. Verbs ending in *oō* in Greek (if they are verbs of mental perception or connected to adjectives denoting moral qualities) denote not the making but the counting or deeming the specific moral quality (C. K. Barrett, *The Epistle to the Romans,* p. 75). This is usually called the *forensic* (court room) use.

5. As Paul's concept of righteousness was drawn from the OT word usage rather than the Greek, so must we see his concept of justification. In the Hebrew OT the equivalent word lying behind justify is *tsadak* which primarily means to "cause to be righteous," that is, *show* to be righteous. It cannot mean to "treat *as if* righteous."

6. Further support for this idea is seen in the fact that the opposite of justification is *not unrighteousness* (1:18-19) which would make justification right living, but *condemnation* (Ro 5:18; 8:34; see Barrett, p. 75 and TDNT). Justification, then, is that act of God whereby He acquits us (1 Co 4:4) of our moral guilt before Him (under wrath) and through grace puts us in a radically different relationship to Him and all His benefits. Perhaps the *Good News for Modern Man* (TEV) captures the thought when it translates: "they are put right with him through Jesus Christ." Hence, justification means basically *standing* with God. It is neither ethical righteousness imputed (KJV) nor imparted but is a status conferred on the ground of faith, not on the ground of merit (see Leon Morris, *The Apostolic Preaching of the Cross* [Grand Rapids: Eerdmans, 1956], chaps. 7 and 8, for a full discussion).

give the sinner (4:5), to place him in a whole radically different relationship to Himself (5:2), and to give him power to become righteous before God. In this new relationship he receives enablement through the Holy Spirit, who brings the Lordship of Jesus Christ to bear on our lives (8:1-9), to worship and serve God in His will (holiness).[7]

This justification Paul further qualifies by the word "as a gift" (Gk. *dōrean*, for nothing). This same word is found in John 15:25 where Jesus says, "They hated Me without a cause" and in Galatians 2:21, "then Christ died needlessly" (i.e., for nothing). It is plain then that by this word Paul is stressing the gift aspect of God's method of putting men right with Himself. They are acquitted (forgiven and introduced to salvation) for no cause or reason in them, that is, they have no merit or virtue nor is any required (Phil 3:9).

2. *Grace* (v. 24). The reason why sinners though guilty can be justified lies in God's grace. This is a key word of Paul's in all his epistles (100 times). In the succeeding chapters this element will be a primary point as he discusses the new life imparted through justification (5:2). Grace (Gk. *charis*) is the free and unmerited favor of God. It is that aspect of God's love which leads Him to bestow on men His free forgiveness even while they are rebellious sinners (5:8; Eph 2:8). Grace, however, is more than God's favorable attitude toward us; it includes also the activity and divine provisions for living fully in the new relationship (Ro 5:21; 1 Co 15:10; 2 Co 12:9). When Paul wants to stress that salvation arises from God's initiative and not from man's work he uses the word *grace* (11:6).

God's grace, while free to the sinner, cannot be made a "cheap" grace, because it cost God the tremendous price of the death of

7. The present tense of the participle translated "being justified" stresses that justification is a *present experience* for all those who are needing the glory of God restored to their lives (v. 23). For the Jews in Paul's day justification was always future, awaiting the balancing of the good works against the evil works of each man (TDNT). The teaching of Jesus (Lk 18:4), as well as Paul's, was radically different at this point. The syntax is difficult at this point: "Because all have sinned (throughout history, not just in the sin of Adam) and all fall short (a present condition of all men due to their sinfulness) of the glory of God (our intended goal from creation), being justified (connect with v. 22, the 'righteousness of God through faith in Jesus Christ for all those who believe')."

His own Son. What has cost God so much cannot be cheap for us. Costly grace confronts us with a call to relinquish our very lives and submit absolutely to the obedience of Christ.[8]

G. Campbell Morgan used to relate an experience he had while preaching this message of free forgiveness in a small mining town in the Midwest. Following the service a miner came up and argued that this kind of salvation was too cheap. Morgan asked him how he got to work each day. The miner replied, "I walk. I live close to the mine." How do you get down in the mine shaft?" Morgan asked. "I ride the elevator," the miner said. Morgan continued, "How much does it cost you?" "Nothing, it's free for us miners," he said. "Well," replied Morgan, "It must be a cheap operation then!" "No," said the miner, "It's free for us, but it cost the company a lot." Then suddenly as if a light had dawned he exclaimed, "Oh, my God, now I see it. Salvation's free for me, but it cost the company a lot, all that God had!"[9]

The important question here is whether grace is purely arbitrary, or whether it rests in some decisive judicial act of God that allows Him to maintain His own holy standards and yet to acquit and deliver sinners.

3. *Redemption* (v. 24). Paul's answer to this question lies in understanding the death of Jesus as a sacrificial death. Two words drawn from the Old Testament highlight this. "Redemption" (Gk. *apolytrōsis*) means basically to buy a slave out of bondage in order to set him free. This imagery arises from both the Old Testament concept of the redemption of the nation Israel from slavery in Egypt (Ex 6:6; 15:13) and through the Passover lamb sacrifice (Ex 12; 1 Co 5:7).

Slavery produced a human condition from which a man could not free himself. It was hopeless unless someone from outside would willingly intervene and pay the price to free him. The release of the Viet Nam prisoners of war may form a close modern parallel. The imagery depicts the evil plight in which man finds himself as a result of his sin. He is in a state of imprisonment from which he cannot break free. He is helplessly under the

---

8. Dietrich Bonhoeffer, *Cost of Discipleship* (New York: Macmillan, 1959), chap. 1.

9. G. Campbell Morgan, *Westminster Pulpit* (Westwood, N.J.: Revell, n.d.), 9:120-33.

judgment of God. But God Himself has intervened, paid the price and effected the release. From the reference to "blood" in verse 25 the price paid can be nothing else than the death of Christ (Mk 10:45, Gal 3:13; 1 Pe 1:18).[10] Christ's death provided the required ransom price to free men from the captivity and dominion of sin and to liberate them to do the will of God. Jesus of Nazareth is Himself the ransom (1 Co 1:30; Titus 2:14).

4. *Propitiation* (v. 25). Paul immediately links the redemption effected through Christ with the concept of "a propitiation in His blood through faith." "Propitiation" (Gk. *hilastērion*)[11] must be understood in the light of the context of Paul's argument in 1:18–3:20. He has established that there is a real wrath of God that extends to all men because of their own willful suppression of the truth of His claims as Creator and Judge. In this context, Paul shows that in the historical death of Jesus ("in His blood") this wrath (anger) of God found adequate judicial *satisfaction.*

God condones nothing because of His holy and righteous nature. Since sin deserves punishment and death (1:32; 6:23), there can be no reconciliation without judicial satisfaction. It cannot be far from the truth if we see in the death of Jesus a substitution (2 Co 5:21; 1 Pe 2:24). He, the righteous one (yet fully human), suffered the just penalty (wrath) for our sins that God might still remain just and the One who can fully pardon the guilty sinner (v. 26). The marvel consists in the act of God's grace where in infinite and consuming love He himself provided the costly satis-

10. There are at least six different Greek words used for "redemption" in the NT (Morris, chap. 1). Paul does not say to whom the price was paid nor exactly how Christ's death provided this tremendous effect. There can be little doubt, however, that Paul's thought included the idea of substitutionary death (Gal 3:13-14).

11. The concept is fraught with problems both linguistically and theologically. Theologically, there are two views, the first, as in the NASB and KJV, sees the term denoting a true sense of propitiation (satisfaction assuaging God's holy wrath against sin) and the second, as in the RSV, which regards the word as conveying only the thought of "expiation" (wipe out sin, removal of guilt). The two concepts are difficult to distinguish, but the former, more in agreement with Paul's argument, stresses specifically the wrath of God which is personally appeased by the sacrificial death of Christ. *Linguistically,* the word may be either a noun or adjective. As a noun it could mean "mercy seat" (LXX word 22 times for the golden lid of the ark where the blood was applied, Ex 25:21; also Heb 9:5) or "propitiation"; as an adjective the thought would be "a means of propitiation." Morris argues cogently for the latter (p. 172); F. F. Bruce *The Epistle of Paul to the Romans* (p. 105) for the former position. It is difficult to settle.

faction (propitiation) for us, which we in ourselves were incapable of presenting (Ro 5:8; Titus 3:4; 1 Jn 4:9-10). Something of this heart of God is captured by Elizabeth C. Clephane when she wrote,

> And though the road be rough and steep,
> I go to the desert to find My sheep.
> But none of the ransomed ever knew
> How deep were the waters crossed,
> Nor how dark was the night that the Lord passed through
> Ere He found His sheep that was lost.

The only adequate response to such love and grace is obedient faith. When one forsakes all his own works and former loyalties and casts himself totally upon Jesus Christ as God's propitiatory gift-sacrifice for his sin, he believes, in the biblical sense. At that point the saving righteousness of God becomes effective in his life (4:16-25).

But, Paul, why did Jesus have to die in order to reveal God's righteousness in the gospel? In verses 25-26 Paul attempts to answer this question. Jesus' propitiatory death first shows that God is really morally righteous. God showed restraint (forbearance; Gk. *anochē*, Ro 2:4) in not visiting wrath upon men's sins in the past ages before Christ came when "He passed over" (v. 25) their sins (not "remission" as KJV). Yet it was not due to moral indifference toward sin that He restrained Himself. Though the "sins previously committed" may be understood as sins in a person's life' before one becomes a Christian,[12] most understand Paul to refer to the sins of men in *former ages* before the governmental act of God occurred in Jesus' death. In days past God did not exercise His full wrath on men for their sins; He was patient and merciful with men (Ac 14:16; 17:30). But in Jesus' death God manifested the truth that He was yet not any less wrathful against sin. The supreme penalty for our sins was borne by Jesus. This allows God to remain God—morally perfect—and yet forgive and receive sinners.

So, too, in the present, God's justice and holy hatred of sin are still maintained even when He, in grace through the gospel, takes

12. C. A. Anderson Scott, *Christianity According to St. Paul* (New York: Cambridge U., n.d.), pp. 64ff.

sinners and puts them in right standing with Himself. Jesus' death vindicates the moral character of God (v. 26). Again (as in v. 24) Paul stresses the present tense of justification, "and the justifier (one who *is* justifying) of the one who has faith in Jesus." He wants to emphasize not only that justification occurs now in this life but also the idea of God's continual *empowering* of men to *be righteous*. Isaac Watts' familiar hymn captures well the sinner's response to such grace:

> When I survey the wondrous cross   .
> On which the Prince of glory died,
> My richest gain I count but loss,
> And pour contempt on all my pride.

> Were the whole realm of nature mine,
> That were a present far too small:
> Love so amazing, so divine,
> Demands my soul, my life, my all.

THE RESULTS OF GOD'S PLAN (3:27-31)

There are two results of this "faith alone" plan of justification. First, it excludes boasting (vv. 27-28). All boasting depends upon some supposed superiority earned through a system of good works (ethical and religious)—that is, pride of accomplishment. The faith system, on the other hand, depends totally on the merciful act of God in Jesus Christ's death. Since God acting in *grace* has done everything, there can be no grounds for human accomplishment. As D. T. Niles has so well put it, "Christianity is simply one beggar telling another beggar where he found bread." If heaven is to be a place where we go because of our good works, we would turn it into hell by going around—as we surely would—boasting of all we did to get there.

Second, this plan of salvation by faith alone establishes the true unity of God as God over all men (vv. 29-30). The Jew would be the first to confess that God is one (*shema*, Deu 6:4). How, then, Paul argues, could He be the one God of both Jews and Gentiles unless He had a plan of righting men with Himself that did not require all men to be Jews (circumcised). This plan is the faith plan that is equally valid for Jews (circumcised) and the Gentiles (uncircumcised).

But, Paul, doesn't what you have said about the faith plan (3:21-30) cancel out the law of God entirely? Paul answers emphatically, no (v. 31). In fact what he has said rather serves to "establish" (confirm, hold valid) the law. While Paul could mean by the word *law* the whole Old Testament (3:19),[13] the more immediate context (faith versus works of law) favors a slightly different view. He probably refers to the charge that by his gospel of grace he is allegedly setting aside the moral commands in the law. Since antinomian (no obligation to keep the moral law) charges against Paul are later raised and dealt with in detail by the apostle (chaps. 6-8), it is likely that he here simply makes the flat statement that the righteousness of God revealed in the gospel fully agrees with the moral nature of God revealed in the commandments of the Old Testament.

These verses (vv. 27-31) bring to a close the most crucial and concentrated argument of the whole letter (1:18—3:31). Before proceeding, it might be well to summarize briefly the two main focal points.

First, Paul has described the human situation from the divine perspective. Men, whether religious or irreligious, moral or immoral, have chosen to glorify themselves rather than their Creator. The man without the knowledge of God in the Bible asserts himself in the form of rebellion against the natural order and his conscience and by so doing claims freedom from God, only to find that in the end he debases himself and becomes inhuman. On the other hand, the religious cultured man with the knowledge of God in the Bible—or at least a sense of morality— asserts his rebellion by, in pride, refusing to repent before God. By substituting the worship of his own self-righteousness, he has failed to keep the true spirit of the Bible which is inward humble submission and obedience to the God of the Bible. Both kinds of people are equally under God's judicial wrath.

Second, all hope is not lost, because God has Himself powerfully acted in history for the acquittal of the guilty. His holy wrath against man's sin was meted out to Jesus Christ in his propitiatory

13. Paul's discussion of the faith of Abraham and of David (chap. 4) would then be taken as a proof of this assertion (see H. P. Liddon, *An Explanatory Analysis of St. Paul's Epistle to the Romans,* pp. 69-70; Barrett, p. 84; Bruce, p. 109).

death on the cross. God shows thereby that He is fully just and
able to put in the right all sinners who trust in Jesus Christ. To
explain this good news, Paul has pressed into service the language
of the law court (justify), slave market (redemption), and the
temple (propitiation). Men put their trust in God's act in Jesus
Christ and experience full pardon, deliverance from sin, and a
new standing before God. In the remainder of the epistle, Paul
will show the implications of this new status before God as it
relates to many different situations.

Abraham and Justification by Faith
(4:1-25)

Paul has established the principle that faith alone secures right
standing before God, not works of human achievement (3:21-31).
He has declared (3:27) that the faith system revealed in the
gospel excludes all boasting based upon human achievement. God
considers the faith of an individual, not circumcision, as the
ground for justification. Chapter 4 expands further on these points
and concludes Paul's major point on justification.

As far as the Jew was concerned, any discussion of the correct
approach to God must consider Abraham, the father of Israel.
Abraham is depicted in Jewish thought as having performed the
whole law before it was given. He was viewed as the perfect example of all Jewish virtues. Thus the case of Abraham was para-
mount. If he was not justified by works, then no man could be;
if he was justified by faith, there can be no other justification for
man. This chapter contains one of the most important discussions
in the Bible concerning the relationship between faith and works.
We will want to note very carefully the helpful material Paul
relates toward the end of chapter 4 stating the more exact nature
of faith.

Paul shows that Abraham was justified by faith and not by
works, as was also David (vv. 1-8). Since Abraham's circumcision
postdated his justification before God, it could not have caused
his acceptance (vv. 9-12). Furthermore, the promise given to
Abraham, that in his seed all nations would be blessed, was given
through the righteousness of faith and had nothing to do with the
law (vv. 13-22). Finally, Paul argues that the same God who

justified Abraham by faith likewise through faith justifies us in
Jesus Christ, who died for our sins and rose again for justification
(vv. 23-25).

ABRAHAM AND JUSTIFICATION (4:1-8)

Paul begins with an objection to his whole view of justification.
Paul, you say faith alone justifies before God, and therefore all
boasting is excluded. What about our father, Abraham? Wouldn't
virtuous Abraham, if he were in fact justified by works (as the
rabbis teach), have something to boast about? Paul replies, Yes,
he would, but in fact, before God, Abraham has no such grounds
for boasting. Whatever you were taught about Abraham's boasting, forget it. The Scripture settles the issue when it says, "Abraham believed God, and it was reckoned to him as righteousness"
(Ro 4:3; Gen 15:6).[14]

Current Jewish understanding of faith included the idea of
meritorious work. Paul interprets the Genesis passage in a fresh
light (vv. 4-8). First, he links together two pairs of opposites,
"Works" and "due" are linked and set off in opposition to "faith"
and "favor" (literally, grace). One who works gets paid, but one
who does not work (and yet gets wages) must be "reckoned"
(counted) as having gotten pay as a gift. Since Genesis says
Abraham had righteousness "reckoned" to him (Ro 4:11), it follows he must have received righteousness as a "favor" (gift by
grace) and not as a result of his works. As Abraham, so the one
"who does not work, but believes in Him who justifies [pres. tense
again] the ungodly, his faith is reckoned as righteousness" (v. 5).

The reference to God justifying the "ungodly" (impious) is
unique. At least two things clearly emerge: (1) justification (and
righteousness) is clearly at its initial stage a forensic (courtroom)
word which does not mean to make ethically righteous but "to
acquit" or "to grant a status of right;" and (2) since it is the un-

14. The Greek word *logizomai* means to count, reckon, estimate, consider,
ponder, credit (William F. Arndt and F. Wilbur Gingrich, *Greek-English
Lexicon of the New Testament and Other Early Christian Literature* [Grand
Rapids: Zondervan, 1963] S.V.). In the papyri it frequently means "to put
to one's account" (James H. Moulton and George Milligan, *Vocabulary of
the Greek New Testament* [Grand Rapids: Eerdmans, 1949] S.V.). The
KJV in vv. 3-11 uses "count," "reckon," and "impute" all for the same verb.
From v. 6 and v. 11 it is clear that what is credited to us is righteousness
(right status or relationship), not faith.

godly (not the ethically righteous) who are justified, Paul is describing a unique divine act of grace without precedent in human affairs.[15]

Paul appeals further to Israel's great king and sweet psalmist, David (vv. 6-8). David is helpful to Paul's argument because while Abraham lived prior to the law, David was squarely under it. David, unlike Abraham, was a flagrant violator of God's law and yet was forgiven by God. Using the interpretive principle that when the same word occurs in two biblical passages, each can be used to explain the other, Paul turns to Psalm 32:1-2 to show that David also teaches justification without works.[16] The "not take into account" (not reckon) of sin mentioned by David is equivalent to "the reckoning (counting) as righteousness" in Abraham's case. Both were acquitted without works because "reckoning" belongs only to the category of favor (grace or gift) and not merit (due). At each new turn in Paul's argument it becomes clearer that justification is not the just pronouncement on human merit (Jewish view), or the imparting of goodness, but gracious forgiveness of sin and release from judgment.[17]

15. Jewish thought also taught that justification was a forensic act of God, but that it only occurred at the last judgment and would be a favorable verdict based on the outweighing of the good works versus bad works (Morris, p. 242). In Greek usage "to justify the ungodly" would mean to *condemn* or punish the ungodly (TDNT). There may be an intended advance in thought between v. 7 where the plural is used ("those") and v. 8 where the singular occurs ("the man"). If such is the case, the first line of the psalm quotation describes God's act of forgiveness which forms the basis of His judicial act of not taking our sin into account (i.e., justification). Thus God justifies the ungodly by first forgiving them, then declaring a new reality to exist. He also transforms and empowers them so that they can act and become what they already are.

16. This is a well-known rabbinical principle known technically as *gezerah shawah* (C. K. Barrett, ed., *New Testament Backgrounds*, p. 146).

17. Can this section of Paul be reconciled with James 2:14-26 where James seems to argue that justification is by faith and works? In the first place, James was probably written before Romans so it could not be an attempt to refute Paul. Secondly, James's use of words "justified," "works," and "faith" is not the equivalent of Paul's. In James justification, as in Jewish thought, looks more at the *end* of one's life and whether the works done were in conjunction with real faith in Jesus Christ (see 2:1). Paul, on the other hand, views justification at the *beginning* of one's life in Christ and counts all works before that as unacceptable meritorious deeds. Works in James are like Paul's "fruit of the Spirit" (Gal 5:22-23); while Paul calls for "a faith working through love" (Gal 5:6), James likewise describes a "faith without works [that] is useless" (Ja 2:20). The essential message is the same, but the context and emphasis are different and must be carefully considered.

CIRCUMCISION AND JUSTIFICATION (4:9-12)

Paul, an objector interjects, Abraham and David were circumcised before this blessing of forgiveness could come to them, weren't they? How then can the uncircumcised ever be justified before God? Isn't it necessary to be circumcised and keep the law? (Ac 15:1).

Paul's answer revolves around the question of chronology. Abraham was in fact circumcised *after* he had been reckoned righteous: "not while circumcised, but while uncircumcised" (v. 10). He had been first acquitted by faith (Gen 15) and circumcised (Gen 17) about fourteen years later! Paul sees a divine purpose in this order. Abraham was to be the "father of many nations" according to the divine promise to him at the time when he believed God and was justified (Gen 15:5; Ro 4:17, 18). If his fatherhood consisted only in the Jewish people (circumcised) how could God fulfill the fatherhood of many nations of the promise? (vv. 17-18). But if his fatherhood consisted mainly in a lineage of those who like Abraham had received the "righteousness of faith" (v. 13), then the Gentiles (uncircumcised) could rightly be called the children of Abraham. He is first of all the father of the believing Gentiles and afterward the father of the circumcision (Jew) providing that they "follow in the steps [lit. Gk. *stoicheō* "join the ranks"] of the faith" (v. 12). Faith is independent of circumcision.

Why then was Abraham circumcised at all if faith is enough? Paul explains that circumcision was a "sign" (outward token) or a "seal" (assurance, confirmation) of the "righteousness of the faith which he had [already] while uncircumcised" (v. 11). When God renewed the covenant agreement with Abraham some fourteen years after he was counted as righteous (Gen 15), He changed his name from Abram to Abraham ("father of many nations"). As a visible seal (confirmation) that Abraham's original act of faith was accepted by God, God gave him the sign of circumcision as an evidence that he was acquitted by faith. Abraham was then to transmit this sign to a covenant people (Israel) who was to receive it as Abraham did, that is, as a seal of righteousness reckoned by faith.[18] Circumcision originally had nothing to

18. A good illustration of this is the old twenty-dollar gold piece. The

do with works of law. Correctly understood, the rite confirms the truth of justification by faith.

PROMISE AND JUSTIFICATION (4:13-22)

Paul already alluded to the promise to Abraham that he should be the father of many nations (vv. 11-12). He elaborates further in verses 13-22 on the relationship between the promise and the law of Moses. *Promise, faith, grace,* and *heirs* are joined by Paul and put in antithesis to law (vv. 13-16). In the first place the law did not come until 430 years after the promise (Ro 4:13; Gal 3:17). Second, the only principle that will insure the literal fulfillment of the promise to Abraham of being a father to "many" nations (vv. 17, 18) is faith. Since only the Jews were given the law, only one nation could participate in the blessing (forgiveness of sins, vv. 7, 9), that is, if the fulfillment of the promise depended on the law observance. Anyway, law works wrath because of sin and would be incompatible with the promise of blessing (v. 15).[19]

What is promise? Promise has the same nature as grace. His point here appears almost the same as in verses 4-5. Promise rests on complete trust in the one who has made the promise. It is not a legal contract where one stipulates pay for labor. Where labor is contracted, the man knows he will receive his due; but where all rests on the promise of the benefactor (grace), a man must believe to receive (as a gift) the promised benefit (v. 16). If law provides the basis of the inherited blessing, "faith" and "promise" have lost their meaning (v. 14).

What is faith? Verses 17-22 help us to understand further about the essential nature of Abraham's faith. Since this faith is like gospel faith, it is quite important. In the first place, Abraham's faith arose as a result of God's Word of promise to him: "A father

seal of the United States was imprinted on the coin as a sign that it was United States currency, but the value of the coin remained the same even if it was melted down and the seal obliterated. Now the same seal can be impressed on an iron slug, but the presence of the sign doesn't alter the intrinsic worthlessness of the slug. If the person who bears the sign of circumcision (Jew) does not have the intrinsic righteousness of faith, the sign is worthless. On the other hand, if a person has the intrinsic righteousness of faith and yet lacks the sign (Gentile), he is still accepted before God.

19. This verse has perplexed many. It certainly anticipates what Paul will develop further in 5:13-14. At any rate it seems parenthetical to his main thought, and the rest of the argument is quite clear.

of many nations have I made you" (v. 17). Authentic biblical faith only exists as response to divine revelation (10:17).

Second, his faith was directed toward God Himself. And Abraham's God was not unknown. He was a God "who gives life to the dead and calls into being that which does not exist" (v. 17). Abraham's God is a God who is the source of all life and resurrection, the Creator. For Abraham to father a child, when he was impotent and Sarah his wife barren, required a God who could act and create life from the natural deadness of the womb. Abraham, at the time of the promise of the child, Isaac, was about one hundred years old and Sarah about ninety (Gen 17:17).

Furthermore, faith has a future aspect in that it also accepts as certain before it is fulfilled what God has promised: "In hope [in God's promise] against [human] hope he believed" (v. 18). He simply in faith took God at His Word. Abraham was "fully assured"[20] and did not waver in unbelief at the promise of God (as those who denied this doctrine of justification were doing), but he gave glory to God (vv. 20-21). He did what those in chapters 1 and 2 failed to do. Abraham acknowledged God as God, the Creator, as such altogether different from creation (holy), powerful where man is weak, living where they are dead.[21] No such trust in works of law can give this kind of glory to God. Such faith God counted as righteousness to Abraham (v. 22). Such faith He will also count as righteousness to us.

ABRAHAM'S FAITH AND GOSPEL FAITH (4:23-25)

The same kind of faith that brought righteousness without meritorious works to Abraham's account also brings righteousness to us in the gospel of Jesus Christ. This trust finds its object in the same living God of Abraham. He is the God who raised up His own Son, not from a dead womb, but from the grave (v. 24). While the faith that brings acquittal and right standing before

20. Abraham's faith (and it was a biblical faith) was not based on doubt or factual uncertainty about God. This is the error of the whole neo-Protestant view of justification by faith. Faith has content and rests upon sufficient historical evidence to place it above reasonable or psychological doubt. See an excellent discussion by C. F. H. Henry, "Justification by Ignorance: A Neo-Protestant Motif?," *Journal of the Evangelical Theological Society* 13 (Winter 1970):3-14.
21. Barrett, *The Epistle to the Romans,* p. 98.

God today is not identical in *content* to Abraham's (promise of Isaac's birth), gospel faith is the same in *quality* (nonmeritorious) and in its object (the living Creator God, who gives men promises and brings life out of death). We are asked to trust not a theological idea or generalization, but the God who acts in history and in the death and resurrection of Jesus. Gospel faith like Abraham's faith involves trust in historical acts of God.

To believe in the God who raised Jesus from the dead is also to believe in the divine explanation of that death, "Him [Jesus] who was delivered up [in death] because of [on account of] our transgressions, and was raised because of our justification" (v. 25).[22] Faith is not a blind leap to a God who is totally unknown. Faith trusts in the God of forgiving grace who is revealed fully in the death and resurrection of Jesus of Nazareth.

Paul has harmonized his teaching about justification with the Old Testament by explaining the account of Abraham and his faith. He has finished his main argument. Paul has talked about (1) the human situation of man under the wrath of God because of rebellion (1:18—3:20); (2) the present and future deliverance of the sinner from this wrath through the gracious and substitutionary death of Jesus (3:21-31); and finally (3) the appropriateness and indispensability of faith as the only way of securing this acquittal before God by his argument based on Abraham (chap. 4). This is truly good news.

Paul at this point turns to consider the life and human situation of those who have by faith entered into this new status of acceptance before God (chaps. 5-8). Is the life of man altered in any way by his new relationship to God? Chapters 5 through 8 can profitably be viewed as Paul's effort to show that a new life actually exists, despite certain apparent problems to the contrary.

---

22. Paul uses identical words for the parallel work of Christ in His death and resurrection. The first "because of" (our offenses) seems to carry retrospective force, i.e., "because of our transgressions" Christ was put to death. The second instance, "because of our justification," could also be retrospective. However, it seems preferable to understand the last expression as prospective, "in order that we might be justified" (Bruce, p. 119; Barrett, *The Epistle to the Romans*, p. 100; Murray, p. 154). In any event no artificial separation of the effects of death and resurrection of Christ should be entertained.

4

The New Situation: Freedom from the Wrath of God

(5:1-21)

CHAPTER 5 marks a turning point in Romans. Paul can now assume the reader has accepted his argument for justification by faith and proceed to spell out the implications of this new relationship of grace in the lives of the justified ones. Paul shifts from argumentative to confessional style, from the second and third persons to the first, and from the indicative-declaratory tone to the subjunctive-hortatory. To accept God's free gift of righteousness also means to accept a new Lordship over the life. Chapters 5 through 8 deal with the nature and effects of this radical new life in the world founded upon the "grace" in which we stand (5:2).

Because God has dealt decisively in Jesus Christ with the twin problems of death and sin (5:12-21), a life of rejoicing and righteousness is for the Christian not a mere fancy but a genuine reality (5:1-11). For example, the Christian is enabled to overcome sin (chap. 6); he is no longer under the law system which he could never fulfill (chap. 7); and he is set free from the dominion of sin and death in order to live a new life of righteousness and hope in the power of the Holy Spirit (chap. 8).

THE BENEFITS STEMMING FROM FREEDOM FROM THE WRATH OF GOD (5:1-11)

Are there any benefits or fruits in the life which result from God's act of justifying us through faith? Paul relates that peace, joy, love, and hope mark the lives of those who have been justified

before God (5:1-11). Finally, in a very difficult section at the
end of chapter 5 (vv. 12-21), Paul portrays an analogy between
Adam and Christ where the oppressive rule of sin, death, and the
law is set over against the liberating dominion of righteousness,
life, and grace.

While certain things are clear in this section and the next it
must be admitted that the precise flow of Paul's thought in this
chapter is difficult. It is clear that positive blessings accrue to the
justified, such as peace (v. 1), joy (exult, vv. 2, 3, 11), love (vv.
5, 8), and hope (v. 2). On the other hand, it is not clear what
lies in the back of Paul's mind to evoke this emphasis. Perhaps
he is thinking of an objector who doubts that the faith method of
justification is safe after all. Can we really be sure, Paul, that
God justifies sinners simply by faith? Such an attitude lurking
beneath the surface of a person's mind could destroy any permanent rejoicing over a new status before God. In the "much
more" expressions (vv. 9, 10, 15, 17, 20), Paul, in using the common argument from the lesser to the greater, appears to be trying
to offset any feelings of *uncertainty* that his teaching may have
produced.

PEACE

The first consequence of having been justified by faith is "peace
with God" (v. 1). This peace is not first of all a psychological
tranquillity or peaceful feeling. Rather, this peace must be the
experience of the factual status of a man who has been justified
before God. It is the opposite of being under the wrath of God
(1:18). Man's relationship to God has been altered in justification
from one who is a rebel against the law of God to one who is fully
acquitted, forgiven, and empowered to a new life. Peace depicts
the consciousness of a new objective status before God the Judge.[1]

1. Some Greek manuscripts at this point read: "*let us* have peace with
God" (in the sense of "enjoy peace"). The change in one Greek letter in
the word (*echomen* to *echōmen*) makes the verb "have" a hortatory-sub-
junctive instead of an indicative. It is difficult to settle the matter. The context strongly favors the indicative over the subjunctive (see John Murray,
The Epistle to the Romans, p. 158; Anders Nygren, *Commentary on Romans*,
p. 193; C. K. Barrett, *The Epistle to the Romans*, p. 101), although some
argue that the third verb (exult in tribulations) in verse 3 favors the subjunctive idea based on an observation of actual Christian experience and thus all
three verbs should follow the mss. which read the subjunctive.

Of course, the inner contemplation of this objective fact can and should produce a real feeling of composure and security. Consider, for example, the results of being under the wrath of God as they are manifested in the life. Men experience alienation from self and others, loneliness, and lack of purpose. To not be any longer under the wrath of God should result in a positive consciousness of reconciliation with self and others and a meaningful reorientation to God's whole created order (2 Co 5:17). Such a peace distinctly alters our life. The thought of this kind of peace leads Paul eventually into a discussion of reconciliation (vv. 10, 11).

GRACE AND JOY

On the basis of this new reality of justification, Paul can now speak of "this grace in which we stand" (v. 2). Being totally accepted by God through faith, the man of faith has continual peace with God—the cessation of hostility—and enjoys living constantly by God's grace. For Paul grace encompasses not only the past free gift of forgiveness through the sacrificial death of Jesus (3:24), but also the whole present and future state of the believer. Such complete provision allows him to continually "exult." The past and the present having been thus secured, the Christian looks forward to the full manifestation of God's grace in the future; he rejoices in the "hope of the glory of God" (v. 2). The hope of glory comes before us further in chapter 8. Note well the nature of the new life. At the same time it is a life both present and coming, something at hand and a reality waiting for its future fulfillment.

Note here Paul's use of the interesting word "introduction" (v. 2). In Ephesians 3:12 the same Greek word is translated to give the picture of a worshiper gaining access to the holy place of God by means of a sacrifice. In nonbiblical literature the term can convey the thought of the admission of ambassadors to an audience with great kings (see 1 Pe 3:18).[2] Our relation to Christ has gained for us this introduction to God's grace.

Following the Civil War, a dejected confederate soldier was sitting outside the grounds of the White House. A young boy

2. TDNT 1:132.

approached him and inquired why he was so sad. The soldier related how he had repeatedly tried to see President Lincoln to tell him he was unjustly deprived of certain lands in the South following the war. On each occasion, as he attempted to enter the White House, the guards crossed their bayoneted guns in front of the door and turned him away. The boy motioned to the soldier to follow him. When they approached the guarded entrance, the soldiers came to attention, stepped back, and opened the door for the boy. He proceeded to the library where the President was resting and introduced the soldier to his father. The boy was Tad Lincoln. The soldier had gained an "introduction" (audience) with the President through the President's son.[3] How much more should we rejoice in our access to the grace of the King of kings.

HOPE AND SUFFERING

Christian rejoicing, however, is not only directed to the glorious future. Paul says, "We also [even] exult in our tribulations" (afflictions) (v. 3). We rejoice in the future hope of the glory of God, but we also rejoice in present trials. Why should trials be the occasion for joy in the Christian's life? Because they turn us away from trust in ourselves to "perseverance." But why is perseverance so valuable? Because perseverance, or endurance, is the attitude that looks beyond the immediate affliction to find its ultimate meaning in God (James 1:2-4).

Trials, rather than destroying our faith, actually develop a "proven character" (v. 4).[4] In a humbling type of experience distresses turn us away from self-trust to complete trust in God. Our persevering attitude in trials brings glory to Him and thus a tried, or proven, character to us (2 Co 11:30; 12:9). When we are brought to the place where we have nothing else but God, we suddenly realize He is all we need. When we thus look totally to God as a result of the trials, we are assured of His approval; and that approval strengthens our hope in the glory of God (vv. 4-5). Andrew Murray has captured the thought:

3. Abraham Lincoln, as cited by Donald G. Barnhouse, *God's River, Romans 5:1-11* (Grand Rapids: Eerdmans, 1958), p. 39.
4. The Greek is *dokimē* which means an object or person who is tested and shown to be reliable, trustworthy, valuable (see 1 Co 3:13; 1 Pe 1:6). In Phil 2:22 the same word refers to the "approved" or "qualified" (for missionary service) person of Timothy.

> First, he brought me here, it is by His
>   Will I am in this strait place; in
>   that fact I will rejoice.
> Next, He will keep me here in His love,
>   And give me grace to behave as His child.
> Then, He will make the trial a blessing,
>   Teaching me the lessons He intends me to learn,
>   and working in me the grace He means to bestow,
> Last, in His good time He can bring me out again—
>   how and when He knows.

I am here (1) by God's appointment, (2) in His keeping, (3) under His training, and (4) for His time. Thus, faith, rather than being insecure because of trials, actually uses suffering to strengthen our hope in God's future glory. It is by suffering that hope is tested and strengthened.

LOVE OF GOD

Further, this hope will not prove to be misdirected hope ("does not disappoint," v. 5). We know this because we already have the foretaste of its consummation—"the love of God has been poured out within our hearts through the Holy Spirit who was given to us" (v. 5). The pouring out of the Holy Spirit seems to vividly recall Pentecost (Ac 2). The love which has been poured out and continues to grip us (Gk. *ekcheō*, to pour out like a stream) is not our love for God (Augustine) but God's love for us (vv. 6-8). The validity of our hope is attested by the experience of the overwhelming of our hearts by God's love. We are made aware of this love by the presence and activity of the Holy Spirit who has been given to us at conversion (see Jn 7:37-39). This is Paul's first clear reference to the Holy Spirit in the epistle. Since everything in the Christian life depends on the Holy Spirit, Paul will develop this truth more extensively in chapter 8. He cannot leave this theme of God's love until he has said something further.

In verses 6-8, Paul elaborates on the nature of God's love which is best described by what it does. The description offers clear proof that God loves men, sinful as they are. God's love is demonstrated chiefly in the cross: "Christ died for us" (v. 8).

Paul is anxious to show us the unique nature of this love. God's love is totally unmotivated by any desirable qualities in the person loved. Paul calls us "helpless" (v. 6), "ungodly" (v. 6), "sinners" (v. 8), and even "enemies" (v. 10). While some men may evidence their love by giving their life for a just man (or cause), what is never heard of is a man dying for his enemy, yet this is precisely what Christ has done.[5]

In verse 9 Paul returns to the original thought of the paragraph of the benefits of justification. Since justification by Christ's blood is now a present reality—"We have peace with God" (v. 1)—the future is more than secured.[6] The "wrath of God" certainly refers to the future "day of wrath" and judgment of God (2:5). While salvation awaits its final consummation in the future, the evidence of God's love and grace shown in our present acquittal should more than assure us of future deliverance from the judgment of God.

Since parallel expressions are used in verses 9 and 10 for "justification" and reconciliation, we may assume they are different metaphors describing the same reality. However, the basic idea in reconciliation goes beyond justification and means to reverse an unfavorable relationship between persons. Men's relationship in sin before God constitutes them as "enemies" and requires the cessation of enmity and estrangement between man and God, or reconciliation: "If while we were enemies, we were reconciled to God through the death of his Son" (v. 10) refers to the past objective removal of the obstacle between God and man. The expression, "much more, having been reconciled [justified], to God . . . we shall be saved by His [resurrection] life," refers to our acceptance of God's reconciliation and looks forward again with certainty, based on the evidence of the cessation of enmity, that we will through the life of Jesus be completely delivered

5. The repetition in verse 7 seems redundant. There is no distinction here between a "good" man and a "righteous" man; both clauses express the same idea (Barrett, p. 106; Murray, p. 167). See J. B. Lightfoot in Murray, p. 33 for the opposite view.

6. "Justified by His blood" (or at the cost of His blood) refers back to 3:25 where the emphasis is on the propitiatory nature of Christ's death. It is essential to the gospel to stress that Christ's life was poured out in death (blood) as the satisfaction for God's wrath against man's rebellion. De-emphasizing the blood aspect of Christ's death tends to eliminate the wrath aspect of God's judgment upon man and the real significance of the gospel.

from God's final wrath (Ro 4:25; Heb 7:24, 25). Note that Paul always links our whole relationship to God (past, present, future) with Jesus Christ.

Verse 11 simply repeats the thought of verse 10 and adds Paul's note of rejoicing in the fact that we who believe in Jesus now possess this reconciliation.[7] Probably this idea of reconciliation, more than any other Paul has used, stresses that in justification there is a reversed relationship to God. Relationship to God affects the whole life of man (Col 1:20, 22; Eph 2:16). For a Christian a whole changed life results from his faith response to God's love gift in Christ (2 Co 5:19-21). Can we do otherwise than rejoice in this whole new situation of reconciliation? The whole matter of reconciliation might look like this pictorially:

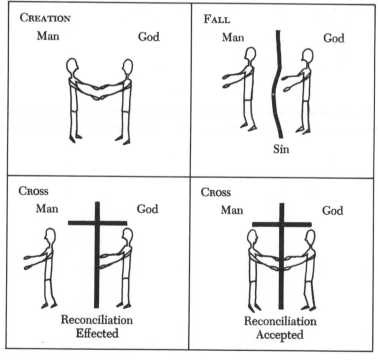

7. It is significant to note that Paul says we have *received* the reconciliation. There is a difference between the English word reconcile and the Greek term (*katallagē*). In English to speak of reconciliation as effected means

ADAM AND CHRIST
(5:12-21)

This passage (vv. 12-21) is generally recognized to be at the same time both the most profound and the most difficult in the whole book of Romans—if not the whole New Testament. Some see the section as an abrupt, unrelated, and generally unintelligible insertion into Paul's main argument. Others strongly insist it is the high point of the whole epistle, in the light of which the whole is best to be understood.[8] Some have also charged, perhaps justly, that it is precisely at this point in the book of Romans where evangelical theology, in failing to sustain interest, has weakened its position.[9]

The master thought of the whole passage revolves around the concept of two representative headships (Adam and Christ) and two consequent groups of mankind where each person is linked solidly to each other and to their respective heads. This explains Paul's constant use of the word "one," as in "one man" (v. 12), "one who sinned . . . One, Jesus Christ" (vv. 16-17), etc. The point to grasp is that Paul is viewing man's condition of fallenness (under condemnation), as well as his condition of savedness (acquittal), not first of all as an individual matter but, in the one instance as well as in the other, a matter of being *in* a representative (1 Co 15:22, 45-49).

Christ has a tremendous historical significance. When Adam departed from God, because he was the representative head of the whole human race, his act was not something that concerned only him as an individual. In Adam's act of disobedience, sin and death became universal in the whole historical human order. On

that both parties (offended and offender) are mutually reunited. On the other hand, while the Greek word may also denote this same idea (see 1 Co 11:11), it may also convey the thought of a one-sided process where the obstacle to fellowship has been removed and the objective reconciliation offered to the offender. God is not Himself reconciled but removes the obstacle to fellowship (God's holy wrath against man's rebellion) in the death of Jesus and now offers to sinful men this reconciliation as a free gift through faith (2 Co 5:17-19). For this view see TDNT 1:255ff. On the equally defensible view of dual reconciliation see Leon Morris, *Apostolic Preaching of the Cross*, pp. 186ff.

8. Nygren, p. 19.
9. Adolf Schlatter, cited in ibid.

the other hand, through Christ, the new representative man, in the same all-inclusive way, and even more so, life has become universal in the historical human order. Death in the Bible is not simply the termination of all bodily functions. Physical death ensues because of man's sinfulness and ultimately negates and condemns human life. It is death indeed because man dies as he has lived in a state of rebellion against his Creator and in alienation from his fellowman.

Life, on the other hand, is not the mere continuation of bodily functions. Instead, life follows from the gift of God's grace (righteousness, acquittal) through relationship with Jesus Christ. It is life indeed because of the blessedness in this human life of being freed from the slavery of sin and death (Heb 2:15), and because it leads on into the goal of an eternal life in this same blessedness.

Our solidarity with our fellows is a reality we often overlook in the assertion of our individuality. John Donne's oft-quoted words eloquently express the truth of human oneness:

> No man is an island, entire of itself; every man is a piece of the continent, a part of the main. If a clod be washed away by the sea, Europe is the less, as well as if a promontory were, as well as if a manor of thy friend's or of thine own were: any man's death diminishes me, because I am involved in mankind, and therefore never send to know for whom the bells tolls; it tolls for thee.[10]

If we ask whether human nature can ever be changed, Paul might answer, no and yes. In Adam the race can never be changed. But a new humanity has come to birth: the old "Adam-solidarity" of sin and death has been broken up and replaced by the new "Christ-solidarity" of grace and life. However, at the present time these two humanities overlap in the individual life of a Christian. Those who were formerly in Adam, even though now in Christ, still bear the sentence of bodily death belonging to Adam's race. But those who are in Christ have assurance that they have received from God that justification which brings resurrection life in its train.

10. John Donne, *Devotions upon Emergent Occasions* (Ann Arbor: U. Mich. Press, 1959), pp. 108-9.

Underlying the whole passage (vv. 12-21) may be the question of how the one individual man Jesus Christ in His death and resurrection could provide such a universal and certain hope of salvation. The subject of the reconciliation of mankind in verses 10-11 has perhaps stirred the question. Paul's answer lies, strangely, not in appealing to the deity of Christ, but to His perfect humanity. Jesus was representative man in *obedience* to God as Adam was representative man in *disobedience* to God. If the first man, Adam, could bring the whole race (in him) into sin and death by one act of disobedience, likewise (more so!) the Son of man, the last Adam, could bring the whole race (in Him) to acquittal and life by one act of righteousness (death on the cross).

In verses 12-14 Paul first emphasizes the headship of Adam. It may be seen in the following diagram:

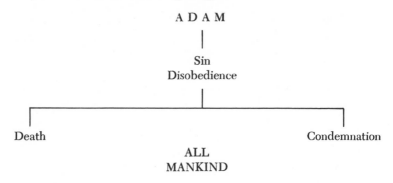

In passing, we may remark on the historicity of Adam, a debated subject in our day. If we insist on the necessity of not the mere idea of a representative in Christ but the actual historical figure of the man Jesus as essential to the gospel, then can we eliminate the need for an actual historical man, Adam, in favor of the idea of a mere symbolical representative? Can the idea, rather than the actual historical reality, form the valid counterpart to the necessary reality in Christ's actual historical significance? We believe it essential to Paul's argument that the first representative man, Adam, was as historically real as the last representative man, Christ.

Paul's expression stating the cause of universal death is: "because all sinned" (v. 12). This could mean that all men originally sinned in Adam as the head of the race (Augustinian seminal view). Another view affirms that all men die because they all commit individual acts of sin.[11] It seems clear that Paul is saying that there is a definite connection between the sin and death of Adam and the sin and death of all men (vv. 13-14, 15, 19). If death passes on to all men simply on the basis of their own individual sins, then it would be impossible to account for the death of infants who do not voluntarily sin. We can best adopt a third view, namely, that all men sin because they are born sinful due to their relationship to Adam, the head of the human race.[12]

Universal sinfulness is evidenced in the fact that even in the absence of any specific divine commandments from the time of Adam to the time of Moses, even though sin as violation of a revealed command was not imputed to men, sin was still universally and pervasively present among mankind and was death-inflicting (vv. 13-14). These verses most naturally support the view adopted above (v. 12) which understands that all men were constituted sinful in Adam's act of disobedience. Paul adds that Adam was a "type" of the one who was to come (i.e., Christ). Perhaps the word *analogy* would better suit Paul's use of the word "type," if understood as an historical counterpart. The only point of comparison between the two men is their representative headships of two mankinds while their respective representative act and its results are contrasted throughout the remaining verses (1 Co 10:6, 11). There really can be no adequate parallel to Christ, but Adam is the closest.

In verses 15-19 Paul sets forth in comparison and mostly by contrast the headship of Christ to that of Adam. Diagrammed, it might look like this:

11. The "for that" of the KJV is *eph ho* which means "because" (NASB). The Vulgate translation "in whom" (*in quo*) is a mistranslation but may reflect a true interpretation (F. F. Bruce, *The Epistle of Paul to the Romans,* p. 130). The "as" at the beginning of the section (v. 12) anticipates the completion of a comparison in a "so." The comparative "so" never seems to come. The sense though is clear from v. 19 where the "as" is repeated and followed with a "so" in a summary of the whole section.

12. Murray, p. 186; Bruce, p. 130; Nygren, p. 214. See also Russell Shedd, *Man in Community* (Grand Rapids: Eerdmans, 1964), especially chap. 3.

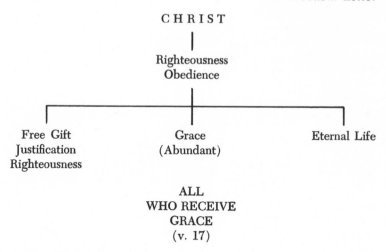

CHRIST
|
Righteousness
Obedience

Free Gift   Grace   Eternal Life
Justification   (Abundant)
Righteousness

ALL
WHO RECEIVE
GRACE
(v. 17)

Throughout, Paul goes out of his way to emphasize the fact that God's grace in Christ operates more inclusively and more intensively than Adam's sin and condemnation. He can only keep saying, "much more," "abounded," "abundance" in reference to Christ's work for man (vv. 15, 17, 20). Those who are touched by Adam's transgression are much more touched by one Man's act of righteousness.

Verse 17 is an important and beautiful verse. It refers to two governments or systems (death and grace) under which all men live: "Death reigned through the one, . . . those who receive the abundance of grace and of the gift of righteousness will reign in life" (v. 17). Man's chief problem is that he lives under the oppressive dominion of both personal sin and a corporate system of sin. Both dominions produce in him the fear of death. But through the "abundance of grace and of the gift of righteousness" (v. 17) he can be released from captivity and enter into a whole new existence of acquittal and life in the man Christ Jesus.

This life is available only to those who "receive" the gift (v. 17). In this way Paul recalls all he has taught about the indispensability of faith (chap. 4). The entire passage (12-21) neither teaches universalism[13] nor strict individualism but representation-

13. Universalism is the teaching that ultimately all human creatures of God will be saved through the universal redemption of Christ. Ro 5:18 and

alism. We got into the mess not by individual decision alone but by relationship to our old head, Adam; we get out of the mess not by individual decision alone but by relationship to our new head, Christ. Note well how Paul teaches emphatically the necessity of faith response or "receiving" this grace in order for justification and life to come to us.

In verses 18-19 Paul continues the contrast between Adam and Christ with the use of the words "all men" and "the many." Again the problem of universalism arises. But Paul's thought is that in Adam's trespass all men actually came under condemnation, whereas in Christ's righteous act[14] all men provisionally come under acquittal but only actually when they by faith receive God's gift (2 Th 1:8-9). The "many" of verse 19 could refer to the "all" of verse 18, but the expression "the many" refers to a group solidarity in a way that "all" men does not (Ro 12:4; 1 Co 10:17). Probably this latter fact guards the biblical doctrine of acquittal from the error of universalism, since only those who are in the "group" solidarity participate in the results of the representative's act. Only those who by obedient faith are in "the many" of Christ's headship participate in being constituted righteous before God (Mk 10:45).

But Paul, haven't you forgotten the most important historical event of all, the dispensation of the law? How does this affect salvation-history? At this point his answer is simple and to the point (later in chap. 7 a more elaborate answer is given): "The Law came in that the transgression might increase" (v. 20). Law "slipped in" (Gk. *parerchomai*) as an inferior part of God's chief plan (i.e., the promise, Ro 4; Gal 3:19). Why then the law? Law was added, Paul states, "that the transgression might increase" (v. 20). Sin is revealed in all of its fullness as rebellion only in the presence of divine law. Actually, law does not remedy the sin problem, it aggravates and even increases it (7:5-11). But the increase of sin through the law cannot defeat God's grace because:

1 Co 15:24-28 are especially appealed to for support of this teaching. Religious liberals, such as Nels Ferre and some neoorthodox theologians such as Karl Barth have in recent days advocated on different grounds the ultimate salvation of all men. See Bernard Ramm, *A Handbook of Contemporary Theology* (Grand Rapids: Eerdmans, 1966).

14. The Greek is *dikaiōma*, "righteous act" (TDNT). The same word occurs also in 5:18 as well as 2:26; 8:4.

"Where sin increased, grace abounded all the more" (v. 20). Finally, the main threads of the section are summed up in verse 21 by contrasting the rule of sin through the tyranny of death versus the new rule of grace through righteousness (acquittal before God) which leads to eternal life through (only through) the Lord Jesus Christ.

To summarize this section (vv. 12-21), we note that our forefather, Adam, as the first *representative man*, plunged the whole human posterity into sin and death. From such a predicament mankind could not of itself escape. On the other hand, as a result of the appearance of the second and last *representative Man* and His unmitigated obedience to God, even to His propitiatory death, there emerged a radically new humanity. This was possible because Jesus was from the beginning the incarnate Son of God. As a man He totally surrendered Himself to God even to death in order that that life which was peculiarly His as the obedient incarnate Son (i.e., eternal life), might spring forth to all His posterity.[15]

The human condition of man in sin in the world can indeed be changed, not by human action but only through divine intervention. Each element in this chapter converges upon the other to guarantee through God's grace the certainty of both the present love of God to us and our future security against any powers that would threaten to annul our eternal salvation. In the light of such certainty anything less than continual rejoicing is a mockery of God's truth.

---

15. "Eternal life" is that distinctive *quality* of the life that was manifested in the human life of Jesus Christ (see 1 Jn 1:2). It is eternal in its *quality* first of all rather than its duration (though it does go on forever), since it is the incarnate life of Jesus Christ. This emphasis keeps us from separating eternal life from the present experience. While it is future in one sense, it is also *now* in part in another sense (see Jn 5:24).

5

The New Situation: Freedom from Sin's Captivity

(6:1-23)

PAUL'S MAIN ARGUMENT and thesis of the letter is finished. He has advocated that all men are under condemnation as rebels against God, but the Creator has intervened on behalf of all men by providing acquittal and forgiveness for them through the substitutionary death of Jesus (1:18—3:31). Furthermore, he has stated that this acquittal before God comes to men individually irrespective of their moral virtues or lack of them. Acceptance before God comes solely by faith which trusts in the God who reveals Himself and who has acted for our salvation in Jesus' death and resurrection (4:1-25). Lastly he has described the grounds whereby they may be continually rejoicing in assurance of their future salvation (5:1-11). Again, such certainty rests not on their moral accomplishments (law keeping) but solely on the grace of God (5:12-21). Paul in fact even teaches that, as sin increases, grace increases the more (5:20).

It is at this point that the apostle moves perilously close to the edge of an abyss—one step to the side and all that he has gained by what has preceded, can be lost. For it would be easy to conclude, if we have understood Paul clearly, that, if the law is subordinate, and if grace is more manifested as sin increases, then why should Christians be morally good? Why not go on sinning that the supply of grace might be increased (v. 1)? Will not God be the more glorified because our continual sin will continually manifest His grace? This is the antinomian (complete moral freedom) error that misunderstands Christian freedom and unfortunately has been present in every era of Christianity including today's. The grace of God in Jesus Christ is indeed freedom (Ro 6:15-18; Gal 4-5), but freedom *from* sin, not freedom *to* sin (1 Pe 2:16).

A notable historical instance of the abuse of Paul's teaching can be seen in the Russian monk, Rasputin, the evil genius of the Romanov family in its last years of power. Rasputin taught and exemplified the doctrine of salvation through repeated experiences of sin and repentance; he held that, as those who sin most require most forgiveness, a sinner who continues to sin with abandon enjoys each time he repents more of God's grace than any ordinary sinner.

In Paul's day the form of the argument that abused the doctrine of justification took two twists. Paul devotes the lengthy section of chapters 6 through 8 to answering these two objections. The first is an ethical objection introduced by the question, "Are we to continue in sin that grace might increase?" (6:1). This is answered in 6:2-14 by Paul's appeal to the reality in the believer's life of a radical inner change witnessed to in baptism and consisting in the fact of the believer's crucifixion and resurrection with Christ.

The second objection is more of a legal problem introduced likewise by a question in 6:15, "Shall we sin because we are not under law, but under grace?" Paul answers this distortion by first appealing to the true nature of Christian freedom, namely, captivity to righteousness (6:15–7:6); second, by showing the true function of the Mosaic law (7:7-25); and third, by illuminating the nature of the life of freedom in the Spirit in chapter 8. These are the most important chapters in the entire New Testament for establishing that the Christian life is continual moral renewal and progressive holiness.

Union with Christ in His Death and Resurrection
(6:1-14)

The charge (v. 1), it may be recalled, was to the effect that since more sin calls forth more grace (5:20), shall we not go on sinning to get more and more grace? Paul's first reaction is abhorrence, "May it never be!" (v. 2).[1] Then he states that such a conclusion embodies an inherent contradiction: "How shall we who died to sin still live in it?"[2] At the outset we can note that this fact of the Christian having died to sin is the fundamental premise of the whole argument in the chapter. The "who" of the verse is a specialized Greek form (*hoitines*) which gives this paraphrased sense: We who in our essential nature are Christians (acquitted in Christ), *we* have died. Death and life are not compatible. To be a Christian means to have died to sin. Therefore, it is a fundamental moral contradiction for a Christian to be still living in the sin to which he has died.[3]

But how did we die to sin? To answer this question, Paul uses three metaphors. He first appeals to the import of our death to sin in the metaphor of Christian baptism. Certainly the truth of their death to sin was known to all the Christians at Rome: "Do you not know?" Yet how much of its real significance did they actually know? It may be difficult to know exactly where Paul depends upon common knowledge and where he goes beyond popular understanding to the fuller implication. But we may assume that they at least knew that to be "baptized into Christ Jesus" was equivalent to the fuller expression to be "baptized into the name of Jesus Christ" (Mt 28:19; Ac 2:38; 10:48; 19:5).

To be baptized into the name of Christ meant to be baptized (placed into) union with Jesus Christ. To be baptized into Moses was to come under the authority of Moses' leadership and to be a participant in all of the privileges of that included (1 Co 10:2). To be baptized into the name of Paul meant to be baptized into the discipleship and dedication of Paul, an idea that Paul passionately rejected (1 Co 1:13, 15). Hence, baptism into Christ means baptism into union with Him, into dedication to Him, and participation in all that Christ is and has done. Now if baptism

1. See note 33 of chapter 2.
2. The rendering "dead to sin" (KJV) misses the force of the definite past tense of the indicative verb by giving the effect of a status of death rather than the specific past event of conversion. The NASB "died to sin" is preferred.
3. To "live" in sin suggests not occasional sin but to have sin as the moral atmosphere which our lives breathe (E. H. Gifford, "Romans" in *The Bible Commentary:* New Testament, 3:125).

means that Christians are united to Christ, it means first of all that we are united with Him in His death, that is, to use a second metaphor we are co-crucified with Him (v. 6).

Furthermore, our union with Christ means that not only are we identified with Christ to the extent that we are "buried with Him through baptism into death" (v. 4), but in the same manner we are also united to Him in His resurrection (vv. 5, 8) so that now we might walk (conduct ourselves) in a new (resurrection) life (v. 4).[4] This new quality of resurrection life is later pointed out to be a kind of life which is lived in full obedience to the glory of God (v. 10).[5]

Paul proceeds in verse 5 to reinforce this fact that to be united with Christ means to participate both in His death and also in His resurrection life: "For if we have become united with Him (Gk. *symphutoi*, grown together) in the likeness of His death, certainly we shall be also in the likeness of His resurrection" (v. 5). The words "grown together" and "likeness" are very difficult to understand. This third metaphor, "grow together," may be understood in the sense of a tree graft. Again, the figure used stresses vital joining or fusing.

But does "likeness of His death" refer to baptism or to the actual

4. The assumption of many to the effect that Paul has in mind by the use of the word "buried" the immersionist mode of baptism is not necessarily warranted. There does not seem to be similar imagery in the uses of "united" (fused) (v. 5) or "crucified" (v. 6). Baptism itself signified full identification with Christ in His death to sin. One could see baptism as immersion if water baptism signified *only* death (under the water) and not also resurrection. Such may actually be the case.

5. From this point onward Paul drops the figure of baptism and speaks directly about our identification with Christ's death and resurrection. One of the major assumptions about baptism upon which these verses depend is that baptism is always linked closely with the conversion experience (faith in Christ) not as the efficacious element in justification, otherwise Paul would have dealt with it in chapters 3-5 (see Ac 10:48; 1 Co 1:18), but more as the seal or symbol of the righteousness given by faith (see 4:11). A true symbol is not the reality itself but points to something beyond itself as the actual reality. But there is a sense in which a symbol participates to some extent in the reality to which it points. Water baptism is the symbol which points to the already established reality of the codeath. While some argue for just Spirit baptism in this passage (W. H. Griffith-Thomas, *Commentary on St. Paul's Epistle to the Romans* [Grand Rapids:Eerdmans, 1946]), almost all commentators understand Paul to be referring only to water baptism. Probably *both* are in view. See the excellent discussion of this passage in James D. G. Dunn, *Baptism in the Holy Spirit* (Naperville, Ill.: Allenson, 1970), pp. 139-51.

death of Christ? Probably neither. It signifies neither complete identity (that which is) nor mere similarity (that which is similar to) but a very close likeness (that which is precisely like). So it refers neither to water baptism nor to the death of Christ itself but rather to the spiritual transformation which takes place at conversion when we become united with a death to sin precisely like Christ's. It is not required that we should die the actual physical death of Christ but to die as Isaac did in the similitude and figure of his death; that is, to die to sin. Thus also the expression, "We shall be also in the likeness of His resurrection" does not necessitate now an actual physical resurrection like Christ's but simply shows that the value of our union with Him now in His resurrection makes possible the distinctively new life of the Christian. The "likeness of His resurrection" is the "newness of life."[6]

It seems that Paul has in mind in these verses *both* the inward reality of death to sin and the rite of water baptism. Water baptism, however, should be viewed in the context of the early church where it was the means of expressing one's faith in Jesus Christ. As such the reality and the rite are closely linked. However, it is also clear in Paul's teaching that it is faith-response to the gospel which effects the reality of salvation and not the rite itself (1 Co 1:17).[7]

More specifically, "our old self was crucified with Him" (v. 6). The old self refers to the whole unregenerate man as seen in Adam: man's life-style under the rule of sin and death, judgment and condemnation (5:12-14). Under this figure the radical and comprehensive nature of the changed life situation of the Christian is highlighted (Gal 2:20; 2 Co 5:17). Such cocrucifixion took place for the purpose that "the body of sin might be done away with" (v. 6). The "body of sin" does not refer to the human body as such. It either refers to the individual human body in its old condition as a slave of sin[8] or, more broadly, it means the old race solidarity of sin and death which all share in Adam.[9] In either

6. Gifford, p. 127.
7. George R. Beasley-Murray, *Baptism in the New Testament* (London: Macmillan, 1962), pp. 271-73.
8. Gifford, p. 128.
9. F. F. Bruce, *The Epistle of Paul to the Romans*, p. 139.

case the emphasis lies in the distinctively new life into which we have been introduced through Jesus Christ.

This old condition was "done away with" (v. 6). The Greek verb for "done away with" is *katargeō*, meaning "to make completely inoperative" or "to put out of use." The very purpose then of being so united to Christ in His death is to bring about our freedom from the slavery of sin. Paul views this from the analogy of being slaves to the master of sin in our old condition, "he who died [with Christ] is freed [Gk. *dikaioō*, 'justified' or 'acquitted'] from [the] sin [master]" (v. 7).[10]

Does this imply that Christians no longer can or do sin? Experience would answer an emphatic, no. Paul also recognizes that bonafide Christians (justified ones) may in fact sin (1 Co 1:2, 9, 11; 3:1-4; 5:5; 6:11). What Paul is teaching is that the desirability and necessity of sin have been broken. The Christian *may* sin, but the fact is that he no longer *must* sin because this power of the sinful human life in Adam is annulled.

But how can the broken power of sin over our lives be actually realized in our day-to-day experiences? Is the Christian life merely a negative activity of ceasing to do things we formerly practiced? Paul answers these questions by focusing attention on the positive side of our union with Christ. This is really the answer to the crucial question posed in verse 1 of why Christians should lead a moral life. In thinking of the death of Christ, our attention is immediately focused also on the historical counterpart of that death, the resurrection of Jesus.

In verses 8-10 the apostle describes the kind of death Jesus died and the kind of resurrection life He now lives. Jesus "died to sin, once for all" (v. 10). Christ died once for all to the power of sin over his life. It is not that He Himself sinned, but in His total identification with us as sinners on the cross, He experienced the power of sin ruling over Him and bringing Him to death (2 Co 5:21; 1 Pe 2:24). He died once in obedience to God, yet under sin's power in order that He might break the power of sin's enslavement over our lives (8:3). Now Christ raised from the dead

10. Some see here (v. 7) a reference to a general maxim that men are no longer liable for supposed sins committed after their actual death (H. P. Liddon, *An Explanatory Analysis of St. Paul's Epistle to the Romans*, p. 111).

lives a life totally for God only. He lives in complete obedience—
He never lived otherwise—to God, yet without facing the prospects of sin and death ever again. So Christians who died this
kind of death (once for all victory over the power of sin) also
share with Christ in this new life (totally for God, of willing
obedience to Him). If this is true, any suggestion that faith-
righteousness leads us to continue living in sin and disobedience
is entirely contrary to the facts of our new relationship to Christ.

But this victory over sin in the life is not an automatic process.
Paul states that we must continually (present tense) "consider
yourselves to be dead to sin [as an enslaving power], but alive
to God in Christ Jesus" (v. 11). The practice of victory over enslaving sin comes not by trying harder or by self-abnegation but
by "considering." This is the same word used to describe God's
"reckoning" righteousness to Abraham by faith (4:3). "In Christ
Jesus" we are newly related to God. This new relationship has
put us in an entirely different position to the formerly enslaving
sin. When a solicitation to do evil (to disobey God) confronts us,
we are to count on the fact that we are now in Christ, part of a
new humanity that is freed from the old captivity that led us to
follow sin's dictates. Furthermore, we are alive with Christ's resurrection life to serve in obedience to God. Christ's victorious
death to sin's power is also our victory; Christ's resurrection to
continual life and obedience to God is also our new life.

But, one may sigh, after all, Paul, aren't we still human? Don't
we live in a world full of lust and evil desires? Paul answers in
verses 12-14 with exhortations based on the truth he has established in verses 1-11. The "lusts" (Gk. *epithumiais*, desires) are
the values that lead us away from obedience to Christ (v. 12).
They are the grave clothes that are carried over from the former
life to the new. Specifically, they are the habits of sin learned in
the old Adamic life style. We are no longer to respond to them
because we are "as those alive from the dead" (v. 13). For the
Christian, life is a great paradox. He is dead to sin but still lives
with it; he is alive with Christ, yet still in the mortal body; he is
fully righteous by God's justification but still a sinner needing to
progress into full obedience to God in sanctification (v. 19). The
Christian lives between two ages. He is called upon to live now

in the old age as if the new age had already come ("as those alive," v. 13). In reality, the believer through justification already participates in the future glory in Christ.

The key to this new life lies in: (1) "considering" (v. 11) and (2) "presenting" (v. 13). To "present" (Gk. *paristanō*) means to place at the disposal of another for service. As Christians we are to stop offering our members (such as eye, hand, foot) to sin as "instruments" against God for establishing unrighteousness. Rather, we are without delay to abandon our whole beings to God as alive in the resurrection life of Jesus and offer our bodily members to God as weapons against evil for establishing righteousness (v. 13). Needless to say, the continual moment-by-moment presentation of our bodily members to God can only be done after we have unreservedly presented our wills to Him. This distinction is reflected in the translation where the two different Greek tenses Paul uses for the two occurrences of the verb "present" in verse 13 are handled differently.[11]

In verse 14, Paul states that sin will not lord it over us because we are "not under law, but under grace." What does it mean to be not under law but under grace? While there are different views, Paul probably does not have in mind the Christian's release from the moral nature of the commandments (which he is arguing against), but freedom from the law as a system of both justification and striving after ethical goodness (sanctification). The law system causes sin to be strengthened and multiplied (5:20) because it offers nothing but condemnation to its violators (4:15; 7:10) due to the weakness of sinful human flesh (8:3). Hence, to be under law is to be under enslavement to sin because law aggravates sin and condemns the sinner, and yet in itself it has no power to deliver the transgressor.

Grace, on the other hand, stands for the whole delivering power and virtue of Christ's death and resurrection and our union with Him in that death and resurrection. Grace was manifested to

11. There is a play on the Greek tenses in the two occurrences of "present" in v. 13. In the first instance the present tense is used with the negative. The sense is "stop presenting." In the second instance the Greek aorist tense is used with the effect of an immediate, decisive, and final act: "abandon yourself at once forever." It should also be noted that "righteousness" as Paul uses the term in this verse carries with it the rarer idea in Paul of ethical goodness.

remove us from the enslavement to sin by providing all that we need to serve God in obedient love. Do we see then how contradictory it is to ask whether we should live in sin that grace may abound?

BONDAGE TO RIGHTEOUSNESS
(6:15-23)

While the moral problem of freedom from law is picked up more specifically in 7:1-6, Paul does begin in a general way to answer this obvious difficulty. He has just stated that we are free from the law and under grace (6:14). An objector might say, well, if that's the case, Paul, can we not ignore the law, and sin (violate law) since the law no longer is over us? Again Paul answers the question as before (v. 2) with an emphatic "may it never be!" (v. 15). This response clearly shows that to be free from the law does not mean to be indifferent toward God's moral commands. Freedom from law is not freedom to sin. Without God's moral law man loses the ability to recognize the seriousness of sin. Law may be powerless to prevent sin, but God's commands at least ensure that sin will be taken seriously. Since God's law reveals His will, the Christian can never be indifferent toward it. There is a sense in which the Christian is not under law and another sense in which he is (Ro 13:8-10; 1 Co 9:21). In our day of moral relativism it is especially important to listen carefully to Paul's teaching. More on this later (13:9-10).

In verses·16-23, Paul describes Christian freedom as bondage or enslavement to the will of God (righteousness). He employs the natural analogy ("human terms," v. 19) of the slave-master relationships to press home his point.[12] When a person presents himself willingly in obedience as someone's servant, he then becomes exclusively *that* master's servant and no one else's (v. 16). The slave-master analogy is quite appropriate since no one could be the slave of two different masters at the same time. The nature of slavery precludes it. Jesus said, "No man can serve two masters . . . You cannot serve God and Mammon" (Lk 16:13; see Jn 8:34). In a man's heart (religious center of human existence)

12. This is certainly Paul's point in verse 19 when he says, "I am speaking in human terms" or in human illustration.

only two options are available for his obedience. A man chooses as his master either sin or God. To choose to be free to follow one's own desires is actually to choose sin as master (v. 12). Sin leads ultimately to eternal death; obedience to God leads to eternal life (v. 23).

Paul is confident that the Romans have responded to that "form of teaching" (or pattern of teaching) preached in the gospel concerning obedience to God through Jesus Christ (v. 17). Note that the gospel came to them with definite content because they became "committed" to it (Ro 6:17; 1 Co 15:3).[13] We see from Paul's mention of this "form of teaching" that the gospel was not Paul's only; it was the common Christian message. The good news not only freed them from captivity to sin, but it also enslaved them to their new master, righteousness (v. 18). They were freed from sin to be servants of God and righteousness (ethical goodness, in this context).

Paul continues his exhortation to the effect that we should no longer put our bodily members at the disposal of impurity (serving one's passions) leading to more and more wickedness (moral indifference), but to offer those bodily members to the disposal of righteousness (the will of God) for "sanctification" (v. 19). The term "sanctification" (Gk. *hagiasmos*, better: "sanctifying") is part of a word group in the New Testament including the words "holy," "saint," "purify," "hallowed," and "holiness." It means first of all to be set apart wholly for the use of service of God. Secondly, it means to acquire, because of this relationship, certain moral qualities of the one to whom we are set apart. Sanctification proceeds from justification, as fruit from the vine, and never justification from sanctification (i.e., the tree from the fruit). The process of sanctification is the work of the Holy Spirit, and Paul will develop this in chapter 8.

Finally, the passage stresses again the contrast between obedience to sin in the former non-Christian life and obedience to God (vv. 20-23). The service done for sin and the service done for

13. Actually the verb is passive in voice and second person plural. The NASB correctly renders: "to which [pattern of doctrine] you were committed." They were delivered to the teachings of the Word of God, which created them in Christ and ruled their life. It is still true, however, that this body of truth was also delivered unto them (see 1 Co 11:23; 15:3; 2 Th 3:6).

God each produces its own reward or fruit and also its own end (final) product. Sin's fruit consists in things of which the Christians are now ashamed and leads ultimately to (eternal) death (v. 21). God's fruit, on the other hand, consists in sanctification (ethical goodness) (Ro 6:19; Gal 5:22-23) and ultimately leads to eternal life (v. 22). To sum up, Paul states that the old sin master (life in Adam, 5:12-14) pays the ultimate wages of death.[14] Sin is a deceiver, it offers life and ends up paying death. As the "wages" are a continuous process, "death" may be thought of as not only the ultimate pay but also as casting its shadow back into the present existence. On the other hand, the free gift of God (not wages) offers finally eternal life in Jesus Christ our Lord (v. 23), which also casts its shadow back into this life.

So the new rule of grace through justification by faith leads not to a life lived in sin but to a new life with Christ in the service of righteousness (God's will). The rule of sin under the law system which enslaved men has now been broken and replaced by the rule of grace. But the Christian takes sin seriously because grace, rather than freeing us to be servants of our own sinful passions, has instead enslaved us to God and His righteousness with the result of fruitful service and ethical sanctification.

The keynote then for the Christian life is single-minded obedience to God's will revealed in Jesus Christ our Lord. The controversial German theologian, Dietrich Bonhoeffer, has written some noncontroversial words about this *costly grace*:

> Cheap grace means the justification of sin without the justification of the sinner . . . who departs from sin and from whom sin departs. Cheap grace is *not* the kind of forgiveness of sin which frees us from the toils of sin. Cheap grace is grace without discipleship, grace without the cross, grace without Jesus Christ, living and incarnate. Costly grace is the grace of Christ Himself, now prevailing upon the disciple to leave all and follow Him. When he spoke of grace, Luther always implied as a corollary that it cost him his own life, the life which was for the first time subjected to the absolute obedience of Christ. Happy are they who, knowing that grace, can live in the world without being of

14. The Greek *opsōnion,* wage or pay, used especially for military service as a *bare* allowance (TDNT); see Lk 3:14.

it, who, by following Jesus Christ, are so assured of their heavenly citizenship that they are truly free to live their lives in this world.[15]

But what about this matter of the law (6:14)? How did we get from law rule to righteousness rule? What about the law then? Isn't it a bad deal after all? Why was the law given? We must hear Paul further in chapter 7 for these answers.

15. Dietrich Bonhoeffer, *Cost of Discipleship*, p. 47.

6

The New Situation: Freedom from the Law's Domination

(7:1-25)

THIS CHAPTER CONTINUES to answer the objection that to be under the rule of grace and not law is to be indifferent toward sin. Paul has already answered this objection in one aspect by showing that the Christian is free from sin only to be a slave of God and righteousness (6:15-23). Previously Paul has simply made assertions about the law: "Now we know that whatever the Law says, it speaks to those who are under the Law, that every mouth may be closed, and all the world may become accountable to God; because by the works of the law no flesh will be justified in His sight; for through the Law comes the knowledge of sin" (3:19-20);. "Do we then nullify the Law through faith? May it never be! On the contrary, we establish the Law" (3:31); "the Law brings about wrath; but where there is no law, neither is there violation" (4:15); "the Law came in that the transgression might increase" (5:20); "Shall we sin because we are not under law but under grace?" (6:15).

Paul's statements about the law seem to contradict one another. On the one hand he obviously takes the law (that is, the Jewish law as contained in the Old Testament to be the definitive expression of God's will for the ordering of human life (2; 3:31). On the other hand, he maintains that the law does not enable man to escape the sinful and death-oriented existence in which he finds himself (3:20; 4:15; 5:13, 20). Chapter 7 provides some clues in reconciling these apparent opposite polarities.

The history of the controversy over the function of the law in the Christian life is long and varied. Luther viewed the law as playing only a two-fold negative role: (1) Its *civil* function is to restrain sin by threatening punishment, and (2) its *theological* function is to increase sin especially in the conscience and show man how corrupt he actually is. Calvin, on the other hand, attempted to synthesize gospel and law and saw its primary purpose for the Christian as *didactic* or *instructional*, to help him understand God's will and excite him to obedience. Paul Althaus, a contemporary German theologian, has in recent days suggested another thesis. He understands the New Testament to teach that God's loving commands which express His desire for our fellowship have through the fall become law, and as such are negative and prohibitive rules that condemn man. Yet through the gospel the same law is transformed once again into the loving commands of God. In this sense he would concur with Calvin that the Christian is free from legalism but not from the command.[1] Not to clarify this distinction between law and legalism can lead to two extremes: (1) modern pharisaism and (2) pure license in the name of "freedom."

Today the relationship of the law to Christian ethics has received renewed interest because of the popular teaching of the situation ethicists who maintain that the only absolute norm for the Christian is love. To the situationist, such as Joseph Fletcher, to be governed by the norm of divine commands is legalism. According to him, if I determine that love (as I understand it) is better fulfilled by setting aside one or all of the divine norms in any given situation, I am at liberty and must set them aside.[2] Since the apostles rejected moral lawlessness (1 Jn 3:4-6), the question of the Christian's relationship to the law or commands may be crucial in understanding who are authentically Christ's disciples today.

1. Paul Althaus, *The Divine Command*, trans. Franklin Sherman (Philadelphia: Fortress, 1966). A short but helpful treatment of the law before and after conversion.
2. Joseph Fletcher, *Situation Ethics* (Philadelphia: Westminster, 1966). A popular treatment of the viewpoint.

THE MARRIAGE ANALOGY
(7:1-6)

The question of why sin will not enslave us because we are now under grace and free from the law (6:14) comes to the fore. It is for Paul the most important and yet the hardest point in his extended discussion. First, the general truth is stated that it is the nature of law (of any kind) to only have power over a person as long as he lives (v. 1). For example, the law of marriage (either Jewish or Roman) binds two people together as long as both are alive. But if the husband (or wife) dies, the law that binds the two in marriage is canceled and in this case the widow is no longer under obligation to the law of marriage. She would be legally considered an adulteress if, while her husband was alive, she was to join herself to another man; but, when her husband is dead, she is no longer bound by the law and may marry another (vv. 2-3).

Thus far this is all Paul has said. His point is not to teach for or against divorce in this context. He simply wants to illustrate the fact that in commonly accepted terms death sets aside marriage law obligations.

But what does it mean? We should not attempt to press Paul's analogy into a full allegory (where every part has an analogous counterpart), otherwise it will not be completely appropriate. In the application of the analogy which he gives in verse 4, the Christian corresponds to the woman in the illustration and the law to the husband. As the law binding a woman to a man is set aside by the man's death, so the law to which men formerly owed allegiance is set aside through our dying with Christ. A death having taken place allows a new marriage to ensue (i.e., to the risen Christ). Whereas we were formerly bound by the law (of Moses), now we have been "made to die to the Law through the body of Christ,"[3] and we are free to be united to another Lord "even to Him who was raised from the dead." The thought parallels chapter 6:5-8 and Galatians 2:19-20: "For through the Law I died to the Law, that I might live to God. I have been

---

3. We must be careful to note that Paul does not say that the law died, but that we died. Again this shows us that the analogy cannot be pressed too far without doing violence to Paul's thought.

crucified with Christ; and it is no longer I who live, but Christ lives in me." Why was death to the law necessary? So that the "fruit" of the Spirit might spring forth (vv. 4, 6).

Why wasn't the law able to bring life and fruit for God? Because before we were Christians ("while we were in the flesh")[4] the passions or impulses connected with sins were aroused in us through the law (v. 5). These passions used our bodily members to produce thoughts and acts characterized by death. It is the same idea which Paul developed in 6:20-22 with the added connection in this context between law and sin. Such was our condition—outside of Christ and grace. "But now" (v. 6) that we are Christians, married to the resurrected Christ, we have been released (v. 2) from the Mosaic law which held us captive. "Newness of the Spirit" (v. 6) is a reference to the Holy Spirit (ch. 8) who effects the newness of life in service to God; while the "oldness of the letter" refers to the legalistic approach to the written tables of the law (2 Co 3:4) which were powerless to effect a righteous life before God because in the context of the whole law system they brought condemnation. But how or in what sense did the law of God hold us "bound"? (v. 6).

Paul with his Jewish contemporaries had believed that in the keeping of the law was found the only way to acceptance and peace with God (Deu 4:1; 6:25; Ro 7:10). As a Pharisee in pursuit of God's justification, he attempted to keep the strict legal observances of the whole law (Phil 3:6). Now as a Christian Paul views the law in a negative fashion as arousing sin (5:20; 7:8) and leading a person to death and condemnation (7:9, 10; 2 Co 3:7, 9). Why had his view of the law been so radically reversed? The only adequate answer lies in his confrontation with the risen Lord on the Damascus Road and his acceptance of Jesus as the Christ of God (Ac 9).

But how did this change his view of the law? Something like this: Jesus was alive! This meant that God had accepted Him and the curse of the cross was not Jesus' own but ours (Gal 3:10-

4. Paul uses "in the flesh" (Gr. *sarx*) in two different senses depending on the context. Christians are in the flesh in the sense of being in the mortal body (2 Co 4:11; 10:3; Gal 2:20; Phil 1:22, 24); yet they are no longer in the flesh in the sense of being dominated by sin, death, and law (Ro 7:5; 8:9; Gal 3:3; 5:24).

13). Paul had kept the law blamelessly, yet he had agreed in the justice of the crucifixion of the young Nazarene carpenter! He kept the law (he thought) and yet was still the "chief of sinners" because he persecuted those who believed on Jesus as the Messiah (1 Ti 1:13, 15). The law then had not made him righteous before God, because he had misappropriated it as the occasion for sinful boasting in his own goodness. The law had worked just the opposite effect in Paul from what he had supposed. Instead of making him righteous before God, it really had condemned him. How then does sin pervert the right use of the law?

The True Nature of the Law
(7:7-25)

Actually Paul found in his experience that the law which promised to promote life, instead provoked sin in him, and as sin increased death ruled. How so? When the law was originally given to Israel at Sinai (Ex 20), it also offered the promise of life for those who did the law (Deu 4:1). Yet in Paul's view "if a law had been given which was able to impart life, then righteousness [acquittal and life] would indeed have been based on law [of Moses]" (Gal 3:21). But something is wrong. The big problem is that all men are transgressors of the law (Gal 3:22). Life, under the system of law, was only guaranteed to those who fulfilled perfectly the requirements of God's commands (Gal 3:12; Lev 18:5).

To break the law in one point was to be a transgressor of law, and no transgressor of law could receive life on the basis of lawkeeping (Ja 2:10). The effect of breaking one of the commandments of the law is not like the effect of breaking one of the bristles on a broom where we can go on sweeping pretty well even with broken bristles. The effect of breaking a commandment is more like that of breaking a pane of window glass; break it in one place and you shatter the whole glass! God does not grade on the curve! For breaking the law the "curse" of the law fell on life (Deu 11:26-28; 27:26; 28:15-68).[5]

5. The law consisted also in a gracious provision for forgiveness of sins through the sacrificial ceremonies (Lev 1-7). When an Israelite had sinned in violation of the law, his sin could be atoned for by the offering of a blood

Paul interprets the curse of the law as ultimately involving condemnation and eternal death (Ro 5:15, 18). Under such a law-
principle of justification our condition was hopeless. But God
intervened through Christ, who, though He was born under the
law, was not condemned by it because He fulfilled it (Mt 5:17).
Therefore, when Jesus died, He bore the curse of the law in His
own body for us (Gal 3:13). God took the condemnation which
the law brought to us because of our violations and nailed it to
Jesus on the cross (Col 2:14; 2 Co 5:21; 1 Pe 2:24). So in Christ's
death we died to the slavery of the law's condemning finger, and
we now serve God through the Spirit without any fear of condemnation for violating one of God's commands (8:1).

Wasn't the law then actually a bad thing ("sin," v. 7)? Paul's
answer is emphatically, no—"may it never be!" "The Law is holy,
and the commandment is holy and righteous and good" (v. 12).
He must steer a close course between the twin perils of legalism
and moral indifference to divine law. On the one hand Paul
affirms emphatically there is nothing wrong with the law ("spiritual," v. 14), yet the law proves in experience to be powerless to
rescue a man from his sinful predicament. The problem is not the
law; it is the sinful nature it has to work on that is the culprit.
Even a Rembrandt is powerless painting on tissue paper. Can we
blame the anchor if the boat drifts when anchored in loose mud?

In verses 7-13 Paul seizes on the tenth commandment, "coveting," to illustrate how the holy command working on the sinful
nature of man actually produces "coveting of every kind" (v. 8).
Sin uses the good command as an "opportunity." The Greek word
(*aphormē*) is often used in military and commercial contexts to
denote the base of operations for an expedition or a war.[6] Sin
launched an attack against man and viciously and deceptively
used the commandment as a foothold for the advance.

When a harmless balloon filled with warm water is brought

sacrifice. But God's purpose for the moral law remained the same until the
coming of Christ (Gal 3:21-22; Heb 9:24-25; 10:1). The latter verse in
Hebrews reminds us that the law did contain a "shadow" of good things to
come in the gracious sacrificial system which pointed toward Christ.
6. W. F. Arndt and F. W. Gingrich, *Greek-English Lexicon of the New
Testament*, s.v. *"a phormē."*

near a coiled rattlesnake, the snake strikes out at the heat and releases its poisonous venom into the balloon. Until the balloon is presented, the poisonous venom lays dormant in the glands of the snake, but the balloon provides the "occasion" for the release of the poison into plain view. Similarly the law, while good in itself, has the effect of drawing out the poison of man's sin into deliberate acts of rebellion against God. In Bunyan's *Pilgrim's Progress*, the pilgrim, Christian, is taken by Interpreter into a large room (the heart) full of dust (sin). A man (law) comes to sweep with a broom, causing the dust to rise up so much that Christian is almost suffocated.[7]

Verses 7-12 describe Paul either in his boyhood experience or in his experience as a Pharisee afflicted with guilt. When a Jewish boy becomes old enough to assume his own responsibility for the commandments (*Bar Mitzvah*), he may discover also a new desire to enter into the prohibited world upon which God has placed what seems to him to be an unwarranted restraint.[8] Thus, in attempting to keep the commands of God, man dies in the experience of disillusionment and disappointment. For instead of receiving life through the commands, he experiences death because he cannot find the power to perform the commandment and is thus separated from his Creator (vv. 9-10). But Paul hastens to emphasize that the fault lies not with the commandment, because it is a true expression of God's will, but with the sinful nature of man which takes the good command and through it brings death to man (vv. 11-12). Sin through the command is revealed in all its rebellious character (v. 13). Like an x-ray photograph, the law reveals the cancer of sin within us. Truly the law is "spiritual" in that it comes from the Spirit of God and is a true expression of His will (v. 14). God's law came that we might recognize sin (3:20; 7:7).

We have deliberately avoided until this point the chief interpretive problem of this chapter which has produced numerous divergent views. Here is the problem. When Paul uses the first

7. John Bunyan, *The Pilgrim's Progress*, new ed. (New York: Dutton, 1954), pp. 31-32.
8. Paul's references to "coveting" (lust), "commandment," "life," "death," and "deceived" in these verses are strongly suggestive of the whole account of man's original fall into sin recorded in Gen 3.

person singular *I* (vv. 7-25) and the present tense (vv. 14-25), is he referring to his own experience as a Pharisee under the law or to his experience as a Christian? While the question of when this experience occurred is not really Paul's main point,[9] it has deeply bothered Christians from the earliest times to the present. In a lecture on Paul's description of himself as being "sold under sin," Dr. Alexander Whyte said,

> As often as my attentive bookseller sends me on approval another new commentary on Romans, I immediately turn to the seventh chapter. And if the commentator sets up a man of straw in the seventh chapter, I immediately shut the book. I at once send the book back and say, "No thank you. That is not the man for my hard-earned money."[10]

If we dismiss the less likely position that Paul's "I" is simply a general reference to mankind or the Hegelian progress of history view of Stauffer,[11] there are three possible interpretations: (1) Paul, the non-Christian Pharisee under the law (Greek fathers, Sanday and Headlam), (2) Paul, the normal Christian (Augustine, Bruce, Murray), (3) Paul, the carnal Christian (W. H. Griffith-Thomas). While it seems impossible to us to adopt any one of the three views without some dissatisfaction, we will discuss and argue for the second view. No doubt the reason there is no unanimity among commentators on this point of interpretation is that the passage relates a psychological experience and depending on our own pre-Christian and Christian experience, we will lean toward interpreting Paul's experience in accord with our own.

In favor of view number one are the expressions in the passage that are felt to be incompatible with the Christian state: "I am of flesh, sold into bondage to sin" (v. 14); "but I practice the very evil that I do not wish" (v. 19); "making me a prisoner . . . Wretched man that I am!" (vv. 23-24). In favor of view number two are the expressions thought to be incompatible with a non-Christian experience: "I joyfully concur with the law of God"

9. Paul's main point is to answer the charge that his teaching about not being under law makes the law sin (v. 7).
10. Cited by F. F. Bruce, *The Epistle of Paul to the Romans*, p. 151.
11. TDNT, s.v. "ego."

The New Situation: Freedom from the Law's Domination 113

(v. 22); "I myself with my mind am serving the law of God" (v. 25); "the good that I wish" (v. 19). In favor of view number three is the fact that the person described seems to desire the good and hate the evil, but he lacks the power to overcome evil and ends in despair (vv. 18, 24). Since there is no reference to the Holy Spirit in chapter 7 (except possibly verse 6), it is obvious to those who argue for this third view that Paul describes himself as a Christian who is trying to live for God in the power of the flesh by law conformity. Thus in the mind of those who feel the section describes the carnal Christian, Paul's main point is the inability of the law in itself (i.e., as a total *system*) to effect fruit unto God.

In our view the main confusion in interpretation has arisen because of attempts to force a chronological or logical sequence on Paul's experience from chapter 7 to chapter 8 rather than seeing the two chapters as complementary. It is precisely because it is Paul's real experience that all the difficulty has arisen. We have lost the point of his teaching by getting overly involved in the precise time when he experienced this despair. It is the truth of the continual presence of sinful nature in the redeemed man that the apostle seeks to describe. When one gets to chapter 8, indeed the picture changes with the emphasis on the life of the power of the Holy Spirit. Yet this new emphasis in chapter 8 is not designed to deny that every Christian experiences to some extent throughout his life the feelings of chapter 7. Paul in chapter 8 gives the complementary and simultaneous experience in our lives.

It is clear that there is a conflict or battle described in verses 15-25 that does not appear in verses 7-13. Paul also changes tenses at verse 15, using the past tense in verses 7-14 and then the present in verses 15-25. Might this not suggest that the first section (vv. 7-13) deals with Paul's past experience under the law as a Pharisee and corresponds to the words in verse 5, "while we were in the flesh . . . to bear fruit for death" while from verses 15 onward he is describing the way the sinful nature operates within him as a redeemed person who desires to do the good. The same conflict (vv. 15-25), hardly possible in one who has *died* (vv. 9,

11), is described by Paul in Galatians as a conflict in the Christian between the Holy Spirit and the sinful flesh (Gal 5:17).

He is burdened throughout the whole section to show that the law is good (v. 12) but powerless because of the sinfulness of man. His inward conflict proves the spirituality of the law. It is not until verse 25, which anticipates the resurrection life, that there is any indication of hope beyond the sorry experience in the chapter. Perhaps a few comments on words and meanings in verses 14-25 will help to draw this tedious discussion to a fruitful conclusion.

In verse 14 "of flesh" means fleshy and hence weak, sinful, and transitory.[12] "Sold into bondage" (literally, under sin) refers to the captivity produced in us by sin working through the good law (see also v. 23). "I do not understand" (Gk. *ginōskō*) of verse 15 reveals that Paul is perplexed by the strange way the law works on his sinful nature: he cannot practice what he desires (the law of God). Instead the apostle ends up doing what he hates, which proves that he agrees in his conscience that the law is good even though he does not do it (v. 16).

The contrast between "I" and "sin which indwells me" in verse 17 should not be made the basis for any profound psychological theory. The statements should be understood as popular terms to describe Paul's personal conflict and not a technical development of a particular theory of psychology.

In verse 18 the sense of the last clause is helped if we read: "but the *power* to perform the good is not." Verses 21-23 contain several references to "law." "The law of God" (v. 22) and "the law of my mind" (v. 23) are definite references to the Mosaic law or commandments. "The principle" (v. 21) and "the law of sin" (v. 23) refer to a type of counterfeit law or principle operating in the sinful flesh which makes war on the true law of God and takes a man captive to do its evil bidding. In verse 23 the expression "making me a prisoner" refers to making military prisoners in the sense that sin, warring against God's will in my life, wins the victory and through law makes me a prisoner (see Lk 4:18; Eph 4:8; 2 Co 10:5). Recent prisoner of war experiences in Viet Nam make this image more meaningful to our day.

12. Arndt and Gingrich, p. 751.

"Wretched man" (v. 24) is Paul's wail of anguish; it is a very strong term of misery and distress. "The body of this death" (v. 24) refers to the human body which through sin and the law has fallen under the dominion and condemnation of death. Paul's misery is due to a frustrated condition but not a divided self. He wants to serve God totally with his innermost redeemed self (vv. 15, 19, 21, 22, 25), but he finds his desire frustrated by the irrationality of his actual performance. He cries out for release from the sinful nature. As Tennyson, in *Morte d'Arthur,* cried, "O for a new man to arise within me and subdue the man that I am." But where can such release be found? Paul knows the answer because he writes as a Christian: "Thanks be to God [release comes] through Jesus Christ our Lord" (v. 25). In another place Paul uses the exact same expression as a reference to the future bodily resurrection of the dead at Christ's return (1 Co 15:57). Ultimate release from this perpetual frustration comes through the future redemption of the body (8:23). Meanwhile, the present work of the Holy Spirit in the believer, which anticipates in a small measure the glorious future deliverance, enables him to partially rise above the weaknesses of the sinful flesh and live unto righteousness (chap. 8).

If the logical or chronological interpretation has been stressed in verses 14-24, the last part of verse 25 will be out of place. If Paul was indeed moving toward a conclusion in the chapter which would prepare his readers for an entirely new emphasis in chapter 8, he most certainly would have ended on the triumphant note of 25a. But he closes the discussion by giving what appears to be his present experience: "I myself with my mind [inward man, his spirit] am serving the law of God, but . . . with my flesh [I serve] the law of sin." By ending thus, he emphasizes that even he himself as a Christian in this world cannot escape the frustrations of living a new life in Christ in a body which, until the resurrection, still bears the marks of the old Adamic race. But chapter 7 is not the whole story of Christian experience.

7

The New Life of the Spirit

(8:1-39)

THE SITUATION PRESENTED in chapter 8 is the contemporaneous but also the complementary side of Christian experience to that described in chapter 7. This new life principle of the Spirit enables those who are justified in Christ ("no condemnation," v. 1): (1) to fulfill the moral law (v. 4); (2) to rise above the operating principle of sin and death (v. 2); and (3) to enjoy life and peace (v. 6). In this chapter Paul describes many of the gifts and graces of the Holy Spirit, who now enables the Christian to experience in part what he will have in full at Christ's return even though at the same time he experiences the frustrations he has described in chapter 7.

Romans chapter 8 is one of the greatest chapters in the Bible. If the Bible were a ring and Romans the jewel in the center, then chapter 8 would be the sparkling point of the jewel. Charles Erdman has splendidly captured the excitement of entering onto this holy ground:

> If the Epistle to the Romans rightly has been called "the cathedral of the Christian faith," then surely the eighth chapter may be regarded as its most sacred shrine, or its high altar of worship, of praise, and of prayer. . . . Here, we stand in the full liberty of the children of God, and enjoy a prospect of that glory of God which some day we are to share.[1]

Truly spoken, for the chapter begins with "in Christ Jesus" (v. 1),

1. Charles Erdman, *The Epistle of Paul to the Romans* (Philadelphia: Westminster, 1925), p. 82.

and ends with "in Christ Jesus our Lord" (v. 39); it begins with
no condemnation (v. 1) and ends with *no separation* (v. 39).

There are two main themes developed in the chapter. Both
focus on the release from captivity which is effected by the Holy
Spirit. First, verses 1-13 develop the thought of *release from the
captivity of sin and death,* while *release from the captivity of
decay* forms the main focus in verses 14-39. Both themes are
closely related. The Spirit of God, whose power enables Christians to rise above the power of the sinful flesh and progress in
sanctification (yet, not without constant struggles), is also the
firstfruit guaranteeing their glorious future inheritance.

RELEASE FROM THE CAPTIVITY OF SIN AND DEATH
(8:1-13)

Paul's long argument in vindication of the moral nature of the
faith method of justification (6:1—7:25) now reaches its clearest
and fullest statement in verses 1-13. Contrary to all the supposed
objections, this method of justification was the only possible
method by which sinful men could be completely forgiven and
released from captivity to sin so that "the requirement of the Law
might be fulfilled in us" (v. 4).

Paul first summarizes the former arguments of the book. He
relates how we have been simultaneously freed from the wrath of
God and freed from the captivity of sin by being made part of a
new way of life which he describes as walking "not according to
the flesh, but according to the Spirit" (v. 4).[2] This new life in the
Spirit (v. 2) becomes possible by the appearance in human flesh
of the Son of God who by His sinless life and sacrificial death
doomed the rule of sin over human nature (v. 3). Jesus now
gives birth to a new humanity of people who walk not according
to the flesh but according to the rule of the indwelling Holy Spirit
(vv. 4-14).

2. The words "who walk not after the flesh, but after the Spirit," found
in the first verse in the KJV are omitted by most modern versions because a
number of early Greek manuscripts omit them. The same words appear at
the end of verse 4, suggesting that a scribe may have accidentally repeated
the phrase in verse 1. However, there is strong manuscript support for the
KJV reading, and it fits admirably into the context if we understand Paul's
thought at this point in the argument.

In verse 1 Paul states in summary and recapitulation, "There is therefore now no condemnation for those who are in Christ Jesus." The "therefore now" probably goes back to 7:6 where, followed by a lengthy explanation of the holiness of the law and the sinfulness of human nature (7:7-25), Paul has stated that we are free from the law's condemning curse, which held us captive, and able now to serve God in the new life of the Spirit. Chapter 8 more fully explains this new life lived by the Holy Spirit. To not be under "condemnation"[3] refers both to justification as release from the wrath of God (chap. 5) and also to our release from the enslaving effect of the law and its curse (6:15–7:6). The Christian can really rejoice because in God's grace and mercy "in Christ Jesus" (in union with Him, 6:3-5) all of our sinfulness and rebellion against God has been forgiven. Our guilt, which was a part of our sinful flesh, has been abolished forever.

Paul states again for us in verses 2-4 why there is no longer servitude to the sinful flesh. It is simply because Christians have been released from the former way of life "in the flesh" by the invasion of a new principle (law) of life lived in obedience to the Spirit (v. 2). How did this new manner of life come to us? It was made available totally through God's own gracious, saving act in the coming and the death of His Son (vv. 3-4). Jesus entered into the world by fully identifying Himself with the sinful human flesh He came to redeem: "in the likeness of sinful flesh" (v. 3). Yet it should be stressed that "likeness" of sinful flesh means neither that Christ was sinful (see 2 Co 5:21; 1 Pe 2:22), nor that He only appeared to be human, but that He came in real human flesh which "looked like" every other person since Adam (sinful flesh) but was different because He, unlike other men, was not under sin's dominion. Christ came "for sin" that is, to deal with sin or to offer Himself as a sin offering (3:24-25; 1 Jn 4:10).

Ultimately the purpose of His coming was to condemn "sin in the flesh" (v. 3). The law, by mere commanding, could not over-

---

3. "Condemnation" (Gr. *katakrima*) when God is the subject refers both to the sentence of judgment and to the execution of that sentence (TDNT). This same word occurs in 5:12-14 as indicating the actual condition of men in Adam, involving them in servitude to sin, disobedience to God, and death. To be removed from these is justification which is more than mere acquittal; it involves also being "set free from the law of sin and death" (v. 2).

come the practice of sin in human nature. It could prescribe the
will of God but provided no power for performing His will in
face of the sinful flesh. Yet it was not the law's fault that sin
prevailed and even increased under its rule. The failure lay in
the "weakness" of the law to effect righteousness in us because sin
ruined our flesh, making it powerless to respond (7:7-25). But
now God has done what the law wanted to do but could not do.
He has condemned the rule of sin over human nature by creating
a new humanity for mankind in Jesus Christ. By living a fully
human life, totally in obedience to God, Jesus broke the rule that
sin had held over human nature ever since Adam. He showed sin
to be not natural to humanness but a usurper. By His own death
Christ provided the means whereby all who are related to Him
can also enter into His same victory over the rule of sin (6:2-14).

This same thought is now repeated in verse 4, where Paul says
that Christ condemned sin in the flesh "in order that the requirement[4] of the Law might be fulfilled in us." The requirement of
the law was that we should be holy before God. The whole law,
Jesus said, is fulfilled in this, "You shall love the Lord your God . . .
your neighbor as yourself" (Lk 10:27; Ro 13:9). Loving obedience both to God and to men was the holy aim in many of the
law's commands.

However, in actual human experience, the law was not able
to produce loving obedience because of the sin-controlled flesh.
But now the believer in Christ has this just goal of the law fulfilled in him due to the simple fact that in Christ he is no longer
living unto himself. Through union with Christ by faith, the
Christian has entered into a whole new way of life. He lives according to the rule and resources of the Holy Spirit of God rather
than the resources of the flesh. This change in relationship is captured well in the following:

> To run and work the law commands,
> Yet gives me neither feet nor hands;
> But better news the gospel brings:
> It bids me fly, and gives me wings.
>
> AUTHOR UNKNOWN

4. This is the same word (Gk. *dikaiōma*) discussed at 1:32; 2:26; 5:16, 18.
The closest parallel is 2:26 where it means "righteous demand or requirement."

The law of the Spirit of life in Christ Jesus (v. 2) is described in verse 4 as walking not "according to the flesh, but according to the Spirit." In verses 5-14 Paul shows what is involved in this new way of living in the Spirit.

But what then becomes of the Mosaic law for the believer in Christ? Does verse 4 teach that the Christian is enabled by the Holy Spirit to keep all the commands which he could not keep as a non-Christian and thus to fulfill the law? *No!* Christians cannot keep the law perfectly either. The point is that the law demanded obedience to God motivated out of love for God. This demand is met through the gospel for those who by the grace of God have been put into a whole new relationship to God through Christ. This is what Paul is stressing. That the Christian will be sensitive to any revealed expression of God's will, including the Mosaic commands, is assumed by Paul, but law-keeping is not the Christian's chief concern. Instead he is to focus on the "new life of the Spirit" (7:6; 8:5-14), not on the old written code. (See 13:8-10 for more on this point.)

Paul now turns to explain this life lived according to the Spirit (vv. 5-14). The Spirit comes to us as a gift (not merited in any way) when we become Christians. Through this gift God's love was poured out into the hearts of Christians (5:6). In 7:6 the Spirit is referred to as the agent of the new life. Jesus Christ is our justification and our sanctification, and it is the Holy Spirit who makes Him real and effective to us from day to day. The "Spirit of God" and "Spirit of Christ" appear to be identical terms (v. 9). So justification can never be separated from sanctification (Christ-likeness). Both are inseparably linked to the grace-gift of God in Jesus Christ. Yet how does the Spirit in our experience effect sanctification?

First, the Holy Spirit produces in us a certain mind-set (vv. 5-8): "those who are according to the Spirit [set their minds on (Gk. *phroneo*, are intent on following)] the things of the Spirit" (v. 5). It may be helpful to note that certain terms Paul uses here denote either different states of existence (Christian or non-Christian) or different patterns of behavior. To be "in the flesh" is to be a non-Christian, under sin's power (vv. 8, 9); on the other hand, to be "in the Spirit" or "in Christ" is to be a Christian.

under the Spirit's power. To "walk according to the flesh" is equivalent to "to live according to the flesh" or be "according to the flesh" and means to conduct our lives according to the standard, values, and resources of the sin-dominated flesh (vv. 5, 12, 13). On the other hand, to "walk according to the Spirit" is equivalent to "according to the Spirit" and "by the Spirit you are putting to death the deeds of the body," and means to conduct our lives according to the standard, values, and resources of the life-giving Spirit within us (vv. 4, 5, 13).[5] The presence of the Holy Spirit redirects our life toward God and creates in us new desires and values. To "set the mind on" the things of the flesh or Spirit means to have one's thoughts, desires, and constant yearning directed toward either the life of the flesh (self) or the life of the Spirit (Christ).

The results follow (v. 6). To have one's mind directed only upon the things of self and this material world means cutting oneself off from the only Source of real human life and results in death now in this life (condemnation and evil) and eternal death to come.[6] On the other hand, to have one's mind directed upon God through the Spirit results in "life" (acquittal and sanctification) and "peace," the conscious enjoyment of reconciliation with God.

Paul further describes the mind directed onto the flesh (non-Christian) in its relationship to God (vv. 7-8). The flesh's interests are such that those who live to please themselves are in fact in a state of hostility against God. Such hostility is evident because the mind directed by the sinful flesh does not and cannot become obedient to the law (will) of God (7:14-25). It follows then that such who live to please themselves cannot live to please God.

The opposite then would be true of those who have been put by grace into the mind directed by the Spirit: instead of disobedience to the law (will) of God there is loving obedience; in place of walking apart from God there is walking with God.

5. It is also possible to be "walking" *in* the flesh (as a weak human being) but not "warring *after* the flesh" (i.e., drawing on the resources, standards, and values of sinful flesh). See 2 Co 10:2-3.

6. "The mind" (*phronēma*) set "on the things of the flesh" is the noun form of the same verb used for "mind" in v. 5.

In verses 9-11 Paul contrasts the state of the Christian ("in the Spirit") with the preceding description of those "in the flesh" (vv. 7-8). In verse 9, "however you," the "you" is emphatic: "but as for *you*." Paul clearly teaches in verse 9 that all Christians are "in the Spirit," which means that "the Spirit of God dwells" in every Christian. In fact, he says, "if anyone does not have the Spirit of Christ, he does not belong to Him" (as a justified one). To be "in Christ" or "in the Spirit" refers to our union with Christ; to have Christ in us (v. 10) or the Spirit in us (v. 4) refers to our ownership by Christ.

The Spirit "dwells" (Gk. *oikeō*, to live in a house) in us in the sense of a person making his home in our lives. The figure of indwelling combines the thought that Christians are people whose lives are directed from a Source outside themselves with the idea that this life Source is also vitally related to them. Three times in verses 9-11 this indwelling of the Spirit is stressed.

What are the effects in our experience of this indwelling Spirit of God? Paul states that, even though the body is dead due to sin, the Spirit is alive because of righteousness (v. 10). What he teaches is a modified dualism in Christian experience. At the present time there is a dual principle operating in the Christian. On the one hand, he still possesses a physical body condemned to death because of Adam's sin (5:15; 6:23). The seed of decay and death is now working in our bodies. Yet for the Christian there is also now another reality at work. Life is also present due to the indwelling of the Spirit given to us through justification. The Spirit enables us to "live" in spite of the fact that the body has been stricken with a death wound (v. 13).[7] The Christian then, while still in the weak, sinful flesh, has been released from its power; while still in the body, which has received a mortal wound from sin, he has a new principle of life working in it through the righteousness of God in Christ. He is totally dead on the one hand, yet fully alive on the other. Such a truth will spare us from

7. Most interpreters have understood the word "spirit" in verse 10 as a contrast to the "body" and refer it to the human "spirit" rather than the Holy Spirit (NASB, "the spirit is alive"). The objection to this latter view is simply that the Holy Spirit is the subject of the whole context and is immediately connected in v. 11 with life (see John Murray, *The Epistle to the Romans*, 294; C. K. Barrett, *The Epistle to the Romans*, p. 162; Anders Nygren, *Commentary on Romans*, p. 326).

either expecting absolute perfection in this life or giving in to complete pessimism concerning the present manifestation of Christ's love and righteousness in our lives.

Furthermore, the presence of the same Spirit, who gives life now to believers living in decaying bodies, also is the guarantee that our bodies, destined to physical death, will be raised from death in the same manner that Jesus' body was raised (v. 11). The Father is the specific agent in resurrection as in the case of Christ (6:4), but as in Christ's case, the Holy Spirit also is an agent (1:4). Later in the chapter Paul will again refer to this future hope of resurrection as the "redemption of our body" (v. 23). Here again we are reminded that just as human nature was not made for sin but the usurper illegally took it over (v. 3), so also the mortal body was not made for death and will be in God's time, because of the Spirit of life, raised to immortal life (1 Co 15:51-53). This is no mere spiritual resurrection. What a glorious truth!

But what about the life now in the body? Has the Spirit nothing to contribute? How does the "life" made possible because of our justification (v. 10) actually manifest itself in our deathbound lives? Paul has already said that the Christian as a Christian is one who walks not according to the flesh but after the Spirit (vv. 4-14). But does this mean that Christians now, since they are "in the Spirit," automatically follow God's will? The answer must be no, for in verses 12-14 Christians are specifically exhorted to "live according to the Spirit." Remember in chapter 6 how Paul stated that because of his union with Christ in death and resurrection the believer was "free from sin" and then he proceeded to exhort them to fight against sin and yield themselves as servants to righteousness? Delivered and yet not delivered. Here likewise the Christian has been shown to be ultimately free from death (vv. 11, 21), due to the Spirit who indwells, but he must in the present life fight the sin and death principle as it works itself out in our bodies.

To live according to the flesh (in separation from God) leads to death both now and eternally. Since Christians have been removed from the servitude to the flesh (self) and put into the service of the Spirit, who is the Spirit of life and immortality, they

are obligated (morally) not to live their lives under the rule of
the sinful flesh. Rather, Christians are to "put to death the deeds
of the body" that they might live (v. 13). Here is the principle
for moving into the practice of holy living. It may be called spiritual neurosurgery. Phillips' translation reads: "cut the nerve
of your instinctive actions by obeying the Spirit." "Putting to
death the deeds of the body" refers to our continual (present
tense) activity as Christians whereby, through the enablement
provided by the Spirit, we strike down in death those sinful practices of the body which are contrary to God's will.

More specifically, how this is done Paul does not say in this
context. The "deeds (habits) of the body" are probably to be
identified with the "members of your earthly body" of Colossians
3:5 which are enumerated as: "immorality, impurity, passion,
evil desire, and greed, which amounts to idolatry" (see also Gal
5:19-21; Eph 4:22–5:14).

While in this context the spiritual neurosurgery is primarily
negative, it assumes that the process is a *renewal*, not simply a destruction. The dead leaves and branches of the sinful practices
fall away only to make room for the "fruit of the Spirit" (6:21; 7:
4; Gal 5:22-23). The weed-killer of the Spirit is applied so that
the grass of the graces of God might be free to grow. So in practice we do not seek mere patience or love or purity (this is a
moralistic approach), but we seek the release of Christ's life, i.e.,
His patience, His love and purity by following the promptings of
the Spirit. The Christian life is an exchanged life. Such a process
leads truly to "life" now as well as eternal and immortal life in
the future.

Verse 14 is transitional. Paul concludes the thought of the previous verses by asserting that all who are thus "being led by the
Spirit of God [to be constantly putting to death the deeds of the
body], these are the sons of God." The truth of the Spirit's leading suggests not general guidance as to what God would have us
to do (vocation) but rather what we should be (character). All
the children of God enjoy this leading; however, it is not op-
tional. Since "leading" often implies the process whereby our
desires lead us (2 Ti 3:6), perhaps the thought of Paul is that
the Holy Spirit imparts new desires and promptings into the

redeemed life to which the Christian develops a sensitivity in responding both negatively (killing process) and positively (in the fruit bearing process).

"Sons" of God includes being children of God but also involves in the Roman world of Paul's day the idea of a new mature stage in the child's development that relates him to his father as a joint heir and master over all (Gal 3:26; 4:6-7). So Paul will turn now to the thought of the future inheritance (vv. 17-18) as soon as he has given evidence to assure his readers that they truly are "sons."

Release from the Captivity of Decay
(8:15-39)

The Spirit, who now relates to us in a new way of life even though we are still in the old human sin nature (vv. 1-14), is also the "spirit of adoption" (v. 15). The Spirit's presence in us now is the "first fruits" (v. 23) of the future deliverance of the entire creation from the bondage of decay (v. 21). It is this assurance of sonship and heirship that the Holy Spirit constantly bears home to us in the Scripture and in our hearts that constitutes Christian hope. Hope leads us to patient endurance even through suffering and persecution (vv. 18-39). This section of the chapter is one of the most beautiful, triumphant, and comforting portions of the whole Bible.

Verses 15-17 continue the thought of the preceding verse by stressing assurance that as Christians we are actually related to God as "sons" and not as those under "slavery." Fear comes from the absence of authentic hope and leads to enslavement by inferior earthly powers which promise deliverance. But Christians have been made true sons of God (adopted)[8] and possess the assurance of genuine hope. The evidence of this sonship relation to God is the inward witness of the Holy Spirit. This witness of our filial relationship to God is seen most clearly in Christian

8. "Adoption" (v. 15) is the Greek *huiothesios*, "legally adopted son" (W. F. Arndt and F. W. Gingrich, *Greek-English Lexicon*, s.v.). It is a term used only by Paul and not found in the OT (LXX) or in classical writers, but the papyri manuscripts use it (James H. Moulton and George Milligan, *Vocabulary of the Greek New Testament*, p. 648; and G. Adolf Deissmann, *Bible Studies* [Edinburgh: T & T Clark, 1901], p. 239).

praying where we cry, "Abba! Father!" The expression, "Abba! Father!" combines the untranslated Aramaic word *abba,* which means "my father" in a very personal, intimate sense (Mk 14:36 with Mt 26:42) with the Greek word for father, *pater.* Only Jesus uses this intimate form of prayer in the gospels due to His unique Sonship (Mk 14:36). When Christians cry out to God, the Spirit of sonship incites them to say as a child would to his father, "Abba," or "my daddy."[9]

Furthermore, "the Spirit Himself bears witness with our spirit that we are children of God" (v. 16). This is an additional witness of our sonship borne directly to our spirit. This consciousness perhaps consists in the undefinable but real conviction through the promises of God that we now belong to God (1 Jn 5:6, 9-12). Note that the Holy Spirit is personal and that He is a distinct being separate from man's own spirit.[10]

As children of God we are "heirs" of God. In fact, the only way we get in on the future inheritance is as "fellow-heirs with Christ" (v. 17).[11] Christ's inheritance is fabulous: "appointed heir of all things" (Heb 1:2). Before Paul goes on to speak further of this future glory which is like an inheritance that we receive solely because of our relationship to someone else, he first mentions a condition for sharing Christ's glory: "if indeed we suffer with Him" (v. 17). Here we discover a further implication of our union with Christ (6:8). As Christ suffered before He entered glory (1 Pe 1:11; Heb 2:9-10), so those who are identified with Him also suffer before they enter the future glory. "In the world you have tribulation, but take courage; I have overcome the world" (Jn 16:33). Yet this is a suffering "with Him" since Christ

9. For some reason certain Aramaic words in the Christian tradition were left untranslated into Greek: "Abba" (Mk 14:36; Ro 8:15; Gal 4:6); e.g., *"Eli Eli lama sabachthani"* (Mt 27:46); *"maranatha"* (1 Co 16:22). Perhaps the precise shade of emotion in the original word or the traditional association was considered too precious to lose through translation. *Abba* was almost never used in prayer by the Jews but was common as a child's address to his own father (TDNT).

10. This point needs to be emphasized especially with the current post-Christian age emphasis on oriental religions where no distinction is made between God's Spirit and the spirit present in all the world.

11. This right of equally shared inheritance even to adopted sons is based not on Jewish law but Roman (E. H. Gifford, "Romans" in *The Bible Commentary: New Testament,* 3:154).

is so united to His body, the church, that when the members suffer for the gospel and for righteousness' sake, He as the Head, also suffers (Ac 9:4; Phil 1:29; Col 1:24; 1 Pe 4:13). Why the suffering of the members of Christ's body must continue, Paul does not reveal (nor does any biblical writer). There is a mystery connected with suffering that God has not been pleased to explain to His creatures in the present. It is sufficient for faith to trust implicitly in God Himself who will ultimately reveal that suffering was in some manner indispensable to the full manifestation of His glory.

In the meantime, Paul shows that there are good reasons for abiding faithful to God even in the midst of sufferings and persecutions (vv. 18-30). Each reason is related to a special ministry of the Holy Spirit. First the Spirit helps by creating a consciousness by his presence of the reality of the greatness of the future glory (vv. 18-25). Second, the Spirit definitely helps us to overcome our natural weaknesses (vv. 26-27). Third is the assurance that all things are working together for our good in the eternal purpose of God (vv. 28-30).

First, in verses 18-25 Paul looks for encouragement to the Christian hope of the greatness of the future glory: "The sufferings . . . are not worthy to be compared with the glory that is to be revealed to us" (v. 18). Just as real to us as our sufferings are now is the certainty of our sharing the future glory of Christ (2 Co 4:16-18). To what does the "glory" that lies in the future refer? First, it involves the release from decay and death of all of the children of God. Second, there follows the release of the whole creation from the captivity of corruption, sin, and death (vv. 19, 21, 23). This freeing from decay not only affects our individual bodies (v. 23), but extends cosmically to the whole created order: "the creation itself also will be set free from its slavery to corruption" (v. 21). Paul brings in the creation to show how great the effect will be of the future revealing of the children of God.[12] So

12. The word "creature" in the KJV in this passage is exactly the same word which is translated in verse 22 as "creation" (Gk. *ktisis*). The latter translation fits the other verses more suitably than the English "creature" which restricts the thought to animate life.

great is this glory that the whole creation is anxiously longing[13] "on tiptoe," (Phillips) eagerly awaiting the revelation in resurrection bodies of the children of God (vv. 19, 23). Why is creation so expectant? Because nature has been so subjected by God Himself to futility that it too might share the same hope of release from decay that will one day come to God's children (vv. 20-21). The hope of man does not lie in cryonics (freezing the dead) but in resurrection.

Paul speaks of the present creation as (1) subject to futility, (2) not of its own will, and (3) subjected in hope. "Futility" (Gk. *mataioteti*) means "to no purpose" or "against the norm, unexpected." It may be Paul's commentary on Ecclesiastes 1:2, " 'Vanity of vanities,' says the Preacher. '. . . All is vanity.' " Nature seems to be imbued with the seeds of futility, decay, and death ("slavery to corruption" v. 21). Creation does not now fulfill its intended goal, which was to be man's wonderful habitat. The forces of nature seem from time to time to work against themselves and man, and do not achieve their intended ends. When drought, floods, hurricanes, or disease destroy vegetation and life, then beauty fades, vitality decays, and joy turns to weeping. This frustration produces what might be called a symphony of nature played in a minor key but with the expectation of a glorious finale. God has Himself subjected the created universe to a form of captivity resulting in this seeming lack of purpose in order to create "hope" in the glorious future release of creation along with the children of God (v. 21).

Paul does not say why God so subjected the universe; it may be tied up with man's sin and the "curse" upon the ground (Gen 3:17; 5:29). He who originally put the creation under man's dominion has now put the creation under slavery to the effects of man's sin and will make it a partaker of man's blessing in the future. So perhaps the next time we see nature frustrate itself in the crabgrass that infests our lawns, or the blight that kills the crops, or the excessive rainfall that ruins the melons, or the killer

13. The Greek word for "anxious longing" is *apokaradokia* from *kara*, "head" and *dechomai*, "to stretch out," so "stretch out the head forward" in eager or anxious waiting (TDNT). Only Paul uses the word (Ro 8:19; Phil 1:20).

tornado, or perhaps even the dilemma of the population explosion, we will think of the eager expectation of creation as it looks in hope toward our future glorious freedom in resurrection and its own deliverance from frustration, suffering, weakness, and decay (Mt 19:28; Ac 3:21, "restoration of all things").

It is important in our day to note how Paul connects man with nature. The fate of nature is bound up with the fate of man. Man cannot solve his ecological problem without at the same time attending to his own problem. Note carefully that man can only find a partial remedy to the problems of ecology (creation) until the ultimate problem of human existence in sinful flesh is remedied by the personal return of Jesus Christ and the creation of new bodies and a new environment (Rev 20:6; 21:1-2). Hence freedom is the significant mark of glorification for both creation and the human body.

But the present experience is no mere bumpy hayride. "The whole creation groans and suffers the pains of childbirth together" (v. 22) and we also "groan within ourselves, waiting eagerly for . . . the redemption of our body" (v. 23). Creation can do nothing but wait, groan (moan), and hope. Christians also do not escape this frustration in their spiritual conflicts. We too then must wait, groan, and hope, but Christians have something the creation lacks, namely, "the first fruits of the Spirit." Firstfruits are the pledge or first installment of the whole harvest which is to come (Lev 23:10; Ro 11:16). The precise meaning of our present trials and apparently meaningless sufferings is not clear, but because of the Spirit's encouragement we can wait to see the glorious outcome. Think of a caterpillar slowly advancing over the weavings of a tapestry. It can see only occasional changes in the color and sizes of the threads, but they would have no apparent meaning even if it could understand. Yet when the caterpillar emerges from its cocoon into a butterfly which can fly above the tapestry and see the beautiful design of the whole, the experiences he had walking over the weavings will be transformed.

Christians are not yet fully redeemed, even though they are fully accepted by God. They possess now a body of death (7:24; 8:10), but they also have received the indwelling Spirit who provides both enablement to rise above the Adamic natural life (lived by control of the sinful flesh) and a guarantee that our bodies will one day be freed through resurrection from death and decay (8:11; 2 Co 5:4). We are real sons of God now and adopted (8:15), but we are not fully the sons of God (adoption, v. 23) until our physical bodies also have been released ("redeemed") from death and decay (including sickness). The Spirit's presence in us is our encouraging guarantee of the greater things to come (2 Co 1:22; 5:5; Gen 24:53)!

In verses 24-25 Paul again poses a paradox. We were really saved in the past moment when by faith Christ became our righteousness, but we were not fully saved because we were saved "in hope" of the future complete restoration. Our present salvation includes the hope of the future resurrection of our bodies (Phil 3:21), but inasmuch as it is not yet realized ("seen") we must wait for it patiently (v. 25; 5:3-5). Faith is the means whereby we are given a salvation which includes hope. Therefore, faith and hope while distinguishable are inseparable in Christian experience. "Hope nourishes and sustains faith," remarked Calvin. Power for living in the present sufferings with Christ lies in the direction of this hope in our future glorification with Christ.[14] Truly the God of the future is greater than the God of the past (from our perspective).

Now the Spirit not only creates hope in us but also provides help for our infirmities (vv. 26-27). The tension between the suffering of the present time and the expectation of future glory certainly marks the Christian life on this earth and calls forth its groaning and longing. If the sufferings of Christ, which include all the forms of frustration and suffering under which we must live in the present age, weigh us down, so also does our "weakness" (v. 26). "In the same way the Spirit also helps our weakness" (v. 26) is Paul's description of the second help we receive in present sufferings. "In the same way" may refer to a comparison between the way the Spirit enables us in present suffering to experience the firstfruits of the certain and blessed future glory and thus wait patiently (vv. 18-25), and in the same way also the

14. On the whole matter of glorification, one should not overlook the excellent book by Bernard Ramm, *Them He Glorified* (Grand Rapids: Eerdmans, 1963).

Spirit relieves our weaknesses by His help.[15] Our main weakness
is spiritual, that is, our struggle to allow the new life of the Spirit
to have freedom in us as we live in a body corroded with sin and
in an environment scented with death.

The English word *helps* translates the Greek compound word
synantilambanō. The root word means "to take hold" (*lambanō*).
The first prefix of the compound (*anti*) means "over against" or
"face to face" while the second prefix (*syn*) means "together
with." The great Greek scholar, A. T. Robertson, suggests the
combined meaning to be: "The Holy Spirit lays hold of our weaknesses along with (*syn*) us and carries His part of the burden
facing us (*anti*) as if two men were carrying a log, one at each
end."[16] The word is found elsewhere in the New Testament only
of Martha's plea to Jesus to tell Mary to get into the kitchen and
help her (Lk 10:40).

Probably the most comprehensive example of how the Spirit
lends a hand to help us in our weakness is in the matter of prayer:
"How to pray as we should" (v. 26). Our problem is not ignorance
of the *form* of prayer (how), but our weakness is an inability to
articulate the *content* (what), that is, what we should ask for es-
specially in sufferings that will meet our needs and at the same
time fulfill God's will. The Spirit lends a hand by "interceding"
for us to God (vv. 26, 27). Christians have two divine intercessors
before God. Christ intercedes for them in the court of heaven in
respect to their sins (Ro 8:34, Heb 7:25; 1 Jn 2:1). On the other
hand, the Spirit intercedes in the theater of their hearts here on
earth in respect to their weakness. The Spirit pleads to God for
our real needs "with groanings too deep for words" (v. 26).
Creation is groaning (v. 22); Christians are groaning (v. 23); so
also God the Holy Spirit groans. As God the Father "searches the
hearts" of His children—sobering but also comforting—He finds in
their consciousness unspoken and inexpressible sighings. Though
inexpressible they are not unintelligible to the understanding of
the Father. Furthermore, these sighings in our heart turn out to

15. It is possible to understand the "likewise" as referring to *our* waiting
patiently; likewise the Spirit on God's part helps our weaknesses (Gifford,
3:157).
16. A. T. Robertson, *A Grammar of the Greek New Testament in the
Light of Historical Research* (Nashville: Broadman, 1947), p. 593.

be spiritual desires in the will of God because in reality they are the expressions of the Spirit's intercession on behalf of our weaknesses (v. 27). In this manner we can understand how God does "exceeding abundantly beyond all that we ask or think" (Eph 3:20).

When one of our preschoolers desires to write to Granny, my wife gives her a sheet of paper and a pencil, and she expresses her feelings in lines, circles, and zigzag marks. They are truly unintelligible signs. When Mother gets the paper back, she adds certain intelligible words to appropriate marks on the paper such as, "Hello, Granny" with an arrow to the first few scribblings, "We miss you" connected to other marks, and finally, "Come visit us soon. I love you, Lynn." Mother truly has interceded for Lynn to Granny, even as the Spirit intercedes for us to the Father.

Finally, verses 28-30 give us the third reason for patiently enduring suffering. It is the firm conviction that under the hand of the Sovereign Lord of all creation, "God causes all things to work together for good to those who love God, to those who are called according to His purpose" (v. 28). God has a plan. Everything in our lives contributes to the realization of that purpose. It is an all-comprehensive plan in that "all" things are included; not one detail of our lives is excluded. It is a cooperative plan in that all things are "working together" in concert; the individual ingredients, as in a kitchen recipe, have no virtue or ultimate significance in themselves apart from the providential combination into the divine pattern. The plan is beneficent in that the goal is "the good." It is also selective in that it applies only to those "who love God" who are in fact those "called" by God into His glorious purpose through the redemption effected through Jesus Christ.[17] Our good, C.S. Lewis points out, is to love God and fulfill His will for our lives.[18]

In verses 29-30 Paul focuses on the main events leading to God's eternal "purpose" for the Christian of ultimate glorification with Christ. He begins before time in the Father's foreknowledge and

17. A textual variant here in some ancient Greek manuscripts reads, "God causes all things to work." While it is possible this is what Paul wrote, the evidence and context strongly support the KJV rendering at this point: "All things work together for good" (Murray, 2:314).
18. C. S. Lewis, *Problem of Pain* (London: Collins, 1940), p. 41.

concludes beyond time in glorification; between these two, within time, comes calling and justification. Please note two prominent features of this plan. First, God Himself is the designer and executioner of each link in the chain. *He* foreknows and *He* predestinates; *He* calls and *He* justifies and *He* glorifies. Man has no active part in the design or execution of the purpose. Man's only part is his response of continual love to God (v. 28).

Secondly, all who begin in this plan by loving God also finish. Those "whom" He foreknew are those "whom" He called; "whom" He called He also justified, and "whom" He justified He also glorified. God starts with one hundred sheep and arrives in glory with one hundred, not ninety-nine. When contemplating the suffering and setbacks of this present life, nothing can be more assuring than to know that the present is only a small segment between justification and glorification in a total plan that has had three stages already fulfilled. It fills us with a sense of humility and worth and dignity beyond all comprehension and a sense of God's ability to meet every challenge that would thwart His purpose in our lives.

The "foreknowledge" (Gk. *proginōskō*) of God refers to more than mere knowledge beforehand (1 Pe 1:2, 20). It emphasizes the fact that salvation was initiated by God in His eternal loving choice whereby He chose us in Christ to be the objects of His loving purpose (see Amos 3:2; Eph 1:4-6). As difficult as it may seem, foreknowledge always depends on God's election or choice and never on our election of God (2 Th 2:13, 14). Those persons whom God chose to set His love upon are the very ones He also determined to "be conformed to the image of His Son" (v. 29). Predestination (Gk. *proorizō*) is almost the equivalent of foreknowledge (v. 30, only predestined is repeated in the chain) but emphasizes the goal or end in view while foreknowledge focuses on the persons involved (Ac 4:28; 1 Co 2:7; Eph 1:5, 11). The goal of God's electing purpose is that Christ might be the eldest (firstborn) of many brothers in glory who bear His very image or likeness (Col 1:18; 1 Co 15:49; Phil 3:21; Heb 2:10; 1 Jn 3:2). Glorification involves receiving the full humanity of Jesus in a redeemed body adapted to full expression of the Spirit.

Those who were predestined before time to this glory were

called and justified by God in time (v. 30). Calling refers to God's gracious direct appeal to our hearts to respond in faith to His free offer of pardon and new life in the gospel of Christ (2 Th 2:14). It too is a word associated with God's election (Is 41:9; 1 Co 1:26, 27); God calls (elects) us out of sin and death by the gospel of Christ. Calling is God's application in time of His election before time (Eph 1:4, 5). Our act of faith in the gospel of Christ secured our actual justification (acquittal and life) which has been Paul's burden throughout the letter. The final link that completes God's plan is our glorification with Christ (v. 30).

All the relative pronouns ("whom") in these verses go back to the first substantive phrase in verse 28, "to those who love God." Paul puts this first because he does not want anyone to miss it. Are these called because they love God, or do they love God because they are called? Theologians have debated this issue for centuries. The point that is important here in Romans is that Paul does not get caught up in this kind of theological speculation. All he says is that those who are foreknown, predestined, called, justified, and glorified are those whose earthly life since their conversion has been one great process of loving God.

Present distresses or reversals can never then be viewed as destructive forces against the Christian. Each fits into the present link in God's unfolding purpose. In some manner they are preparing us for the future revelation of His glory in the redeemed and in the whole creation. Reversals and distresses may pull us down. Yet on the other hand the contemplation of the reality of the future salvation (vv. 18-25), together with both the help of the Holy Spirit in our weakness (vv. 26-27) and the firm knowledge that all our experiences are working for our good in God's eternal plan (vv. 28-30) all combine to cause our spirits to rise in triumphant praise to God. It is He who has put us into an eternal relationship to Himself and freed us from all accusation (vv. 31-34) and all possibility of separation from His love in Christ Jesus (vv. 35-39).

Verses 31-39 conclude with the highest rung in the ladder of comfort which, from verse 18 onward, writer, like reader, has been mounting. Paul wants to apply this knowledge of certainty and security to the believer to elicit from the believer a feeling of confident assurance. God is for us (in forgiveness and acceptance in Christ). Who can legitimately accuse us before Him, for is He not the very One who, to show His love for us, sacrificed the greatest gift He could, His very own Son (vv. 31-32)? In the phrase, "He who did not spare His own Son," we can see an allusion to Abraham's offering up his only son, Isaac, whereby he showed his intense love for God (Gen 22). In the present instance God Himself is seen as expressing His supreme love for us in not even sparing His own Son from death. If God has already so proved His love to us (5:8), how can anything that happens to us be considered less than the evidence of the outworking of His good (v. 28)? Dwight L. Moody once illustrated this concept by remarking that if his friend, Mr. Tiffany, had offered him as a gift a large, beautiful diamond, he would not hesitate to ask Mr. Tiffany for some brown paper to wrap up the diamond.

Who can accuse us if God, who is the highest court of appeals, has already acquitted us (v. 33)? Who can condemn us to suffer the penalty and burden of a broken law if Christ Himself, the Judge of man (Jn 5:22), has died and risen and is interceding for us to God (Ro 8:34; Lk 22:31-32; Heb 7:24-25)? Grace and grace alone has brought us into this certainty of acceptance with God.

If no person can accuse us, who or what then can separate us from the eternal love of Christ for us? "Shall tribulation, or distress, or persecution, or famine, or nakedness, or peril, or sword?" (v. 35). Paul has already experienced all of these except the last and has found that his faith and hope were not destroyed but enlarged (5:3-5). As far as the "sword" (death) is concerned, Paul could refer to the Old Testament (Ps 44:22) history of the persecution of God's people not as something marking God's disfavor but rather as (1) received for Him, " for thy sake," (2) continually, "all day long," and (3) delivered unto death, "as sheep to be slaughtered" (v. 36).

Can any or all of these things in any amount ever detach us from the love of Christ? *No!* Paul answers, because in fact it is *"in* all these things" that God works out His plan for good (v. 28) and causes us to overwhelmingly conquer through Him who loved us" (v. 37).[19] No earthly affliction or infliction can disturb this confidence in God's love for us.

But further, Paul is also convinced that no factor of human existence (life or death), nor unseen spiritual power (angels, principalities), nor the expanse of space (height, depth) nor the course of time (present, to come), nor anything in the whole universe of God (any other created thing) can cut us off from this unbelievable love of God, the Father, manifested at the cross and poured out in our hearts when we received the grace of God (vv. 38, 39; 5:5). Yet in all this glorious victory we are reminded to not forget the means or the focus of such triumph since it is "through Him who loved us" (i.e., Jesus Christ) and "in Christ Jesus our Lord" (vv. 37, 39). An early fifth-century Christian witness well illustrates Paul's jubilation:

> When Chrysostom was brought before the Roman Emperor, the Emperor threatened him with banishment if he remained a Christian. Chrysostom replied, "Thou canst not banish me for this world is my father's house." "But I will slay thee," said the Emperor. "Nay, thou canst not," said the noble champion of the faith, "for my life is hid with Christ in God." "I will take away thy treasures." "Nay, but thou canst not for my treasure is in heaven and my heart is there." "But I will drive thee away from man and thou shalt have no friend left." "Nay thou canst not, for I have a friend in heaven from whom thou canst not separate me. I defy thee; for there is nothing that thou canst do to hurt me."[20]

SUMMARY OF ROMANS 5-8

From chapter 5 through chapter 8, Paul has been establishing the "new situation" in grace of those who stand acquitted before God. He has argued that they are not only forgiven but brought to a radically new relationship of life and righteousness before God through the grace which is in Christ (chap. 5). Paul has

19. "More than conquerors" is the Geneva Bible rendering (1557) of the Greek *hypernikaō* which Paul has used to express the superlative (*hyper*) victory (*nikaō*) of the Christian over all of life's threatening evils. We "easily win the victory" or we "come off as super victors" might also capture the force of Paul's word. The word occurs only rarely in pre-Christian literature (Arndt and Gingrich, s.v.).

20. See Henry Hart Milman, *History of Christianity* (New York: Crowell, 1881), 4:144.

spoken to the twin moral problems of continued sin in the Christian's life (chap. 6) and the end of the dominance of the law for those who are in Christ (chap. 7). Finally, he has expounded the main principles of the new life in the Spirit as the counterpart of the old way of life under the law (chap. 8). In his final hymn of victory (8:31-39) Paul has sung his heart out in adoration to the unqualified faithfulness of God from which nothing can ever separate us.

This unshakable confidence in God's ability to keep his promises raises the final problem of the letter. Paul, it might be asked, didn't God make promises to the nation of Israel in the Old Testament? Doesn't your gospel as it has developed historically show that God has rejected the Jew and thus broken His covenant to them? The fact is that the majority of people in the nation of Israel are not believers in the Messiah. Paul's answer to this grave problem is given in the following section (Ro 9-11).

8

The Faithfulness of God: The Challenge of Jewish Unbelief

SOME UNDERSTAND this section on the Jew to be parenthetical to the main thought of the letter. We will argue that chapters 9-11 form an essential link in the whole argument of God's righteousness by faith and fulfill a necessary and climactic function to the whole doctrinal section. The problem Paul encounters at this point in his doctrine is two-fold. First, if in the universal preaching of the gospel of Christ the priority of the message went "to the Jew first" (1:16), why then has the Jew so little share in this salvation? Hasn't the history of Jewish unbelief in Paul's gospel shown that it is basically incompatible with the Old Testament revelation?

Second, what has happened to the specific divine promise of blessing given to Abraham and his seed? If the majority of the Jews are found to be rejected because they cannot accept this new faith which Paul preaches, how can God remain faithful and fulfill His Word of promise to Abraham? Or stated differently, doesn't the gospel as Paul preaches it nullify the whole Old Testament privilege of Israel as a people, which even the apostle himself has previously affirmed (3:1-2)?

Paul's answer to this seeming discrepancy between his message of the gospel and Jewish unbelief lies in two broad directions. He shows on the one hand that the Jew's unbelief is not due to God's unfaithfulness but their own faithlessness. If they are rejected, it is because they have first rejected God (chaps. 9-10).

But this does not exhaust the answer. Paul also describes the outworking of a divine "mystery" in Israel's unbelief. Through Israel's unbelief, God's mercy and compassion will see unparalleled manifestation (chap. 11). More specifically, the promise to Abraham was not intended to be fulfilled to all Abraham's descendants but to a chosen seed or believing remnant both of Jewish and Gentile stock (9:6–10:21). Yet even though the integrity of God to His promises is fulfilled in the remnant, God also has in mind the eventual restoration of the whole people of Israel through their faith in Christ and through them a tremendous blessing for the entire world (11:1-36).

Paul's Sorrow over Israel's Unbelief
(9:1-5)

Paul's sorrow (9:1-3)

Paul seems to move from the peak of joy in the last chapter to the valley of sorrow in these opening verses. The great apostle to the Gentiles (11:13), who repeatedly has had to speak against the Jewish concept of justification by works held by his fellow countrymen, shows that he is not a feelingless renegade from his own people. Paul is continually and deeply grieved in his heart over the unbelief in Christ exhibited by his fellow Jews. Three times he appeals to the absolute sincerity of his feelings (v. 1). So intense was his sorrow over their failure to receive Jesus as Messiah that he wishes that he might even be "anathema" (accursed)[1] from Christ if it would mean their reconciliation to Christ (v. 3). While this was not possible, his genuine love for those who were his "kinsmen according to the flesh" (not brothers in Christ) prompted this agonizing expression for their spiritual welfare. Do those who stand opposed to the gospel in our day so grieve our hearts?

The Jewish privileges (9:4-5)

Paul has already mentioned the "advantage" of the Jew in 3:1-2

---

1. The Greek word *anathema* corresponds to the OT *herem*, "devoted to destruction" and often translated "accursed" (see Jos 6:17; 7:1; 1 Co 12:3; 16:22; Gal 1:8, 9). Like Moses of old (Ex 32:31-32), Paul wished to lose his own salvation for the salvation of his fellow Jews.

(actually only one was mentioned: the oracles of God). Now he elaborates eight privileges of being a Jew, against which his sorrow is intensified. To whom more is given more is expected and the deeper the sorrow when failure results. The eight-fold advantage is (1) the "adoption" was Israel's calling to sonship with God as their Father in the exodus (Ex 4:22, Ho 11:1); (2) the "glory" was God's visible manifestation whether in cloud and pillar of fire (Ex 15:6, 11) or in the sanctuary (Ex 40:34-35); (3) the "covenants" were five-fold: Abrahamic (Gen 15), Mosaic (Ex 20), Palestinian (Deu 29), Davidic (2 Sa 7), and new (Jer 31); (4) the "giving of the law" was at Sinai (Ex 20); (5) the "temple service" was the divine worship associated with the tabernacle; (6) the "promises" usually associated with the covenants included the main feature of blessings through the coming of the Messiah; (7) the "fathers" refer to the godly patriarchs (11:28); (8) the "Christ," who came through the Jewish descent (v. 5).

The last part of verse 5 has been the subject of much debate because of the way it may be punctuated (the Greek has no punctuation). One punctuation makes the expression a final doxology to God the Father: "May God, who rules over all, be for ever praised" (TEV). This is highly unlikely because a doxology at this point (that Christ came from unbelieving Jewish descent) would be totally inappropriate.[2]

The other punctuation refers the "who" to Christ but differs on whether "God" should be referred to Christ which precedes or to "blessed" which follows: "who (Christ) is over all, God blessed for ever" (ASV, NASB); or "Christ Who is God over all, blessed for ever" (Phillips). Either of the latter two renderings is preferable to the former because they refer Paul's doxology to the dual nature of Christ as being on the one hand Jewish flesh but on the other hand "over all" in His nature as Lord.[3]

---

2. E. H. Gifford, "Romans," in *The Bible Commentary: New Testament,* 3:169.
3. See John Murray, *The Epistle to the Romans,* vol. 2, Appendix A for an excellent discussion of the problem. Murray adopts the traditional KJV rendering as superior to others.

THE PROMISE, GOD'S ELECTION, AND ISRAEL'S PAST HISTORY
(9:6-29)

Paul has sharpened the problem of Jewish unbelief in verses 1-5. If such privileges and promises were given to the Jews by God, how can they now be largely cut off from the blessings of the Messiah by unbelief? If God makes a promise, can't He keep it? What becomes of God's righteousness which the gospel proclaims if God's truthfulness and faithfulness have apparently failed in connection with God's Word to Israel? If God has reneged on His promises to Israel, how could the Christian be certain that He would not change His mind toward him? If the promises of God are revocable, then how can one have joyous confidence in God's eternal plan through Christ? Both the validity of the promises and by implication the character of God are at stake.

Paul gives four lines of argument to answer this challenge. The first concerns the nature of God's promises as being rooted in the free and righteous elective purpose of God in Israel's history (9:6-29). Paul will show from Israel's history that God's promise to Abraham was intended to be fulfilled only to those whom He sovereignly "called."

It is important at this point to get some background in first century Jewish views of election. Problems which for years have entrenched theologians in chapters 9 and 10 might have been avoided if this material had been considered more seriously. Furthermore, by being preoccupied with these theological debates, many have also missed the real point of chapter 11.

The Jewish argument is well summarized by Berkeley Mickelsen in his commentary on Romans in *The Wycliffe Bible Commentary*.[4] Paul's Jewish opponents would present this view: "We have circumcision as a sign (Gen 17:7-14) that we are God's elect people. Members of God's elect people will not perish. Therefore, we will not perish." Rabbinical evidence shows that this was the attitude of most Jews in Paul's day. Hermann L. Strack and Paul Billerbeck have prepared a *Commentary on the New Testament* in which they bring together parallels from the Tal-

4. Berkeley Mickelsen, "Romans," in *The Wycliffe Bible Commentary*, ed. C. F. Pfeiffer and E. F. Harrison (Chicago: Moody, 1962), pp. 1209-10.

mud and Midrashim that shed light on the New Testament.[5] In Volume IV, Part 2, they have devoted an entire excursus (#31) to the subject of *Sheol, Gehenna* (place of punishment), and the *heavenly garden of Eden* (paradise). The following translations include names of tractates of the rabbinical writings from which their ideas about these places are drawn.

> Rabbi Levi has said: In the future (on the other side—what the Greeks called the spirit world) Abraham sits at the entrance of Gehenna and he allows no circumcised ones from the Israelites to enter into it (i.e., Gehenna). [Midrash Rabba Genesis, 48 (30ª, 49)].[6]

In this same context the question is asked: How about those who sin excessively? The answer is: They are returned to a state of uncircumcision as they enter Gehenna. The next translation deals with the question of what happens after death to an Israelite.

> When an Israelite goes into his eternal house (=grave), an angel is sitting over the heavenly garden of Eden, who takes each son of Israel who is circumcised for the purpose of bringing him into the heavenly garden of Eden (paradise). [Midrash Tanchum, Sade, waw, 145ª, 35].[7]

Again the question is raised: How about those Israelites who serve idols? As above, the answer is: They will be returned to a state of uncircumcision in Gehenna. Here is a translation that looks at the Israelites as a group:

> All Israelites who are circumcised come into the heavenly garden of Eden (paradise). [Midrash Tanchuma, Sade, waw, 145ª, 32].[8]

It is clear from these quotations that most Jews believed and taught that all circumcised Israelites who have died are in paradise and that there are no circumcised Israelites in Gehenna.

To the claim that the Lord could not reject his elect people, Paul first of all replies by emphasizing God's freedom, righteous-

5. Hermann L. Strack and Paul Billerbeck, *Kommentar zum Neue Testamentum aus Talmud und Midrach*, 4 vols (Munich: Beck, 1922-28).
6. Ibid., 4.2.1066.
7. Ibid.
8. Ibid., 4.2.1067.

ness, and sovereignty. God acts freely, acts in righteousness, and acts sovereignly because he is free, righteous, and sovereign in His own eternal being.

THE PROMISE AND ABRAHAM'S DESCENDANTS, ISAAC AND JACOB (9:6-13)

Has God not kept His Word to Israel? No, Paul asserts: "But it is not as though the word of God [the promises] has failed" (Gk. *ekpiptō*, "to be in vain," "to lose validity") and by implication God's own faithfulness (v. 6). The reason why Paul asserts that the promises to Israel have not really been empty is that the promise has always been linked to the purpose of God determined by election or calling (v. 11). From the very beginning onward in Israel's history God has been selective in the application of the promise. He says, "They are not all Israel [true spiritual seed] who are descended from Israel [physical lineage]" (v. 6). The promise is valid only to those for whom it was intended.

Paul, in verses 6-13, uses two cases in the beginning of Israel's history to demonstrate that when God gave the promise of blessing to Abraham and his descendants, He did not have *all* the descendants of Abraham in mind. In the first place God chose Isaac rather than Ishmael to continue the promise made to Abraham: "Through Isaac your descendants will be named" (Ro 9:7; Gen 21:12); and the Word said, "Sarah shall have a son" (Ro 9:9; Gen 18:10). In an argument parallel to that elaborated further in Galatians 3 and 4, Paul argues that the descendants of Ishmael through the bondwoman Hagar are of the flesh and not the heirs of the promise. His point is that God moved toward fulfilling the promise through selection as in the case of Abraham's children.

But were not Abraham's children (Isaac and Ishmael) born of different mothers? God probably chose Isaac, it might be suggested, because he was born of Abraham's full wife, Sarah. To show that God's election has no reference to merit derived from the status or relationship of the mothers, Paul shows the same principle operating in *one* mother, Rebecca, and the birth of her twins, Jacob and Esau. God's election has nothing to do with the merits of special lineage or of an individual's own works. It all depends on God's sovereign will. God selected Jacob ("the older will serve the younger," v. 12) to continue the lineage through whom the promise was to be fulfilled even though such recognition was contrary to the Near Eastern custom of the right of inheritance going to the firstborn (vv. 10-12).

In verse 13 Paul appeals to a passage in the prophets to further support the practice of God's selection, "Jacob I loved, but Esau I hated" (Ro 9:13; Mal 1:2, 3). Love and hate in this context do not have to do with God's personal emotional hatred or love but with the *choice* of the one over the other to continue the fulfillment of the promise.

My children play a game involving various colored marbles. They inform me that I am to be interested only in marbles of a certain color, and I am not to try and take the others of different colors. In words similar to Malachi's they say, "Daddy you *hate* blue (marbles), and you *love* red (marbles)." Thus I choose (love) the red marbles for my purposes and leave (hate) the blue ones alone for other purposes. God's purposes in salvation, however, are never carried out without respect to a man's response of belief or unbelief. Paul will get to this point later (vv. 30-33), but first he must answer two objections to his concept of election.

GOD'S SOVEREIGNTY AND GOD'S JUSTICE (9:14-29)

The most natural objection to Paul's teaching on God's sovereign election (if correctly understood) is that it seems to make God unfair since He chooses one and not the other (even before birth in Jacob's case) without any regard to their works. So an objector might say, "There is no injustice [unrighteousness] with God, is there?" (v. 14). Paul's answer is disappointing but instructive. He simply abhors the idea ("May it never be!") and shows that God does exercise His mercy in absolute freedom of choice. Paul assumes throughout that God is just and His actions of election are also consistent with His justice.

To support his view of God's justice in His free choices, the apostle turns for further evidence to the Words of God to Moses and Pharaoh (vv. 15-18). If anyone in Israel's history should have been chosen for his good works, it would be the great lawgiver, Moses, but it is to Moses that God says, "I will have mercy on whom I have mercy" (Ro 9:15; Ex 33:19). Not even Moses was shown God's mercy except on the basis of God's own choice to bless Moses (v. 17). All God's acts toward man are on the basis of His mercy; man deserves nothing, because he is in rebellion. If God comes to man in mercy, man's status and blessing before God cannot be due to man's willing or achieving. This is Paul's whole position on justification by faith (chaps. 1-8).

What about Pharaoh himself (Ex 4:16-21)? It was precisely because Pharaoh hardened his heart that Israel was oppressed, and God could show His power in the exodus and proclaim His name to all ages through the Passover celebration (v. 17). Upon whom He wills He shows mercy, and "He hardens whom He desires" (v. 18). The hardening of Pharaoh's heart which resulted from his unbelief (Ex 4:21; 7:3; 9:12) was designed to show God's mercy. God's sovereignty even extends to the callousing of men's hearts. But even this severe action was a means to the end of showing His mercy. Pharaoh first hardened his own heart following the first five plagues, then God hardened Pharaoh's heart in the last five plagues.[9]

In the diatribe fashion (see 2:1) Paul utters the actual words of another objection, "Why does He still find fault? For who resists His will?" (v. 19). The objection is discerning and devastating. If God sovereignly hardens men's hearts like Pharaoh's, how can He justly judge them as hardened sinners since no one can resist His sovereign will? It is the problem of human responsibility and God's justice. Again Paul's answer is even more disappointing in one sense than the former but perhaps also more instructive. He does not answer the charge but simply says in the strongest way that man's position as a creature does not qualify him to contradict the Creator (vv. 20, 21). Man must be silent! Just as a potter may fashion his clay as he pleases (Jer 18), so God has perfect liberty to make of humanity what He pleases. As the pottery cannot answer back challenging the design of the potter, so neither can man (Is 29:16).

But someone may object, man is not a pot and he *will* ask ques-

9. Carl F. Keil and Franz Delitzsch, *Commentaries on the Old Testament*, 13 vols. (Grand Rapids: Eerdmans, 1949), 1:453-57.

tions! But Paul's reply rejects this kind of question because it presupposes the centrality of *man* and to try to answer it would tend to lower God to human reasoning and attempt to justify God theoretically. Rather, Paul affirms the centrality of God and will not lower God's actions to fit man's reasoning. His response demands that first of all God be acknowledged as God (1:21). Ultimately, as the potter is responsible for the vessel he fashions, so God is, finally, responsible for what He does in history.

Verses 22-24 expand the thought of the potter having the absolute right to make vessels for whatever end he wishes either for aesthetic ends or for more common, menial ends ("honorable use . . . common use"). Paul further draws upon the potter analogy but begins to narrow down the sense to his immediate concern. God makes "vessels [instruments] of wrath prepared for destruction" (v. 22)[10] and "vessels [instruments] of mercy, which He prepared beforehand for glory" (v. 23). Verse 24 makes it plain that Paul has *individuals* in mind: "Even us, whom he also called." Further, "calling" in the whole epistle refers to the individual call to salvation and justification (8:30). One cannot then, regardless of the difficulty, weaken at least the latter part of the chapter's emphasis on individual election and calling (regardless of the earlier portions) to that of mere national or corporate election. Paul's very point is to the opposite effect, that is, God has by grace selected some out of the nation to whom He will manifest His mercy (forgiveness), and He has fitted others to receive His wrath (deservedly because of their unbelief, vv. 30-33).

But lest we charge God with arbitrary rigor, it should be noted that Paul's burden is to show that God's deliberate design in election was to show forth His mercy (v. 23). In order to do this, God exercised much longsuffering (patience) toward the vessels of wrath (Pharaoh and the unbelieving Jews and Gentiles, in Paul's day by not immediately destroying them but giving them opportunity to repent before His final power and wrath is revealed (2:4-5).

10. The Greek verb is *katartizō* which means "to suit," "to fit," "to establish," "to foreordain" (TDNT). The verb interestingly is passive in voice, which may suggest Paul is softening the active role of God in thus making such a vessel (although ultimately God is responsible). In verse 23 the vessels of mercy are directly prepared (active voice) by God for glory.

Paul's main point seems to be that when unbelief and hardening arise as in the case of Pharaoh and the majority of Jewish people in Paul's day, God has a purpose in history (as well as for the individual). This purpose is first of all to reveal His wrath against rebellion and thereby proclaim to the world His power. Second, through unbelief God will cause His mercy to be brought upon those whom He calls. Ultimately, then, history is redemptive in its purpose. In glory and in wrath through election God is working out His purpose in history of manifesting His righteousness.

In verses 25-29 Paul appeals to the Old Testament prophecies for the principles which substantiate his claim by references to God's announcement to choose an elect company of both Jews and Gentiles to participate in His mercy. To show that God had in mind to "call" (to salvation) Gentiles, Paul quotes Hosea 2:23 and 1:10, which originally applied to apostate Jews as "not My people" and "not beloved," to the effect that God would call to Himself those who were not His people (by application, Gentiles) and make them "sons of the living God" (vv. 25-26).

Furthermore, Paul quotes Isaiah to show that the Old Testament predicted that God would "call" not the *whole* nation of Israel through His promise, but only a remnant would be saved (Ro 9:27-29; Is 1:9, 10, 22, 23; 11:11). Again in Isaiah's day God's wrath was poured out through the Assyrians on a disbelieving nation (v. 28), but God moved also in electing grace to preserve a remnant or seed (v. 29). So in all God's dealings with men the promise of blessing (forgiveness) relates to the chosen seed who are of faith; and if unbelief prevails, it does not thereby nullify the Word of God.

ISRAEL'S FAILURE HER OWN FAULT
(9:13—10:21)

Paul has argued that Israel's unbelief cannot invalidate God's Word because God's promise is based on the principle of election. He now turns to the human side of Israel's failure, their own unbelief. If God has elected some in sovereign grace to fulfill His Word, He has not thereby invalidated human responsibility. His election is not unrelated to man's belief. Israel's stumbling was due to her own misguided effort in attempting to please God through law obedience rather than by faith. "Christ is the end of the law for righteousness to everyone who believes" (9:30–10:4).

Furthermore, this faith righteousness which Paul proclaims, unlike the law, is easily available to all who will hear its Word (10:5-13). Yet Israel has heard this universally preached Word of Christ and has turned from it in disobedience as the prophets foretold. They are therefore fully responsible for God's rejection of them (10:14-21).

THE CAUSE OF THE JEWS' FAILURE (9:30–10:4)

While the Jew has not lacked enthusiasm for God ("pursued righteousness," "zeal for God," 9:31; 10:2), his commendable sincerity has not helped him before God because it was selfishly misguided. The Jewish moralist, in attempting to attain acceptance before God by keeping the law, has, in fact, not attained this acceptance (righteousness) as did the believing Gentile. Why? Because, as Paul has already argued through the first part of the letter (chaps. 1-8), all men are sinners and cannot approach God on the basis of good works. A man can come to Him only in humble acceptance by faith of God's provision in Christ (vv. 30-32).[11] This "stone of stumbling" (i.e., Christ and faith righteousness; 1 Pe 2:6-8) was prepared by God and foretold by Isaiah, the prophet (Ro 9:33; Is 8:14; 28:16). If the image of running is still in Paul's mind, then the picture of a runner tripping over a hurdle and losing the race vividly captures his point (vv. 32, 33).

The misinformed zeal for God of his Jewish kinsmen intensifies the tragedy of their rejection. It is Paul's earnest desire that they may realize their error and turn to Christ for deliverance from their sin (10:1-2). Charles Erdman commented that there would be no lack of converts to the Christian faith if all who profess to follow Christ felt for the spiritual welfare of their fellow countrymen this deep concern expressed by Paul for his own people.[12]

11. The use of "law" of righteousness in verse 31 is similar to the use of law in 3:27; 7:21, 23; 8:2 and means principle or rule or order.
12. Charles Erdman, *The Epistle of Paul to the Romans*, p. 101.

The error of the moralist begins with his failure to judge himself correctly in view of his own moral and spiritual shortcomings. Supposing himself to be all right or as good as others, he develops a spirit of proud self-seeking, which is the root of sin. He ends up by boasting in his own moral achievements (v. 3; 3:27). In seeking to establish before God his own righteousness, the moralist overlooks God's way of righteousness which comes through faith in Jesus Christ. It is an ironic tragedy—zeal for God, but rejection by God. These statements of Paul should forever settle the thesis that sincerity in place of truth suffices before God. Sincerity indeed may be indicative of a right attitude toward God, but not necessarily, as the present case reveals. Nor can ignorance be pleaded as an excuse before God because no man is totally ignorant of God's truth (1:19-20).

Christ is an "end" (Gk. *telos*, goal, termination) of the law to obtain justification to all who have faith (v. 4). When one submits to Christ as God's means for justification, it puts an end to the attempted (but futile) seeking for justification through the moralistic approach of law.[13]

THE RIGHTEOUSNESS OF FAITH (10:5-13)

In these nine verses the righteousness which comes through law (v. 5) is contrasted with the righteousness based on faith (vv. 6-13). The latter is not only available (vv. 5-8), and universal in its appeal (vv. 11-13), but rests upon the historical fact of Jesus' death and resurrection (vv. 9-10).

What about obedience to the law? Was not the keeping of the law the prerequisite for having life (Lev 18:5; Lk 10:28)? If God gave the law and commanded total obedience to it, can it be maintained that obedience to it would have no relevance? Paul seems to argue in verse 5 that Moses taught that the achievement of righteousness before God on the basis of obedience to the law was at least a theoretical possibility. However, Paul argued earlier in the letter that the law came in to increase the trespass (5:20).

13. "End" of law here should not be viewed as teaching either that the law was fulfilled in Christ or that the *aim* of the law was to be a pedagogue until Christ (Gal 3:24), both of which are true. Rather, Christ is the end or *termination* of the law both in the sense of 7:6 as well as in the sense that the believer no longer seeks for justification in the law.

It may not be impossible to reconcile these two opposites if we remember that when a man attempts to keep all the law he discovers that he is powerless to do it and thus judged sinful by the same law through which he sought acceptance and life (Deu 27:26).

The Jews' (and all moralists') real mistake, according to Paul, is not that they do not take the law seriously but they fail to take it seriously enough. Moralists count on two illusions. They believe on the one hand that on the ledger of life certain good works in the credit column will in the long run cancel out many of the debit marks in the other column and ultimately put them in the black before God. On the other hand, they also hold to the false belief that whatever does not balance up will be overlooked by God's indulgence. But God does not keep any such credit books of good versus bad, because He has an entirely different way of balancing out the debit column. Righteousness comes only through faith in the Lord Jesus Christ.

In verses 6-8 Paul combines references to the Old Testament law (Deu 30:11-14) with statements about the gospel. It is clear that the words "do not say in your heart" (v. 6) are aimed at the attitude of unbelief in the gospel. What is not so clear is Paul's use of the phrases "who will ascend into heaven?" and "who will descend into the abyss?" which are borrowed from the Deuteronomy passage. Does Paul mean that the words which were originally applied to the law in the Old Testament have equal significance when applied to faith in Christ? Moses' warning in Deuteronomy is against the taunt of unbelief expressed when a man claims that the revelation of the law is too difficult (impossible) to fulfill because it is inaccessible (in heaven or beyond the sea). Likewise, Paul sees the danger of unbelief in the gospel as evidenced in a man demanding before he will trust Christ to actually have firsthand empirical proof of the incarnation ("bring Christ down") and the resurrection ("bring Christ up from the dead").

But faith operates on the basis of the *Word* of divine witness proclaimed in the message of Christ and therefore salvation-faith is immediately possible when one hears the gospel message. How important this truth is that connects the truthfulness of the historical facts of Jesus' death and resurrection with the preached Word of the gospel witness. This means that when I believe the gospel message by faith I do not need to actually witness or be able to infallibly verify those historical events to have their certainty and efficacy immediately applied to my life.

Verses 9-10 describe the two-fold content of this faith righteousness: namely, (1) "If you confess with your mouth Jesus as Lord" (the divine king from heaven); and (2) "believe in your heart that God raised Him from the dead." The kind of faith which grants forgiveness and acceptance before God consists basically in two articles. Along with acceptance of Jesus as Lord goes the second, God raised Him from the dead. The resurrection is a crucial fact because it marks out Jesus, the Lord from heaven, as absolutely distinct from any other lord. He is the one in whom alone the Father has accomplished his redeeming work for man (Heb 1:3).

No special point should be made in verse 10 over the dual use of "heart . . . righteousness" with "mouth . . . salvation." The biblical idea of the heart refers to the religious center or core of our life and should not be limited to only the affections or emotions. What the heart believes will be uttered by the lips. As Paul says elsewhere, "No man can call Jesus Lord, except by the Holy Spirit" (1 Co 12:3; Mt 12:34). To "confess" means to declare, avow, profess, proclaim. It seems evident that the "confession" is to be made out loud before men, with the mouth, not by some other action.

Along with an affirmation from Is 28:16 to the effect that one who trusts in the Lord will not be "disappointed" (or "disillusioned"—TDNT), Paul strikes the note of the universality of this faith salvation in verses 11-13. Everyone (Jew and Gentile) who calls upon the name of the Lord shall be saved (Joel 2:32). The Old Testament foretold of this universal salvation available to all who evidence their faith in the Lord. Calling upon His name is an act of worship.[14] But why, then, haven't the Jews believed? Why have they been rejected in favor of the Gentiles? Paul now turns to this problem.

14. Murray, 2:58.

152 The Freedom Letter

THE FAILURE OF FAITH (10:14-21)

Perhaps ignorance of the gospel is the problem? In verses 14-15 Paul constructs a five-link chain to emphasize that ignorance is not the cause of the Jews' failure. Men will only call (for salvation) upon one in whom they believe. Faith must have a proclaimed conscious object, which requires a message and a messenger. Finally, a genuine messenger or an apostle who is commissioned by the Lord Himself must be "sent" (Gk. *apostalōsin*) (v. 15). This last link is confirmed by a reference to the Old Testament where God approvingly mentions the ministry of *sent ones* (apostles) to Israel for salvation purposes (Is 52:7).

Paul abruptly breaks the chain at this point and raises the issue of Israel's unbelief, "However, they did not all heed the glad tidings" (v. 16). The hearing of the message was only beneficial when it was received by faith (Heb 4:1-2). "Those beside the road" writes Luke, "are those who have heard; then the devil comes and takes away the word from their heart, so that they may not believe and be saved" (Lk 8:12). Even Isaiah confirms the truth Paul is stating by predicting that the message (report) concerning the Messiah would fail to be accepted (Is 53:1).

In verse 17 Paul summarizes ("so") his main point by affirming the connection between the message proclaimed by Christ's apostles and faith which calls upon the name of the Lord for salvation. Saving faith, then, arises in response to the message (Word preaching) about Christ (His lordship and resurrection, v. 9).[15] Faith has a perpetual relationship to the Word and cannot be separated from it any more than can the rays from the sun whence they proceed.

Now in verses 18-21 Paul speaks more pointedly to why Israel failed to respond to Jesus Christ. Perhaps they, in fact, did not have opportunity to hear the gospel of Christ? Paul answers quite emphatically to the contrary, "Indeed they have." The language of Psalm 19:4, which Paul uses to describe the universal satura-

15. The Greek here would permit the thought either of the Word about Christ (obj. gen.) in the sense of the apostles' preaching, or the word originated by Christ in the sense that the substance is His Word (subj. gen.). In either case the authority of the Word is emphasized. It is the very Word of Christ (Jn 3:34; 5:47; Eph 5:26; 1 Pe 1:25).

tion of the world with the gospel message, has raised an important question (v. 18).

Does the revelation of God in nature, to which the Psalm refers, carry with it the gospel message? In this case Paul would be saying that the Jews heard the gospel in the witness of nature. While this sense is possible, the context argues for a different meaning. Just as the revelation of God in nature is universal (Ps 19:4), and makes no distinctions between Jew and Gentile, so the historical revelation of God in the gospel of Jesus has gone forth with universality to all places and to all peoples. Israel indeed had heard the proclaimed message in the first century at least. They could not plead ignorance of Christ. The faithful obedience of our first century brethren in spreading the message of Christ to their known world regardless of the cost certainly should convict us.

Finally, the apostle discusses a further reason offered to explain why Israel failed to embrace Christ by asking, "Surely Israel did not know, did they?" (v. 19). The sense of the brief question is sharpened if we more accurately translate "know" by "understand." Perhaps the gospel preachers spoke unintelligibly and Israel misunderstood their message? Again the answer implied is no for both the law (Moses, v. 19) and then the prophets (Isaiah, vv. 20-21) declared that God was going to work significantly among the Gentiles ("not a nation;" "nation without understanding") and as a result the Jews would be "jealous" and "angry" (v. 19). Such strong emotional response could not but be the result of first of all a clear understanding of the universal character of the gospel message which puts Jew and Gentile on equal footing.

Furthermore, the Gentiles' response was immediate and grateful, from a people who were not even associated with the Lord (v. 20; Is 65:1). Yet, to Israel, God through the prophet declared (Is 65:2) that He had unceasingly stretched forth His hands in unwearied love only to have his pleading met with rebuffs (see also Mt 23:37-39). Surely there is a great mystery surrounding why man rebels against his Creator.

It seems clear from this chapter that the Jews' failure to respond to Christ's Word lies neither in their lack of knowledge nor in their failure to grasp the meaning of the message. Their rejection goes back to their own choice of unbelief and disobedience. It is not because God has withdrawn His love and promises to them.

ISRAEL'S FAILURE NEITHER TOTAL NOR FINAL
(11:1-36)

Since the Jews have rejected the gospel of Christ, does this mean that they have been entirely rejected by God for salvation? Has the plan of God in calling this nation of people been frustrated by their obstinancy? Who will now do what God intended Israel to do? Paul's answer is two-fold and very definite. First, God has not totally rejected the Jewish people from salvation. Paul is exhibit number one that God still has a believing remnant, though the majority are rejected because of their unbelief (11:1-10). Second, God is not through with this people as a whole nation, but He has planned a glorious revival among them sometime in the future (11:11-29). There two aspects of the Jews' present and future are both introduced by a separate question in verses 1 and 11.

JEWS' FAILURE NOT TOTAL (11:1-10)

Paul asks, with all that he has just said in mind (10:18-21), "God has not rejected His people, has He?" (v. 1). The form of the question in the Greek expects a negative answer, so he answers immediately with the strong negative, "May it never be!" (see 3:4). The principal reason for his confidence in God's favor toward Jewish people is that he himself comes from pure Jewish ancestry and yet believes in Jesus as the Messiah. The existence of Jewish Christians in the world proves that God has not rejected the total Jewish community.[16] "God has not rejected His people whom He foreknew" (v. 2) reflects the language of Psalm 94:14 (1 Sa 12:22). God remains ever faithful to His covenant prom-

---

16. "Jewish Christians" is a term used to describe a person of Jewish cultural and religious heritage who has come to believe in Jesus as the Messiah (the divine king of Israel). There is a more modern trend developing, especially in the state of Israel, for Jewish Christians to drop the name Christian and refer to themselves simply as Jews who believe that Jesus is the Messiah, the *Mesh*e*him*. The term "Christian," we should remember, was not used of the followers of Jesus until many years after His death and resurrection and at first only by pagans in derision of the way believers in Christ lived (Ac 11:26). The important fact is not the name but whether you belong to and follow the Lord Jesus Christ. Jewish conversion presents a special case of Christian conversion and must be so recognized.

ise to Abraham (Gen 22:17-18) and has set His love ("foreknew," see 8:29) upon an elect Jewish remnant of those who believe, which constitute "His people" at the present time.

Paul turns in verses 2-5 to one of the many cases in the Old Testament where the nation in large measure had turned away from God's will, yet there were still those who followed him. It forms a parallel to the problem of unbelief in his own day. Elijah's circumstances in the revolt against God incited by Jezebel forced him to conclude that he alone of the whole nation was still a true follower of the Lord (1 Ki 19:10-14). Yet God's Word came to him and revealed that there were some seven thousand others whom God had "kept" for Himself who were still obedient to Him (v. 4). Paul identifies himself with Elijah in his aloneness and also in the mild but encouraging rebuke of the Lord, who reminded the prophet that there was a chosen remnant out of Israel that constituted the true Israel through whom God's covenant purposes would continue (9:6-8).

"In the same way then [as in Elijah's day], there has also come to be at the present time a remnant [of Jewish Christians] according to God's gracious choice" (v. 5). Since the remnant can only exist by God's choice, it must be by grace and not on the basis of man's works. Paul digresses briefly in verse 6 to emphasize his main argument that appeared earlier in the letter (3:27—4:25). God deals with men only on the basis of His grace (hence, man's faith) and not their works. Grace and works are mutually exclusive principles in winning acceptance before God. If God's election is the basis of the remnant's existence, then it must be based on God's grace which precedes all human works, otherwise grace ceases to be grace, and works cease to be works. In other words, if we confuse such opposites as grace and works, words lose their meaning (Eph 2:8-9; Ro 9:11).

But what of the "rest" of the nation of Israel who were not the remnant? Paul says they were "hardened" (v. 7) in accordance with the Old Testament predictions in Moses' writing (Ro 11:8; Deu 29:4), and in David's statements (Ro 11:9-10; Ps 69:22). Hardening is a divine judgment arising out of unbelief (Ro 11:20; 9:17-18; Heb 3:12-13; Mt 13:14-15). Unbelief brings blindness, insensitivity, bondage ("bend their backs," v. 10), and social discord ("table become a snare," v. 9). One cannot refuse the divine grace without at the same time positively opposing God (Mk 9:40). Such opposition brings God's active judgment in the present life much in the same manner as the three-fold reference to divine judgment ("God gave them over") in chapter 1.

The expression in verse 7 to the effect that Israel did not obtain what it sought for can mean nothing less than that the majority of the people did not obtain righteousness or justification before God (9:30; 10:3). The elect remnant obtained the justification by faith, but the rest did not. Here is further evidence that although Paul has groups of people in mind in these chapters (9-11) he is also in certain places talking about the relationship to God in salvation of individuals who make up these groups.

JEWS' FAILURE NOT FINAL (11:11-32)

If the majority of the Jewish nation stumbled over the gospel, even though a remnant believed, does this mean that God is through with the people as a whole or as a nation? Paul's question in verse 11 is very important: "They did not stumble so as to fall, did they?" That the Jews have "stumbled" into unbelief and disobedience the apostle has already clearly stated (9:32). But what does he mean by the phrase, "so as to fall"?

Some understand the "fall" to refer to Israel's final rejection as a religious community in the sense that God has purposed ("so as") as a whole they should never recover. The negative reply, "May it never be!" would then deny that this was true. Furthermore, the latter part of the chapter (vv. 12, 25-27) would also support this idea that God is not finished with the nation as a spiritual community when it refers to the future salvation of "all Israel."

The chief problem with this view is that it does not do justice to the rest of verse 11: "But by their transgression [stumbling] salvation has come to the Gentiles, to make them [Israel] jealous." In this use of the words, "by their transgression" (Gk. *paraptōma*, trespass, sin, 5:15), the reference is clearly to their stumbling into sin and unbelief.

Another sense, then, for the word "fall" is preferred. Paul's real question is whether the Jews' stumbling into the sin of unbelief was purposed by God so that they might lose their covenant relationship involving not only a future redemptive purpose but also a present purpose. Paul answers in strong abhorrence to the effect that they have not fallen down completely and proceeds to state two present divine purposes in Israel's stumbling: (1) that the gospel of salvation might go to the Gentiles and (2) that as a result of Gentile blessings the Jews might be stirred to jealousy and desire to come to Christ (11, 14). Both purposes are merciful in their design. This much, then, is clear. The sin of the Jews is temporary, and while it lasts, serves a particular gracious divine purpose.

In the first instance the immediate result of the Jewish rejection of Christ was the historical turning of the apostles to the Gentiles (Ac 13:46; 18:6; 28:28). Thus even in her disobedience, Israel still fulfills her calling as a link bweeen the Christ and the nations. Second, as a result of the conversion of the Gentiles, the Jews will be stirred to jealousy over the working of God among those who were formerly not His people. Paul's own ministry to the Gentiles can be viewed as ultimately a means of reaching at least some of his fellow Jews with Christ's gospel by making them jealous (vv. 13-14).

In verses 12 and 15 Paul contrasts and compares the present effects of the Gentile conversion with the future effects of Israel's conversion:

	JEWS	GENTILES
PRESENT	"Transgression" (v. 11): "failure" (v. 12); "rejection" (v. 15).	"Riches for the world" (v. 12); "riches for the Gentiles" (v. 12); "reconciliation of the world" (v. 15).
FUTURE	"How much more their fulfillment" (v. 12); "'their acceptance . . . life from the dead" (v. 15).	"Fulness of the Gentiles" (v. 25).

Paul sees a glorious future for the people of Israel as a nation and through them a tremendous blessing for the whole world.

This latter truth is highlighted in verse 15 by the difficult expression "life from the dead." The phrase probably does not describe the resurrection from the dead (most commentators since Origen) or the revival of the nation of Israel. Rather, it should be understood as a figure to describe some future glorious vivified condition of the whole world which occurs as a result of Israel's conversion.[17] Whatever tremendous thing Paul has in mind, it can only be described as the difference between death and life (v. 25).

To develop his argument further that the nation of Israel will still enjoy a future restoration as the people of God, Paul selects two analogies in verse 16. The "first piece" or "firstfruit" of the dough was a small portion of the newly kneaded lump that was set aside and, after having been baked into a loaf, offered to the Lord (Num 15:19-21.)[18] The consecrated offering of a part of the dough to the Lord was to sanctify, or set apart for God's purpose (make "holy"), the whole mass of dough. But who are the firstfruits of Israel? Some refer them to the Jewish remnant of whom Paul has been speaking in the context (v. 5). In this view the few Jewish Christians, like Paul himself, would be the pledge that the whole nation would eventually be saved.[19]

Most commentators, however, prefer to understand the firstfruit to mean the ancient forefathers (patriarchs) of Israel (v. 28). Because the first Jewish people were holy, that is, the patriarchs such as Abraham, who were truly consecrated to God, the people which came from these godly forefathers of the covenant form a whole with these patriarchs. Even though temporary unbelief and rejection has overtaken the nation, the covenant people will yet appear in the future in their real character and purpose as God's people. The temporary and partial unbelief of even a number of generations of Israelites, Paul would argue, cannot annul the continuing holy purpose of God destined for this people as a whole.

In the second metaphor of the "root" and "branches" of a tree, Paul further stresses the same point (v. 16). The tree bears the

17. Murray, 2:83-84.
18. The Greek *aparchē* (firstfruit) occurs a number of times in the NT: Ro 8:23; 16:5; 1 Co 16:15; 15:20, 23; Ja 1:18; Rev 14:4.
19. C. K. Barrett, *The Epistle to the Romans*, p. 216; and F. J. Leenhardt, *Romans* (London: ET of CNT, 1961), p. 286.

same character as the root. If the root (Abraham, Isaac, etc.) is holy (belonging to God), so are the branches (whole nation springing from the root). It is in the character of Israel as a covenant people, whose origins are good, that Paul sees the hope for their future restoration as a whole nation. Just as the believing wife or husband sanctifies (makes holy) the whole covenant marriage union of a believer and unbeliever, so that the children are not considered illegitimate or rejected by God (1 Co 7:14), so the believing forefathers of the Jewish people sanctify the whole covenant posterity in the sense that they are destined to fulfill God's purpose as a covenant nation.

Verses 17-24 continue the figure of the tree with its root and branches. In this section Paul is concerned to ward off some dangerous misconceptions about his teachings that might arise in the minds of the Gentile Christians to whom he is writing. Because the Jewish people are likened by Paul to branches from a holy root (v. 18), it might be argued that their present unbelief and rejection cancels out God's covenant with the patriarchs and denies any future for the Jews as the people of God. Paul, haven't they blown it by what they did to Christ? Didn't they get what they deserved because of their unbelief? Hasn't God now taken us Gentiles to be his new people in place of the ancient Jews? This raises the important question concerning what kind of attitude Christians should have toward nonbelieving Jews. A number of important facts must be considered, and each seriously, if we are to develop a correct attitude toward these ancient people and toward ourselves as Christians.

Paul first stresses the humble position of Gentile Christians. Extending the imagery of the tree (v. 16), Paul states that even though a portion (historically) of the Jewish people have stumbled into unbelief, their trespass has only resulted in the breaking away of some of the branches and not in the uprooting of the whole tree, for the root is holy. Christians should not, then, feel that God is finished with the Jewish people as a nation. They are, despite their temporary rejection, still God's covenant people.

There is a very common misconception among Christians today. Some have disregarded as visionary all predictions of a future national resurgence of Israel as a spiritual entity, and appropriate the promises made specifically to the nation of Israel in the Old Testament to themselves in some spiritual sense as the distinctively new people of God, the new Israel. This belief still persists even though the present political state of Israel (since 1948) is forcing some serious reconsiderations. Instead Paul sees one continuous covenant people of God under the figure of the "olive tree." The root, or stock, from which believing Jews and Gentiles all receive their spiritual strength and nourishment, is found in the patriarchs who bear the original promises of salvation in Christ (Gal 3:16). The branches are either individual believers or generations of believers who derive their life from the continuous covenant family of God to which they belong.

The branches are of two kinds: (1) the original branches are the Jewish people, some of which have been "broken off" because of their unbelief in God's promise (v. 20), and (2) the "wild olive" branches are Gentile believers that are grafted into the covenant family of God. Paul's use of "wild" olive tree (v. 17) and the reference to grafting "contrary to nature" (v. 24)[20] further stress the humble position of Gentile Christians who were not originally even part of the tree.

Paul warns the Gentiles as a group not to gloat over the fallen branches (unbelieving Jews). There are two reasons for this: (1) Gentile believers are enjoying the blessings of God because they have been made part of the covenant promises given to the patriarchs of Israel and not the other way around: "it is not you who supports the root, but the root supports you" (v. 18); and (2) the Gentiles stand in relationship to God because of faith. If they begin to exhibit pride in their position, God will remove them from the tree in the same manner He removed the proud, unbelieving Jews (vv. 19-22). Faith (absence of pride, 3:27-28) alone provides man his only hope, peace, and security. The proper attitude of man toward God is always reverent "fear" (v. 20).

These lessons are greatly needed today. What could be more unscriptural than for Christians to despise or discriminate against

20. Though the normal process of grafting involves placing a good, strong shoot on a weaker stem to transfer the strength of the better tree to the poorer, Paul's phrase "contrary to nature" recognizes this and shows that he was familiar with the normal horticultural process but wished to use this analogy to press home his point.

unbelieving Jews? Not only have Christians inherited the blessings which were brought into the world by Jews, but did not even Jesus say, "Salvation is from the Jews" (Jn 4:22)?

Furthermore, Gentile Christians must not be skeptical about the problem of continuing Jewish unbelief, since it is much more natural for God to put the Jew back into his own inheritance than it is for God to save the Gentiles (vv. 23-24). It must be remembered that Paul is talking about groups of people or generations and not individuals as such.

Paul now turns more directly to the prediction of the future Jewish revival in verses 25-27. He still wishes to further warn Gentile Christians against congratulating themselves for being wiser than the Jew, wiser, since they responded to the gospel whereas the latter rejected it. It should never be forgotten by Christians that Israel as a nation and as a spiritual entity has a glorious future in the outworking of God's purpose in history. Since there are several important terms in these verses and each has its own problems, it may be well to discuss each briefly.

1. The *mystery*. "Mystery" is Paul's characteristic way of referring either to a past secret purpose of God which has now been uncovered and made known to men (Ro 16:25; Col 1:26-27; 2 Th 2:7), or to a future purpose that is made known now for the instruction and attitude of the believer (1 Co 15:51). The mystery is this: a partial (not total) hardening (not blinding) has occurred in the present among the Jewish people because of their unbelief (v. 7) and will continue until the fullness of the Gentiles is brought about, and then all Israel will be saved. Paul here speaks of the nation of Israel and not every last individual in the nation. He says in effect that the nation's blindness to Christ is "partial," not total, temporary, not permanent ("until").

2. The *fullness* of the Gentiles. What does "fulness" (v. 25) mean? A number of views are possible. In verse 12 Paul refers to the "fulfillment" (Greek is same in both) of Israel as the opposite of their diminishing (only a remnant is now saved). So the fullness of the Gentiles could mean their "full number" in comparison to the small number who up to Paul's time were converted. The fullness might be reached whenever in any generation the final person filling up the total number is converted. But

in the light of what the same word ("fulfillment") means in verse 12—no longer a redeemed remnant but a converted mass—it seems better to understand "fulness of the Gentiles" to indicate some sort of sweeping revival in the future resulting in the conversion of most of the Gentiles just prior to the great harvest of the Jews.

Others attempt to relate the fullness of the Gentiles to fulfillment of the "times of the Gentiles" spoken of by our Lord in Luke 21:24. The sense would be, "a partial hardening has happened to Israel until the fullness of the times of the Gentiles has come." Israel's acceptance is preceded by the moment in which God put an end to Israel's oppression by the Gentile nations.[21] But "Gentiles" in Romans 9-11 almost always means Gentile Christians (9:24, 30; 11:12-13), and "times of the Gentiles" has an oppressive, unfavorable connotation, while "fulness of the Gentiles" like the "fulfillment of Israel" (v. 12) has the sense of a favorable divine blessing.

One further modification of the first view deserves mention. The fullness of the Gentiles might have reference to geographical fullness, that is, it would refer to the full complement of the Gentiles, or the Gentile nations as a whole.[22] This note of universality of the evangelization of the Gentile nations is sounded by Christ in the Olivet discourse when He says. "And this gospel of the kingdom shall be preached in the whole world for a witness unto all nations, and then the end shall come" (Mt 24:14). Again, the reference as in the first view, would be to some great evangelization effort of Christianity reaching all the Gentiles that will precede the conversion of Israel and in some way be related to that later event. It need not mean that every Gentile would be converted, but enough would be to refer to the whole ethnic group or entity. The main objection to this modification, as we understand it, is that "fulness" refers more definitely to conversion than to mere evangelization.

It seems preferable to us to adopt the first view while admitting there are still unresolved ambiguities.

3. *And thus.* It may appear that this little "and thus" (v. 26)

21. Ernst Käsemann, *New Testament Questions of Today,* trans. W. J. Montague (Philadelphia: Fortress, 1969), p. 144.
22. Erdman, p. 127.

is not important, and to isolate it smacks of pedantry. But if we make the text read "then" or "after this," we will not totally distort the sense of Paul, but we may miss the deeper thought. The use of "and thus" stresses some *logical* (not temporal) connection between the fullness of the Gentiles and the salvation of all Israel. The "and thus" might refer to the manner of Israel's deliverance, that is, that Israel will be saved by means of the coming Redeemer. described in the following words, "The Deliverer will come from Zion" (v. 26). But probably it is better to see the term as referring back to the whole mystery explained in verse 25: the strange detour by which Israel's partial unbelief continues until God brings in the fullness of the Gentiles.[23] Whether the Gentile fullness will provoke Israel to emulation or some other means will be used is not clear.

4. *All Israel* to be saved. Finally, what is meant by "all Israel" (v. 26)? Some understand Paul to be referring to *spiritual* Israel composed of both believing Jews and believing Gentiles (Gal 6:16). This interpretation was held by a number of early and later church fathers (Theodorus; Augustine, in some texts; Luther and most of the reformers).[24] However, the context and exegetical factors strongly favor an alternate view.

Paul's entire usage of the word *Israel* in this section of the book (chapters 9-11), especially in chapter 11, and even the preceding verse, make it virtually certain that he is denoting the ethnic Israel or Jewish people which could not include Gentiles. This more limited use becomes clear by also noting the subject of the following phrases: "their fulfillment" (v. 12); "they do not continue in their unbelief, will be grafted in" (v. 23); "their disobedience . . . these also now have been disobedient . . . they also may now be shown mercy" (vv. 30-31); and, "all in disobedience, that He might show mercy to all" (v. 32).

"All" Israel, then, must refer to the forgiveness of the whole Jewish people or nation, the whole ethnic group in contrast to the saved remnant of Jews in Paul's day and ours. It is the whole people, rather than a small part, that will be converted to the Messiah (so teach Origen, Chrysostom, Ambrose, Augustine in

23. Käsemann, p. 146.
24. H. P. Liddon, *Romans,* p. 217.

City of God, and Jerome).[25] In other words, the "partial" hardness will be removed.

In verses 26 and 27 Paul appeals to the Old Testament to support his position that the nation will one day be saved. He quotes from Isaiah 29:20, 21 and 27:9 which refer to the day when the Messiah (the Deliverer) will remove all ungodliness from Jacob (Israel) and forgive the whole nation their sins. This fact supports Paul's contention that God will one day restore the whole nation in the blessings of the new covenant. It is not certain whether the reference in Isaiah to the Messiah's coming refers to His first coming and the still future implication to the nation of that coming, or whether Paul had in mind the second coming of Christ. Either will do justice to the context.

Further, the existing fact of Israel's present unbelief does not militate against Paul's view of the full salvation of the nation in the future because Israel has a unique paradoxical relationship to God: they are at the same time both "enemies" and "beloved" of God (vv. 28-29).

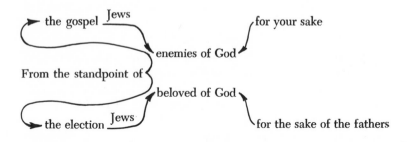

On the one hand they are enemies of God because they have rejected the gospel message which is of divine origin. But on the other hand, they are beloved of God because of His covenant-electing purposes for the nation. The latter phrase in each instance shows the eternal purpose in God's actions: "for your sake" explains why the majority of Jews are under God's wrath: it is

25. Ibid.; this view is also held by Murray; F. F. Bruce, *The Epistle of Paul to the Romans;* Erdman. For a strong case arguing the same view, see Peter Richardson, *Israel in the Apostolic Church* (New York: Cambridge U., 1969), pp. 126-47.

because in God's providence the Gentiles were to be extended the call to salvation. "For the sake of the fathers" (the patriarchs, Abraham, Isaac, Jacob) explains why Israel will yet be blessed and received as a people. God's covenant promises to the patriarchs concerning their national blessing through salvation in the Messiah have not been abrogated despite the unbelief of many of the Jews. In verse 29, Paul emphatically states, "The gifts and the calling of God are irrevocable," that is, God's covenant promises are irrevocable because of His own faithfulness (3:3). This in no way overlooks the fact that individual Jews are either in or out of right relationship to God on the basis of their faith or that they are not accountable in judgment before God.

In verses 30-31 Paul reiterates the truth he has already stated several times. The salvation of the Gentiles was occasioned by the unbelief of Israel (v. 30). But Israel's salvation will be occasioned not by the Gentiles' return to unbelief but by means of the great mercy shown to these non-Jews (v. 31).

Finally, in verse 32, Paul concludes by drawing our attention to the relationship between man's disobedience and God's mercy. It is only in the context of disobedience that mercy can operate. Both Jew and Gentile are consigned to disobedience, but God's purpose is to show mercy. Paul is not teaching that all men individually will be saved but that God's mercy is extended to all people without discrimination (Gal 3:22).

PAUL'S PRAISE (11:33-36)

Paul has been granted a small window into God's great plan for man. He stands back in awe and wonder. He worships Him by exclaiming, "Oh the depth of the riches both of the wisdom and knowledge of God! How unsearchable are His judgments and unfathomable His ways!" (v. 33). God's ways and thoughts are unfathomable to created intelligence. His exhaustless grace and goodness (riches), His providence (wisdom), and His understanding (knowledge) elude all attempts to trace out their causes or their directions because God is Himself the inscrutable origin of these characteristics (v. 34, from Is 40:13). Only poetry can do justice to this idea:

Thy way was in the sea,
And Thy paths in the mighty waters,
And Thy footprints may not be known (Ps 77:19).

This is the reason for worship and the occasion for faith. This is ever God's ways with us: to reveal enough of Himself and His plans that we may glimpse the wisdom and movement of His ways and stand in awe, but only enough to reserve the mystery of His being just beyond the veil of our deepest gaze.

Furthermore, no one stands in relationship to God as a bene-factor or innovator. God always acts in grace and love toward man; therefore, man can never build up a store of merit: "who has first given to Him [God] that it might be paid back to him [man] again?" (v. 35, from Job 41:11).

Paul closes with a burst of praise to the sovereign God: "For from Him [source] and through Him [agent] and to Him [goal] are all things" (v. 36). He is the center of all the created, histori-cal, and personal order. God is the Alpha and the Omega (the A and the Z), the beginning and the end, the first and the last (Rev 4:11). If in this one case of His dealings with Israel, we can catch a glimpse of the vindication of His mysterious providence, in other cases we can wait for the explanation of His wisdom and the final evidence of His love and mercy. Surely, then, to *Him* alone belongs the glory forever and ever. So be it!

This is the expression of a faith which trusts when it cannot un-derstand, which loves when it cannot explain, which reasons cor-rectly that nothing but good can ultimately come from God to those who accept His grace through the Lord Jesus Christ.

ADDITIONAL NOTE ON CHRISTIANITY AND CONTEMPORARY ISRAEL

This is not the place for an extended discussion of modern Is-rael in its prophetic, political, and religious aspect. But it seems hardly appropriate to write a modern commentary on these chap-ters and not say something about the relationship of Christianity to the newly formed political state of Israel.

PEOPLE AND COUNTRY

We have seen by careful exegesis that Paul clearly teaches a revival among the Jewish people when they are restored as a people to the blessings of God in the olive tree. The question is whether this future restoration must also involve the ancient land of Canaan, or Palestine.[26]

There is no doubt that in the Old Testament God's promise to Israel as a people is connected explicitly to one particular land area, Canaan (Gen 12:1; 13:12; 17:7-8; Deu 30:1-10). Dispersion and separation from the land is the repeated mark of God's judgment for Israel's disobedience, and the restoration to the land is the mark of God's grace to the nation (Deu 28:64-66; 30:1-10; Is 62:4; Eze 36:8-12, 28, 33-36; Amos 9:11-15; Zec 8:1-23; 10:9-10). The latter two passages especially emphasize how closely the salvation of Israel as a people is connected to the land of Palestine.

But why Jerusalem and not Amman or Dacca or Rome? Could it be in part because Palestine forms the division between East and West? The Westerner looks at the Bible and senses its Eastern imagery and symbolism. While in the eyes of Easterners, the Bible is Western because its doctrine of creation secularizes the world. Israel is truly in the center (navel) of the earth (Eze 38:12). To a certain extent this mixing of Eastern and Western cultures has produced the current conflict in the Middle East between Westernized Jews and Easternized Arabs and Palestinians. There are also internal problems between the African-Asian Jews and the European-American Jews in Israel.

Yet the focus on Jerusalem (and Palestine) in God's plan must in large part be traced back to the Abrahamic and Davidic covenants as the outworking of the full realization of God's promises to them (Gen 12:1-3; 2 Sa 7:16).

Again, in the New Testament words of Jesus there seems to be further continuity with this same Old Testament thought. Jerusalem's destruction in A.D. 70 is not to be the last stroke in the connection of land and people, for Jesus predicts, "Jerusalem will be trampled under foot by the Gentiles until the times of the Gentiles be fulfilled" (Lk 21:24). This last of the great prophetic discourses reiterates with certainty that no matter how insurmountable the difficulties, land and people will one day be re-

26. I am here following the excellent summary of Käsemann, pp. 147ff. I do not think this author can by any standards be labeled "dispensationalist."

united, and Israel will fulfill its destiny in Palestine. Perhaps
Scripture is not clear as to whether this return precedes their
national conversion or follows it. It is clear that there is coming
a time within this age, in which God's faithfulness will triumph
over Israel's unbelief, and Israel will realize her destiny as a
people, in Palestine, as the great evidence of God's saving activity
in the world.

THE POLITICAL STATE OF ISRAEL

The chief question for the Christian concerning the present
state of Israel (established in 1948) is whether this has any connection with the predictions of Israel's national conversion and re-
union with the land of Palestine. It is a difficult and complex
question to answer, but one that is notably significant. When the
Christian considers the way in which the State of Israel came
into being, he may wonder if God could have had any direct hand
in it.[27] If God is not directly involved in the formation of the
present State of Israel, it would be difficult for Christians to
maintain any special significance in it over any other temporary
nationalism. Yet God has in Israel's past history overruled their
questionable activities to accomplish in them His own purposes.
Take the Jacob and the Joseph narratives as an example.

However, since I have no direct way of knowing which of
these alternatives is actually the case, my position as a Christian
toward the present state of Israel is somewhat ambivalent. Theologically, if I decide that God is preparing or actually beginning
the process of Israel's restoration, I may be drawn in my sympathies to them and desire their welfare in the land. Yet I must
also at the same time be repulsed from them morally whenever
there is injustice toward the Arabs (especially Christian Arabs)
or other peoples. Just because the Christian feels that Israel has
a future in Palestine does not mean that he cannot be critical of
any unethical and criminal acts committed by the Israelis.

The same attitude should hold true for the person who feels

27. George Giacumakis, Jr., "The Israeli-Arab Conflict in the Middle East"
in *Protest and Politics*, ed. R. G. Clouse, R. D. Linder, and R. V. Pierard
(Greenwood, S. C.: Attic Press, 1968), pp. 227-50; also "Christian Attitudes
Toward Israel" in *The Cross and the Flag*, ed. Clouse, Linder, and Pierard
(Carol Stream, Ill.: Creation House, 1972), pp. 203-15.

that the present state of Israel is not God's doing but merely man's. He cannot lightly dismiss or overlook acts of injustice done by Arabs or their leaders to their own people or to Israelis. In the present conflict the Christian must not identify totally with either the Arab or the Israeli political position. Both peoples have rights to the land historically. Instead he must be the reconciling ingredient between the two parties. Above all the Christian must treat all men as human beings, created in the image of God, worthy of respect and loving compassion.

THE MILLENNIAL KINGDOM

While there are numerous worthy Christian views on the question of a future divine earthly kingdom of peace established in history, it seems quite appropriate to think of this kingdom in association with the restoration of Israel as a people. The Old Testament views this kingdom of peace as occurring within history and centered in Israel (Is 2:2-4; 4:1-6; 9:6-7; Zec 14:8-11). Furthermore, in the one universally agreed upon clear passage in the New Testament (Rev 20:7-9) touching the question, a recovered Israel is seen as the center of the kingdom. The importance of discussing the whole modern utopian kingdom idea in the context of the biblical data on a restored Israel cannot be overestimated in the light of contemporary Marxist, Reichian,[28] or the Valhalla and all fools' paradise concepts.[29]

PROSPECTS OF WORLD REVIVAL

It has been shown exegetically that the interpretation of Paul's thought favors the view that there will be an extensive expansion of Gentile Christianity just prior to and in connection with the conversion of Israel. Are there signs that our era may be close to this? Of course, while any answer to this question must be speculative, there are several interesting facts to note. A noteworthy revival of large scope can be observed among American youth that appears to have prospects of growing to a worldwide movement and is already creating a "Jews for Jesus" movement

28. Charles Reich, *The Greening of America* (New York: Random, 1970), chap. 9, n. 3.
29. Käsemann, p. 153.

within its wake. As subjective as it may seem, there are numerous leaders in the evangelical church who feel we are on the brink and may be into a great worldwide revival.[30]

Finally, one is greatly impressed that in Israel today the Bible is the center of cultural focus. Each young person must memorize in Hebrew the entire historical books (Genesis through Chronicles) plus the prophets (Isaiah through Zechariah) before he can graduate from high school! While largely of historical and moral emphasis, this preparation of Jewish minds and hearts might in the future play a significant role in the nation's conversion to the Messiah. There is also a significant openness in Israel today toward discussing the relationship between Jews and Christians.

Thus Paul has dealt decisively with the major objection to his doctrine of God's faithfulness raised by Jewish unbelief: Israel has stumbled due to their own unfaithfulness, not God's, and furthermore God is working out in the Jewish people's unbelief a divine mystery which will magnify His mercy in an unparalleled manner (chaps. 9-11).

Paul's main argument of the book is now completed (1:18—11: 36). There yet remain several areas of more immediate concern pertaining to the outworking of this new life in Christ as it touches the real world of the Roman Christians.

---

30. Bill Bright, *Come Help Change the World* (Old Tappan, N.J.: Revell, 1970; Rufus Jones, "Will the Church Miss It?," *Bulletin of the Conservative Baptist Missions* (Fall 1971); Robert E. Coleman, "The Coming World Revival?," *Christianity Today* 15, no. 21 (July 16, 1971): 10-12; "The New Christians," *Christianity Today* 15: 20-23; "The New Rebel Cry: Jesus Is Coming!," *Time* 97, no. 25 (June 21, 1971): 56-63; "Jews for Jesus," *Time* 99, no. 24 (June 12, 1972): 66-67.

PART 3

The Christian Way of Life

9

The Christian Way

(12:1–15:13)

As IN ALL his other letters, Paul first sets forth the theological facts of Christianity and then follows out these truths into several concrete matters of actual Christian living in the world. In earlier chapters the apostle has already struck the note of moral renewal of the entire life. Such new life is inseparably wed to God's action of forgiveness (chaps. 6-8).

It should be carefully noted that Paul, unlike many preachers today, bases his call to Christian character upon Christian doctrine; he traces the expression of Christlikeness to belief. We will not find in Paul the often repeated but erroneous sharp distinction between "doctrine" and "life." Exhortations to live a certain type of ethical life which do not grow out of and find their basis in the gospel facts and redemptive message are mere moralisms, impotent to effect the real transformation of the moral life. To make any significant difference, then, between Paul's doctrinal sections and the practical sections manifests a failure to grasp this relationship. Furthermore, it should also be noted that the sections of doctrinal teaching embody ethical teaching and the sections of ethical teaching before us implicitly or explicitly teach doctrine.

But now the question could be put to Paul; just what, precisely, is the relationship between all this theology and doctrine and my actual Christian experience and conduct?

More specifically, Christian ethics is the application of Christian redemption or what is called sanctification. Our conduct springs from union with Christ (6:1-4). Jesus Himself constitutes for

us both the form and through the Spirit the actualizing or transforming power of the Christian life-style. Our motivation for
this life of discipleship lies in the desire to be obedient to Christ
which is an essential element in faith (1:5), and as an expression
of our deep gratitude to God who has shown to us His forgiving
and justifying mercy.

In the following chapters, Paul sketches the specific relevance
of the obedience of faith in Jesus Christ to the more general but
actual situations of life. Three major themes are touched upon:
(1) the relations of Christians to one another (12:3-13); (2) the
relations of Christians to non-Christian society (12:14–13:14);
and finally (3) a special problem in the relationship of believers
to one another, arising from their differences in cultural backgrounds (14:1–15:6). While the somewhat loose connection in
thoughts through the chapters emphasizes the spontaneity of
the Christian ethic as it confronts the complicated spectrum of
ethical situations, there is nevertheless an underlying regularity
in the application of the principle of life in the new being in
Christ, which is to walk in love.

THE LIVING SACRIFICE
(12:1-2)

Paul begins with the foundation of all Christian living. In these
two verses we find the secret that unlocks the unlimited possibilities of genuine Christian life in the world. Calling the Christians
in Rome brethren, the apostle appeals to them to make the supreme offering of complete dedication to God.

Paul bases his appeal on the "mercies of God" (v. 1). The best
clue to the meaning of this statement is found in the "therefore"
which indicates that Paul grounds his present appeal on what he
has previously said in his letter. God's mercy means God's merciful activity toward sinful man through Christ which Paul has
been expounding in the previous sections of the book and especially in chapters 9–11 (see 11:32). A Christian, then, is one
who has experienced the mercy of God.

But what are Christians to do? They are admonished, "Present
your bodies a living and holy sacrifice." The language draws upon
the sacrificial ritual of the Old Testament offerings: "present"

(offer on the altar), "sacrifice," "holy," "acceptable to God." Straining for some adequate image of the proper response of the believer to God's mercies, Paul, as previously (3:21), thinks of the sacrifices and especially the burnt offering (Lev, 1:3-17). When an Israelite wanted to express his devotion to the Lord, he selected an appropriate animal or bird and brought it to the tabernacle to present it to the Lord. He laid his hands on the head of the animal, signifying substitutionary identification, and killed it, whereupon the priest burned the entire carcass upon the sacrificial altar. The offering was "holy" to the Lord in that it was wholly His (priest did not get any part). This act of worship and service was an "acceptable" odor to the Lord (Eph 5:2).

By "body" Paul does not mean our personalities or selves but our physical bodies with all their functions (6:6, 12; 8:10, 11, 23).[1] We are to serve God in these temporal earthen bodies, not in some imagined other-worldly vision or fancy. By stressing the sacrifice of the body Paul may have been countering certain latent Greek philosophical ideas which taught the deprecation of the body and man's eventual liberation from its captivity. Perhaps some thought that because the "body is dead because of sin" (8:10), it could not be acceptable to God for service.

"Spiritual service of worship" is more difficult. The word "service" (Gk. *latreia*) means to serve God by sacrifice. Since the whole cultic service of the priests in the Old Testament was viewed as a service before God, the same term has both the connotation of service to God and worship of God. Under the new covenant, in this age, every believer is a priest and can serve God by the sacrificial offering of his body in an act of worship to Him (1 Pe 2:9).

This service is further described as "spiritual" (Gk. *logikē*). While the Greek word Paul uses is related to the Greek word for "reason" or "rational" (Eng., logical), the meaning may come closer to the thought of something that is true, or has inner reality in contrast to the merely external, material form. Worship in

1. Paul may not mean to exclude the self or person from his use of *body,* but there is no warrant to follow Bultmann and others here to see only the self. Man is a whole being from the biblical view, including the body as a prime ingredient.

both Judaism and pagan ritual tended toward the outward, more material form.[2] The Christian, in contrast to these external ritual religions, is to present his physical body as an act of true, inner, Spirit-directed service to God (Ro 1:9; Phil 3:3; Jn 4:23, 24).

The complete abandonment of our bodies to God's service constitutes the indispensable foundation or core of Christian living. Such a commitment should be made as a decisive, accomplished event, as the Greek tense of "present" suggests. All future decisions and actions will constantly be made in keeping with this initial step. Perhaps the best analogy is marriage. From the first act of each giving themselves totally to the other there follows a whole life lived together in the context of that original pledge.

We are simply kidding ourselves if we are trying to do Christian things and yet have never pledged ourselves fully to Jesus Christ. God's grace is free, but it is not cheap, for God gave us the most costly gift He could give, the suffering unto death for our sins of His own beloved Son. The discovery of this gift is like finding an incomparable pearl or a million-dollar treasure in our backyard (Mt 13:44-46). What lesser response to this love and mercy of God would be enough? As Isaac Watts has written,

> But drops of grief can ne'er repay
> The debt of love I owe;
> Here, Lord, I give myself away,
> 'Tis all that I can do.

As the late Sam Shoemaker has stated, to be a Christian means to give as much of myself as I can to as much of Jesus Christ as I know.

In verse 2 Paul describes the general nature of the growth process which is the natural and inseparable outworking of our supreme act of divine service related in verse 1. "This world" means this world which "is passing away" (1 Jn 2:17) and probably should be rendered as "age" (Gk. *aiōn*). The term *age* in biblical teaching views the present world as under the control of various alien powers such as sin, death, the flesh, covetousness (Gal 1:4). Its chief characteristic is lust or selfishness (1 Jn 2:

2. F. J. Leenhardt, *Romans,* p. 303, cites some examples of the word from Hellenistic Jewish texts where it denotes what is interior, what concerns the deepest being of man, in contrast to what is formal, external, or theatrical.

15-16). The world, or present age, has much more to do with attitudes and values than things; it is much more related to selfishness than certain kinds of activities. This age will pass away (1 Co 7:31); it has no permanence; it is only fashionable; it acts out a part and holds the stage, but it is without real being. Once a man realizes this, how foolish it is to join in with this "flick" which is projected on such a shaky screen. There is something better in Christ.

Paul warns his readers not to be "conformed" to this age. The word means to be poured into the mold of something and thereby to shape the outward appearance, to rubber stamp something. Phillip's translation has: "Don't let the world around you squeeze you into its own mould." Or in keeping with our previous thought it may be translated, "Stop letting this age give you your lines in its flick."

But Paul does not stop with the negative as do so many Christians. He goes on to admonish that they should allow the new age of the reign of God to break into their lives and "transform" (literally, metamorphose) them. Paul's word here is the same term found in the "transfiguration" of Jesus (Mt 17:2). He uses the word to describe the "changing" of believers into the image of Christ by the Holy Spirit as they reflect the glory of Christ (2 Co 3:18). This is no mere imitation of Christ but the outworking of the divine presence and power in the life. That the "mind" needs "renewal" shows how radically different Paul's idea of the mind is from Greek thought, which exalted the mind to almost divine status. The mind here, however, implies much more than man's intellectual activities but refers to the deepest springs of human existence and includes both man's willing and knowing faculties. Since the writing of Charles Reich's, *The Greening of America*, it may be more contemporary to call this "consciousness." It is a whole way of viewing the world and our experiences.[3]

The purpose or goal of this constant renewal of the mind is that you might "prove what the will of God is" (v. 2). To "prove" does not mean to test whether God's will is good or bad, but it

3. Charles Reich, *The Greening of America*, p. 14. Perhaps "Consciousness IV" would be appropriate to describe the changed world outlook of the truly renewed Christian mind; see Harry Blamires, *The Christian Mind* (London: SPCK, n.d.).

means to "try and approve" the will of God. In the consciousness of a person who is being transformed by Christ's Spirit, there lies the possibility of actually recognizing and doing the will of God in every human situation (Eph 5:9-10). In the testing and affirming of what is actually the will of God, the believer will also discover that it is precisely equivalent to the "good," to the "acceptable," and to the "perfect" in God's eyes in each situation. By following out these terms in Paul's usage a further clue can be obtained as to what precisely constitutes the will of God.

Here then in the first two verses is Paul's way of restating Jesus' call, "If any one wishes to come after Me, let him deny himself, and take up his cross, and follow Me. For whoever wishes to save his life shall lose it; but whoever loses his life for My sake shall find it" (Mt 16:24, 25). There will be found a constant tension in the Christian life between the present age in which we live and the age to come which has, in some measure, through the Holy Spirit already broken into our lives. There is a wrong way of staying in the world, just as there is a wrong way of fleeing from it.[4]

Christianity is change—radical, revolutionary change at the center of human consciousness. Paul's thought strikes devastatingly at every form of Christianity which is stagnant, complacent, proud of its accomplishments, or not radical enough to stand in judgment over every aspect of its relationship to the current age—whether political, social, personal or ecclesiastical.

THE CHRISTIAN COMMUNITY

(12:3-8)

In the practical outworking of our deeply personal relationship to Christ, we will be confronted immediately with the fact that Christianity involves a people. One cannot be Christlike alone. Every Christian is united inseparably to all Christians in the one body in Christ (vv. 4, 5). Paul, in an epistle to the Corinthian believers, has already elaborated more fully on this thought (1 Co 12).

4. One good modern exposition of discipleship is Dietrich Bonhoeffer, *The Cost of Discipleship*. One does not have to agree with all of Bonhoeffer's theological conclusions to reap a rich profit from his understanding of obedience to God.

Furthermore, this section of Paul's letter illustrates the out-working of the first principle of Christian ethics stated in verse 2. Such may be the force of the word *for* at the beginning of the paragraph. One of the characteristics of this age which Christians are not to copy is pride (v. 2). Pride always has reference to others and must be seen as one of the prime roots of dissension. Paul may have had some knowledge of one group of Christians in Rome who thought they were better than others (11:18-21; 14: 1-4). So he exhorts, "to every man among you not to think more highly of himself than he ought to think; but to think so as to have sound judgment, as God has allotted" (v. 3).

Humility, contrary to general opinion, is not assuming the least role, or taking the lowest notch on the totem pole. Rather, humility is an attitude and action which results from taking an honest look at where we best fit into the whole of God's work as He has determined by His gifts to us. Paul himself, for example, exercises his gift as an apostle by exhorting the Roman Christians prefacing his exhortations with the words, "Because of the grace that was given me" (15:15). Pride assumes or desires more prerogative than God has given to us. It is an exaggerated self-esteem. False humility, on the other hand, tends to assume a lesser role than the Lord has assigned. Therefore, each person is to "have sound judgment" or to hold a balanced viewpoint of his harmonious contribution to the whole body (vv. 4, 5).

The "measure of faith" (v. 3) certainly should be understood as the same as "gifts that differ according to the grace given to us" (v. 6) and corresponds to Paul's similar statements about gifts in 1 Corinthians 12 and Ephesians 4. Gifts of the Spirit are given to every believer. These spiritual enablements are differentiated and yet interlaced within the church so that there is a preservation of the beautiful relationship of the uniqueness of each individual contribution together with the importance and necessity of the community of the redeemed for the mutual edification and maturing of each individual person (Eph 4:13-16).

An individual Christian must not then think of himself as the whole church but as a petal to the flower. In realizing this truth I must constantly affirm two things: (1) I, or my group, do not have all the truth or all the gifts, and (2) the other person or group may have truth and gifts I do not have. So to be whole I must have fellowship and dialogue with all true Christians worldwide. Paul enumerates seven such gifts in this passage. The list should not be thought of as exhaustive or without special significance in Paul's mind with respect to the Roman Christians' needs and problems.[5] It is interesting to ask why no special "charismatic" type gifts are mentioned as they are in the Corinthian correspondence (1 Co 12; 14).

Prophecy is mentioned first (v. 6). In the other lists of gifts "apostle" takes preeminence even over a prophet (1 Co 12:28; Eph 4:11). Since no apostle had apparently yet ministered to the Roman Christians (15:20), Paul omits mention of it. The prophetic gift in both the Old and New Testaments involves the receiving of a message from God and communicating it to men. Frequently, but not always, the prophet predicted future events (Ac 21:10, 11) as well as giving the Word of God for the contemporary situation.

The church stands in need of this ministry today. Those who can sensitively discern the movement of God in contemporary events and are able to apply the biblical revelation dynamically to our times may be modern day prophets such as Francis Schaeffer.[6] Of course, their words are not infallible and must always be evaluated critically in the light of Scripture (1 Co 14:29), especially by those who have the gift of "discerning of spirits" (1 Co 12:10).

The prophet is to use his gift "according to the proportion of his faith." This expression might mean that the prophet must speak in agreement with the faith, that is, scripture doctrine. However, it is better in the context to understand the exhortation as a further subtle reminder by the apostle that the prophet is not in pride to go beyond his appointed authority, but should exercise his gift in exact agreement with the divine grace of enablement which has been given to him. The same warning would hold

---

5. One should study more than a single tradition in the interpretation of the gifts; e.g., John Walvoord, *The Holy Spirit* (Wheaton, Ill.: Van Kampen, 1954), chaps. 19, 20; and Donald Bloesch, *The Reform of the Church* (Grand Rapids: Eerdmans, 1970), chap. 9, form a good comparison.
6. Francis A. Schaeffer, *Death in the City.*

true for the other gifts as well. Those who minister their gifts should be neither negligent nor pretentious.

The next gift mentioned is "service," or ministry (v. 7). This gift should not be thought of as one involving merely a call to be a preacher or missionary but means all forms of service, especially to the needy (Ro 15:25, 31; 2 Co 8:4). It may also refer to the deacon's work (Ac 6:1-3; 11:29; Phil 1:1; 1 Ti 3:8, 10, 12, 13). This gift and its ministry should not be regarded as less spiritual because it deals with material needs. A man or woman (Ro 16:1) may give full time to such services without coveting higher or allegedly more spiritual ministries (1 Ti 3:13).

"Teaching" (v. 7) involves more systematic explanation and application of Christian truth than mere preaching, such as Paul has given in this letter to the Romans (Ac 13:1; 15:35). While all prophetic preaching contains explanation (1 Co 14:2, 21) and all teaching should have contemporary application, the prophet is more concerned with proclaiming a direct Word from God to the immediate historical situation, whereas the teacher will explain and relate this Word to the rest of Scripture and its great themes. The effective ministry of the Word of God needs both gifts. If they are not found in one man, which is rare, then provision should be made for a dual ministry.

As for "exhortation" (v. 8), Paul may have reference either to the gift of ministering consolation (Gk. word is the same) to those in affliction or to the gift of exhorting men to arouse their spirits and encourage their hearts toward God and His will. Both aspects are related. Have you ever left the presence of some Christian, saying to yourself: Oh how thankful to God I am for that person's life; how glad I am to be a Christian! I believe this is the ministry of exhortation that we all need in a day of recurring waves of less than zealous Christianity.

The one who "gives" (or contributes) is to do it with "liberality," or better, with "unmixed motive of the heart" (2 Co 8:2; 9:11, 13; 11:3; Eph 6:5; Col 3:22). While it is possible to understand Paul's words for "liberality" to mean to distribute "liberally," the idea is more that gifts of money given by the individual to the needy should be for the single purpose of showing Christian love in meeting the needs of those lacking and not to gain

merit before God or status before men. So hidden from men's
eyes should these deeds be that Jesus said, "Let not your right
hand know what your left hand is doing" (Mt 6:3). How different this sounds from so much Christian giving where everyone
knows who the liberal donors are! I am reminded in contrast to
this of the cornerstone plaque affixed to a large building complex
now used by a well-known Christian organization in California:
"Purchased by a Christian and donated to the glory of God."

Next, Paul refers to those who "lead." The Greek word for
lead used here may mean "to care for." That "leading" and "caring
for" are dual meanings for the word is explained by the fact that
caring for the needs of people in the early church was the obligation of the elders or leading members (1 Th 5:12; 1 Ti 3:4-5;
5:17). The emphasis is not so much on authority or power as on
pastoral care.[7] Jesus emphasized this aspect as the chief role of
a leader (Lk 22:26). Caring for the flock is to be done with
"diligence" or zeal, which may explain why a special recognition
for this diligence is recommended by Paul elsewhere (1 Ti 5:17).

Finally, one who "shows mercy" as the expression of the Holy
Spirit's gift should do these deeds cheerfully and brightly. Calvin's remark captures the spirit of the exhortation: "For as nothing gives more solace to the sick or to any one otherwise dis-
tressed, than to see men cheerful and prompt in assisting them;
so to observe sadness in the face of those by whom assistance is
given make them to feel themselves despised."[8]

While it is extremely encouraging in our day to find so many
individual Christians exercising a variety of Spirit-ministered
gifts, it is sad to see so few Christian churches that provide any
structure in the church meetings for the spontaneous ministering
of gifts to one another. To counteract this deficiency one church
on the west coast has recently begun a Sunday evening meeting
called a *Body-Life* service. After nearly a thousand people pack
into the Peninsula Bible Church in Palo Alto, California, the
leader gets things started by saying, "This is the family, the body
of Christ. We need each other. Let's share." One after another,

7. TDNT, 6:702.
8. Cited by John Murray, *Epistle to the Romans*, 2:127.

persons all over the auditorium stand and speak. A divorced mother of three tells how God put food on the table that week. A glassy-eyed girl requests prayer for her older brother who is blowing his mind with LSD and won't stop. The leader asks a former "acid head" to go stand by her and lead out in prayer for the brother. A woman gives the keys for the family's second car to a student who has expressed a need for transportation for work. Other needs, insights, helps, prayers, comfort, and good news are shared, and at times laughter, applause, or hushed moments of anguish accompany the events. When the offering is taken, those in need may also take from the plate up to ten dollars![9] Somehow we feel that this must come closer to the New Testament meaning of the gifts than most of our churches have experienced.

THE LAW OF LOVE APPLIED
(12:9-21)

At this point Paul seems to change the subject matter and offer a number of ethical injunctions or general rules for Christian conduct.[10] Each command appears permeated by the underlying principle of showing love first to the brethren in Christ (vv. 9-13), and then to all men, even to those who treat Christians as their enemies (vv. 14-21). In this section as well as the following, Paul seems to be integrating and applying Jesus' teaching found in the Sermon on the Mount (Mt 5-7) as well as selected Old Testament ethical injunctions. Two main overarching principles govern Christian conduct: love and peace. In these exhortations there is really no system of ethics propounded, but nevertheless all of life comes under the direction of the renewed mind in Christ (v. 2). Little comment is needed except at certain points in the exposition.

Paul heads the list with love, as he does elsewhere (Gal 5:22

9. Edward Plowman, *The Jesus Movement in America* (Elgin, Ill.: Cook, 1971).

10. The series of imperatives in English, "abhor," "cleave" are participles with imperative force in Greek and probably follow the Rabbinic Hebrew use of participles for expressing not direct commands but rules and codes (see C. K. Barrett, *The Epistle to the Romans*, p. 239). If this is a correct explanation of the linguistic phenomenon, then these commands could represent a Semitic source originating in a very early Jewish Christian church.

If love is true and genuine and not just a put-on or facade, then everything else to which Paul exhorts the church will follow. The great identifying mark of the Christian life-style and the final compelling apologetic for Christianity is the love that Christians have for one another (Jn 13:34, 35). This love must be especially visible to the world. One area of acid test is the way we walk toward other brothers who differ with us. We must truly regret our differences that cause friction among us and must show a costly love by practicing consciously our love for each other regardless of the inconvenience or loss to us personally or to our group.[11]

"Abhor [shrink back from] what is evil; cleave [stick in total devotion] to what is good" (v. 9) underscores the dual nature of the world in which Christians live. Christian love must at times constructively negate some things in the world and affirm others. Furthermore, this love should embrace fellow Christians as if they were members of the same family with all its emotional and affectionate ties (v. 10). Genuine love for others in our common family in Christ will incite us to "give preference to one another" or to "take the lead" in honoring the other before any honor comes our way (v. 10), each being readier than the other to recognize and honor God's gifts in a brother (Eph 3:8). This exhortation can have tremendous healing effects in the fractured church of today, especially if we will apply it to groups of Christians other than our own and in honor prefer them above ourselves!

Verse 11 contains three exhortations which seem to relate to the problem of Christian apathy. "Not lagging behind in diligence" is more literally "not hesitant in zeal" and relates to Christian enthusiasm in using God's gifts to multiply His harvest (Mt 25:26, 27; 2 Ti 1:6, 7). The same warning against discouragement appears elsewhere (Gal 6:9; Heb 12:3). To uncover this problem, the question could well be asked: Are there any issues in my life which I am concerned over? Have I ceased to get excited over anything anymore?

"Fervent in spirit" surely relates to both the former injunction and to the following command to serve the Lord. While "spirit"

11. Francis A. Schaeffer, *The Mark of the Christian* (Downers Grove, Ill.: Inter-Varsity, 1970).

could refer to the Holy Spirit, it is not necessary here, for the inner human spirit of the Christian is surely "set aglow" by the fire of the Spirit (Ac 18:25). The final order concerning "serving the Lord" suggests how this zeal is to be channeled to avoid apathy in our Christian lives. When the Christian becomes overly depressed in any type of work or service, and zeal ebbs, it may be due to the fact that the priority of the Lord's service has slipped from his mind. These are general exhortations designed to keep God's people from indolence and apathy.

Three further brief commands are linked together in verse 12: "rejoicing in hope, persevering in tribulation, devoted to prayer." Power for living now lives in the direction of the Christian's future hope (8:18-27). Because God has granted to us in His promises such a strong vision of His future kingdom and the resurrection, our present lives are to be lived as if this kingdom had already arrived.

Such living in hope will bring a radical criticism and judgment upon the present world order and result in the world's reaction and very often persecution. In these afflictions the believer must be steadfast and not relinquish his trust in God. No greater resource for strength in trials and joy in his hope can be found than in prayer which should be entered into as serious work, as part of the battle of spiritual warfare.

Being "devoted to" prayer emphasizes the persistence in prayer that distinguished the prayers of the early Christians from the merely religious performance of prayers of the contemporary Jews and pagans. "Devoted" to prayer catches well the force of the Greek word which means to stick diligently with something and attend to it (the same word is used in Eph 6:18; Ac 1:14; Lk 11:1-13; 18:1-8; Col 4:2).

Paul continues with the exhortation about "contributing to the needs of the saints" (v. 13). The force of the verb denotes "sharing in" or "partaking of" the needs of brothers in Christ. We are to feel a oneness, as in the same family, with those who suffer afflictions and deprivations for the name of Christ. When we truly follow this exhortation, it will be natural for us to also *meet* those needs if it is in our power.

If, on the other hand, these needy brethren come to us, we will receive them with open homes and hearts. "Practicing" hospitality does not quite catch the more intensive force of the verb which means "to actively pursue." Christian hospitality demands a special effort that goes beyond the mere inconvenience of non-Christian people; we cannot choose our time or our guests. Hospitality in the early church was a prime example of "contributing to the needs of the saints" (see also 1 Pe 4:9; Heb 13:2; 1 Ti 3:2; Titus 1:8). Perhaps we should see the test of this ministry today in terms of whether our homes are open to the more "hippie" type of young Christians or "Jesus people."

In verse 14 the character of thought abruptly changes. That there is a change can be noted for two reasons. First, the subject changes from general exhortations or commands stressing mainly relationships of Christians to other Christians to admonitions dealing with the Christian response to non-Christian attitudes and actions. Also, the grammatical structure of these verses changes from Greek participles to imperatives and infinitives.

"Bless those who persecute you; bless, and curse not" (v. 14) reminds us definitely of our Lord's words (Mt 5:44; Lk 6:28). Such a response demands the exercise of radical Christian love expressed toward one who has made himself our enemy by persecuting us. To bless means more than mere words since the utterance must come from the heart and will be followed by the appropriate action as occasion affords. When we "rejoice with those who rejoice, and weep with those who weep" (v. 15), we as Christians identify with all men in our common humanity as fellow human beings. We must and should be truly able to empathize with them after the example of our Lord (Lk 15:1-2). The early church father, Chrysostom, poignantly observed how much easier it is to weep with others than to rejoice with them. It is at the point of a man's sorrows and joys that he is most deeply himself. At this point the Christian is to identify in love with him.

In verse 16, Paul continues by admonishing Christians to cultivate a loving harmony and practice of humility in the company of non-Christians. "Do not be haughty in mind, but associate with the lowly" is a difficult passage and unfortunately ambiguous in the Greek. Does the "lowly" refer to men or things? If the latter, then the thought is that we are not to cherish selfish ambitions, but to give ourselves over to humble tasks (Phil 4:11; 1 Ti 6:8, 9). If "lowly" refers to men, then the sense is that we are to give ourselves over to association with the less attractive, more lowly people in the world. There is no final way to decide between the two views. Both are worthy Christian goals. In either case one line of thought would lead to the other.

The force of the exhortation, "Do not be wise in your own estimation" is that we must not be conceited (Pr 3:7). Such words strike at the very heart of an opinionated person who cherishes his own ideas and judgments as if they themselves were the absolute truth and refuses to acknowledge the opinions and thoughts of others. Furthermore, we should not be misled by our own preferences which often incline toward that which flatters our pride, namely, the distinguished and brilliant. There is a way of clinging to the truth which is no more than a way of clinging to oneself.

Finally, in verses 17-21 of the chapter, Paul interacts more specifically with the question of Christian response to hostility from non-Christians. As in the teaching of Jesus concerning nonviolence and nonretaliation (Mt 5:38-42), Paul's concern is with the question of private, personal, and individual relationships and reactions. In chapter 13 he will consider what response toward hostility and evil is correct for civil authorities.

Love will never retaliate or "pay back" blow for blow for harm done (Pr 17:13), but on the contrary will "respect [take thought] for what is right [Gk. means "good"] in the sight of all men" (v. 17). Christian conduct should be recognizably commendable before non-Christian men (1 Th 5:15; 2 Co 8:21). Many Christians today, in contrast, are far more concerned with how their behavior strikes their Christian friends than whether it is acceptable to the non-Christian consensus.

This rule of behavior does not mean that the Christian will turn to the world for his norms of conduct, but in seeking the will of God for each ethical situation, he will consider what is right and just in the sight of all men as part of the basis for his decision (v. 2). In practice, the believer must weigh the consequences of whatever action he takes against the effects of the testimony that results to the nonbelieving community for or against the Christian message (1 Co 10:31-32; Mt 5:16). This principle takes into account that God's law is operative in the hearts of all men, however dimly they perceive or recognize His norms as they formulate their concepts of right and wrong (2:15). The Christian, however, is always to obey God's law instead of man's wherever conflict arises.

By so acting, the interests of peace and good will among men are promoted (v. 18). There is, however, a qualification: "If possible, so far as it depends on you," or if the possibility of peace can be brought about by you. Peace cannot be secured at the cost of God's truth or if others refuse to cooperate (Mt 10:34-36; Lk 12:51-53; Ja 3:17). The Christian should do everything in his power to be the reconciling salt in the hostilities between men in the world. If conflict arises where the Christian is involved, let it only arise because of the Christian's stand for the truth of God and justice. Strife or conflict should never be sought or initiated by the Christian.

In verses 19-21 the apostle answers a possible objection to his peace way of life (v. 18). Someone might say, won't this approach play into the hands of evil men, favoring their scheme and allowing them to go unchecked in their wickedness? Wouldn't it be better to set them straight forcefully and put an end to their injustice? Paul says, no! The essence of sin in human relations is for an individual man to assume the place of God and take justice into his own hands. A man cannot presume to do this, because not only is he limited in his information and understanding, but when his own personal interests have been hurt he will invariably distort justice in favor of his own selfish concerns.

Therefore, the individual Christians must not try to "get even" with the other person who has wronged him. Instead he must commit himself in trust to the administration of God's justice upon the unjust person, that is, "God's wrath" (2:5, 8; 3:5; 5:9; 9:22). God's wrath is being presently directed toward evil doers both directly (1:18-25) and indirectly through the civil authorities (13:4, "wrath") and will be completely manifest in the future final judgment (Ro 2:5, 6; Rev. 20:11-15). Paul quotes Deuteronomy 32:35 to support this principle of nonretaliation which should be the rule of God's people.

But the Christian must do more than be passive toward personal animosity; he should also take positive steps to manifest that he does not harbor vengeance against the offender. While he does not pay back evil for evil, he does pay back good in return for the harm: "If your enemy is hungry, feed him, and if he is thirsty, give him a drink" (v. 20). Here Paul seems to call to mind Jesus' admonition to love the enemy (Mt 5:44 and Lk 6:27), but he actually quotes Proverbs 25:21, 22. "Burning coals upon his head" does not refer to coals of judgment (hence a way of getting back at the other) but the fires of shame and remorse burning the conscience of the offender and hopefully bringing about repentance and reconciliation to the offended. By following this unnatural but loving course of action, the Christian will not be conquered by evil men in his life of promoting peace (v. 18). He will instead conquer such evil fostered against him by good (acts of love) toward the evildoer, more than he could through acts of vengeance (v. 21). Thus evil is more permanently dealt with when the heart of the evildoer is changed and his resentment overcome than if he were merely brought to justice.

THE CHRISTIAN AND CIVIL AUTHORITIES
(13:1-7)

It is important at the first in this highly controversial passage to establish the link, if any, in thought with the preceding section. This teaching on government appears somewhat abruptly (without connecting particle) between two exhortations pertaining to the exercise of Christian love and peace (12:9-21 and 13:8-10). Arguments can be advanced for a logical connection with the preceding in either the idea of "vengeance" and "God's wrath" (12:19 with 13:4); or with the thought of not being conformed to the world or any of its institutions (12:2); or as answering the problem as to whether the Christian is to view the state as evil because it renders evil for evil, which the Christian is not to do.

While these logical connections may not be absent, they are largely matters of conjecture. Actually the local historical conditions in Rome itself may have had more to do with the inclusion of this section on civil authorities than the previous subject material. Such a view would also be in keeping with the more spontaneous nature of the exhortations in chapters 12-16. In any case we should not think of this section on civil government as a parenthesis in his exposition.

Adopting the historical explanation may be better for several reasons. In the first place there is good evidence that, at the time Paul wrote Romans (early A.D. 57), there was considerable hostility mounting between Rome and the Jews. In A.D. 49 the emperor Claudius finally had to expel all the Jews from Rome due to the continual disturbances and riots caused by one Chrestus (or Christ).[12] A further inscription of the times may show that this trouble was caused by the preaching of the resurrection of Jesus in Rome by believing Jews and the countercharge of unbelieving Jews that the body of Jesus was removed from its tomb by the disciples (Mt 28:11-15). This tomb-robbery allegation could explain why the trouble resulted in Rome in connection with "Chrestus" between Jewish Christians and nonbelieving Jews and also why Claudius wrote an ordinance about this same time (curiously found in Nazareth) forbidding tampering with graves on punishment of death.[13]

In addition, Jewish revolutionary activities (by zealots) against Rome during this period are well-known. Since Jesus was a Jewish Messiah, the Roman government was likely to suspect all followers of Jesus as having revolutionary tendencies. Therefore, any insubordination to the authorities among groups of Christians could be interpreted as a revolutionary threat to Roman rule on the part of the whole Christian movement.

Furthermore, there is evidence that due to either pagan or Jewish backgrounds certain Christians entertained perverted theological notions of Christ's kingship and lordship and its relation

12. C. W. Barrett, ed. *The New Testament Background,* p. 14. Acts 18:2 records that the Jew, Aquila, and his wife, Priscilla (Prisca in Ro 16:3) were expelled by Claudius from Rome. They were probably Christians before they met Paul.

13. Ibid., p. 15; also E. M. Blaiklock, *The Century of the New Testament* (London: Tyndale Press, n.d.), p. 42. The inscription was discovered in 1932.

to the kingdoms of this world (see Mt 22:17).[14] Was obedience
to Christ as King compatible with obedience to the civil institutions? This question also involved the further problem of the
extension of Christian liberty under Christ's lordship to include
freedom from all other authorities of any kind (1 Pe 2:13-17).

In the actual text of 13:1-7 four general principles concerning
the relationship of the Christian to government can be summarized: (1) there is a binding Christian responsibility toward the
authority of the governing rulers as well as toward the authority
of Christ; (2) human government is a *divine* institution; (3) the
purpose of government is twofold: to promote the good in society,
and to restrain and punish criminals; and (4) loyalty in general
to the government and support of its needs should be the correct
attitude of every Christian.

More specifically, Paul first states in verses 1 and 2 that all
Christians ("every person") with no exceptions are to be obedient
to the "governing authorities." They are to do this because all
past rulers ("no authority except from God") and present government officials ("those which exist") have been appointed by the
will of God (Dan 2:21; 4:17, 35; Jn 19:11). Furthermore, to
resist the government agent in the discharge of his duties is to
resist the command of God and incur, therefore, God's judgment
ministered through the penalty imposed by the authorities (v. 2).

The "authorities" are most certainly the government officials in
the Roman commonwealth.[15] At the time of Paul's writing (early
A.D. 57), Nero was emperor of Rome (A.D. 54-68). Though it is
true that Nero was cruel, lustful, and murderously vicious, yet he
had the aid of two provincials (Burrus and Seneca) who were
relatively honest and promoted a model government during the
first five years of Nero's reign (during the time Paul wrote this
letter). It is amazing that the apostle wrote these words on

14. See H. P. Liddon, *Explanatory Analysis of St. Paul's Epistle to the
Romans*, p. 246, for illustrations from Jewish and Ebionite sources to the
effect that government authorities were the expression of the evil and devil-
ish power of the universe.
15. Although Oscar Cullman (*The State in the New Testament* [New York:
Scribner, 1956], pp. 93ff.) has shown that philologically the word "powers"
or "authorities" in Paul's writings has a dual reference to both angelic powers and government rulers (see Col 1:20; 2:15), it does not seem to fit the
evidence in this passage. (See Murray, 2:252ff. for criticism of Cullmann.)

obedience to government after being himself recently mistreated by the Roman authorities at Philippi (Ac 16:37). Peter also wrote much of the same type of exhortation to Christians later in the reign of Nero (1 Pe 2:13-17, c. A.D. 64). "Will receive condemnation" is more literally, shall receive "judgment" from the rulers, not external damnation (v. 2).

Paul goes on to describe the reason why the punitive power given to the civil authority can be used (vv. 3-4). God has appointed government officials to a two-fold duty which reflects the general purpose of the state: (1) government must not destroy or subvert the good of society but protect and promote it: "do what is good, and you will have praise from the same" (v. 3); "for it is a minister of God to you for good" (v. 4); and (2) the civil power must deter crime and bring to punishment those who foster evil in society: "it does not bear the sword for nothing; for it is a minister of God, an avenger who brings wrath upon the one who practices evil," (v. 4). Christians who do good and not evil should have no fear of the civil powers.

"Praise" from the ruler (v. 3) simply implies approval with no necessary reward involved. Evangelicals could do better in emphasizing this theme rather than always the punitive aspect of government. "Minister of God" (two times, v. 4) refers to the discharge of God's appointed civil authority (vv. 1, 2) and has no reference to implications concerning the salvation of the ruler. Such a term strongly counteracts any tendency to attribute evil to the existence of the state *per se*, as some are advocating in our day. That the ruler is a minister of God "to you" argues that government exists for the good of the Christian community, as well as for the non-Christian (v. 4). The state, then, is not just an entity for unbelievers, but God's grace to the church is in some measure mediated through its protection and good benefits.

The "sword" that the ruler bears refers to more than the mere symbol of his authority but also suggests his right to wield it to enforce justice, and if need be to inflict death (Mt 26:52; Ac 12:2; 16:27; Heb 11:34, 37).[16] "For nothing" means for no purpose or

16. The "sword" is the power possessed by all higher magistrates of inflicting the death penalty for certain crimes and is known technically as *ius gladii* (Tacitus, *Histories* 3:68, cited by Barrett, *The Epistle to the Romans*, p. 247).

for no use. The ruler does not just wear the sword for effect merely, but he may also use it in administering justice. The ruler is further described in this service to God as an "avenger" (note that this is the same Greek word as "vengeance" in 12:19) for wrath (i.e., God's wrath, 12:19). What Paul expressly forbids to the individual Christian (vengeance) is here attributed rightfully to the civil powers. There is no inconsistency in this because God's method of dealing with evil is not through individual vengeance but through His own justice as ministered by the state, though the state is recognizably imperfect and occasionally in error.

We understand from this that the government ruler has authority from God to promote the good and punish evil as God's own servant in these civil matters. Such recognition lays a two-fold moral obligation upon Christians to comply with civil authorities (v. 5). First, because to resist the state by doing evil would incur their "wrath" or force which, as we have argued, is in fact an expression of God's vengeance upon evil (v. 5). Second, our "conscience" toward God would smite us because we have violated His ordained authority over our lives in this area (v. 5).

It should be remembered that our conscience is not a standard in itself but involves a mechanism that is set by knowledge of the right and wrong obtained from an external source. The Christian conscience is to be developed by God's Word, His Creation order, and the promptings of the Holy Spirit. Therefore, whenever the civil power commands us to violate God's will, we must refuse on the same grounds of conscience toward God (Ac 4:19, 20; 5:29). Peter says, "Submit yourselves for the Lord's sake" (1 Pe 2:13). It is this matter of conscience toward God that leaves open the possibility of resistance and even disobedience to government.

Finally, Paul pushes one step further and suggests that since government is ordained by God, the Christian should participate in its continued existence by supporting the various needs of government, such as taxes, tolls, duties, assessments, and respect for officials as servants of God (vv. 6-7). "Devoting themselves" to taxes (v. 6) is the same word used in 12:12 for the Christians being "devoted" to prayer. If Christians would exercise the same concern over prayer that the Internal Revenue Service does over collecting our taxes, no telling what might happen in today's church! "Tax" is the direct tax such as income and real estate tax, while "custom" refers to indirect taxes on goods such as sales and custom taxes. This description in no way limits or justifies a particular form of tax or the amount assessed.

It seems clear that Paul's position on the relationship of the disciple of Christ to the governing authorities is the same as that of Jesus. Both are opposed to the zealot's revolutionary concept. In his oft-quoted words, Jesus deftly balances the two authorities, "Render to Caesar the things that are Caesar's; and to God the things that are God's" (Mt 22:21).

Paul's theological position concerning the civil authorities leaves several contemporary questions unanswered. We can do no more here than attempt a passing comment or two.

WHAT IS THE BEST FORM OF GOVERNMENT?

Paul does not commend or condemn any particular form of government nor does the rest of the New Testament. From a Christian perspective, any form of government is better than anarchy and as such is worthy of our loyal support. We must remember that Roman government with its wedding of the pagan gods and emperor worship presented no more of a special problem to Christians in the first century than would living as a Christian under an atheistic form of communism today.

It should also be noted that Paul didn't know about participatory democracies or republics, since Rome did not allow all of its subjects to vote or run for office or participate in decisions that affected the people. If such had been Paul's situation, he might have exhorted much more of a positive involvement in government than simply paying taxes and complying with the rulers. Which form of government is better than others must be settled on the level of political and economic theory informed by Scripture but not on the theological level.

SHOULD GOVERNMENT POLICY EVER BE CRITICIZED?

Is it possible to be loyal to the civil authorities in obedience to Romans 13 and at the same time be critical of certain acts or policies of government officials? Apparently Jesus felt free to criticize not only the Jewish civil leaders (Jn 18:23), but also the Roman ruler Herod Antipas in referring to him as the "fox" (Lk 13:32). Paul likewise accused one of the members of a grand jury, who commanded him to be hit on the mouth, of being a "whitewashed wall," although he apologized when he learned that the man who issued the order was the high priest (Ac 23:1-5).

These examples are few but are sufficient to show that the principle of a critical attitude toward certain civil acts and policies is not foreign to Christianity. Such criticism should always be aimed at improving and not subverting the government or questioning whether a particular officer rightly represents a government. The Christian must say both yes to the state and no to the state. A Christianity tied too closely to the civil authorities soon finds itself being used as a tool to sanction the particular policies and acts of a government which uses the church to win citizen approval.

WHAT ABOUT CIVIL DISOBEDIENCE?

It is clear that the New Testament teaches that obedience to God always takes priority over obedience to the state regardless of the consequences (Ac 4:19, 20; 5:29). While a direct command of the state to disobey a direct command of God—say in the case of idolatrous worship—presents little problem, the question arises whether resistance and even disobedience to the government may be the right action when our conscience toward God dictates to us in less direct matters. For example, Paul apparently resisted, or even disobeyed, the Roman official's command to leave prison secretly because he judged that he had been treated unjustly by the Philippian civil authorities (Ac 16:35-40). He could not have had a direct command from God to not leave prison secretly.

There are many vexing questions in regard to civil disobedience, and conscientious Christians have been divided over this issue down through history.[17] This much can be said. Paul does not

17. Daniel B. Stevick, *Civil Disobedience and the Christian* (New York: Seabury, 1969). Stevick argues that the scriptural ambiguity on this question has pervaded the church from earliest times to the present.

qualify his request for obedience to the civil powers in Romans 13. However, he does indicate that the proper role of government is in promoting good and punishing evil, and refers to the role of "conscience" toward God in our actions. It can be assumed that if either of these two conditions are not met there is ground for resistance or even disobedience. The state is not absolute in its demands over us, nor is it infallible or always on the side of justice. The question of when and how the state should be resisted or disobeyed will never find unanimous consensus among Christians. The question must be constantly studied and discussed as we bring all of our decisions to the bar of careful scriptural examination and Christian conscience. Whatever action is taken must be responsible and conscientiously fully Christian.

SHOULD A CHRISTIAN EVER PARTICIPATE IN POLITICAL REVOLUTION?

This question is extremely important in a day of worldwide revolutionary movements, especially among young people. Political revolution is a more extreme form of civil disobedience directed at the destruction of the established structure of a particular form of government and the ultimate replacement of it by a new form of rule. Paul does give instruction as to what a Christian should do when a revolution has occurred: "Be in subjection to the governing authorities" (13:1). At what point this new government is the "governing authority" he does not discuss because such discussion lies more in the area of moral and political thought than theological direction for Christian behavior.

Furthermore, Paul indicates that the ideal government functions as God's servant when it promotes "good" and resists "evil" (13:3). If, in the judgment of a majority of its people, the existing government is largely suppressing good and promoting evil, has the civil authority abdicated its divine orders and thus proven no longer worthy of the Christian's obedience?

Whatever our answer to these vexing questions for the Christian conscience, it must be affirmed that because our ultimate (though not exclusive) loyalty belongs to the kingdom of God, we can never be identified totally with either a proposed revolution or the established form of government powers. Our position in Christ will lead us to be critical of, but not aloof from, all human movements. There can be no "Christian" revolution. One should also realize that much of the revolutionary movement in our times arises from a Marxist philosophy of history and not a Christian world-view.

DOES PAUL ADVISE THE CHRISTIAN TO GO TO WAR?

It should be clear from what has been said on the exegesis of the text of Romans 13:1-7 that Paul is not talking about whether governments have the divine right to wage war or not. The "sword" is the right to punish offenders of the civil government even by death. Whether this right also extends to punishing evildoers who assault the government from without can only be an inference from this passage and not a direct teaching.

From very earliest times the church has been divided over whether killing in warfare under obedience to one's government constitutes a violation of the sixth commandment against killing. One group of Christians (pacifist) sees such killing as disobedience to God's will and refuses to participate; another group (believers in a just war) believes that governments must from time to time defend themselves in punishing the evildoer through warfare and have therefore a right to expect its citizens to obey and bring the offenders to justice by whatever means is necessary.

While Paul does seem to consent to the legitimate use of force by the civil ruler within his realm, which presents a problem to the pacifist position against violence of any kind, he does not forbid or justify killing in warfare. This difficult question must be settled by bringing other factors to bear including scriptural principles (Old and New Testament) and moral concerns. If I as a Christian agree that obedience to the state involves going to war, this does not relieve me of bringing appropriate moral criticism to bear on the military activities of my country.

FURTHER INSTRUCTIONS ON LOVE, VIGILANCE, AND HOLINESS
(13:8-14)

In this section Paul shows how the great command of Christ concerning love relates to the divine commands under the old covenant. He argues that the old and the new are mutually

complementary, the former hinting of the latter, and the latter
revealing the former (vv. 8-10). At the close of the chapter Paul
turns to exhortations to holiness motivated from a consideration
of the nearness of Christ's return and the consequent urgency to
act (vv. 11-14).

In verse 8 Paul calls upon Christians to "owe nothing to anyone," which is understood by some to refer back to verse 7 concerning paying our taxes. In any case this exhortation refers to
unpaid debts and not to borrowing money (Ex 22:25; Mt 5:42;
Lk 6:35). All of our obligations are to be paid up except one:
the perpetual debt of Christian love to one another. This sole
perpetual obligation is not at variance with the obligations of the
divine commands of Moses, because "he who loves his neighbor
has fulfilled the law." The neighbor (v. 9), who often becomes
the one like-minded to ourselves, is literally, "the other one who
is different" from us (Gk. *heteros*, the other who is different).
This guards Christian love from mere mutual admiration.

In verses 9 and 10, Paul explains further the connection between the law and Christian love. He cites the following commandments of the Mosaic tables as the epitome of law (the order
varies somewhat): adultery, killing, stealing, and coveting. He
says that these and any other commands of God (positive and
negative) are summed up in the statement, "You shall love your
neighbor as yourself" (v. 9, from Lev 19:18; Mt 22:39-40). Paul's
point simply is that the essence or chief point of all the commands
is to promote loving action toward the other person. He is stressing that law and love serve the one and the same end, to do no
harm to the other person (v. 10).

To pit love against law as some have done in our day is to miss
Paul's whole point.[18] Where love prevails the things which the
law forbids do not occur (see Gal 5:23). Note carefully that the
apostle does not institute a new legalism of "love—righteousness"

18. Joseph Fletcher, *Situation Ethics,* pp. 69-75. Fletcher's strong antithesis between law and love violates Paul's whole emphasis and lies at the
heart of Fletcher's strong relativistic love-only ethic. As Edward L. Long,
Jr. has noted, Fletcher's approach borders strongly on a new legalism which
has replaced the old Pharisaic "works/righteousness" with the new "con-
text/righteousness." (See Paul Ramsey and Gene H. Outka, eds., *Norm
and Context in Christian Ethics* [New York: Scribner, 1968], pp. 281ff).

to merit justification as the situation ethicist does, but in Paul's teaching the fulfilling of the law is a valid divine expression of love for the neighbor. Since the law required love to the other person, Paul teaches that "love is the fulfillment [or 'fulness'] of the law" (v. 10). It is only love that makes the law fulfill its purpose. The Christian who walks continually in love fulfills all the demands of the law.

The thought changes in verses 11-14. The apostle turns to a final ethical exhortation pertaining to the urgency of adorning the life of holiness in Christ. Verse 11 gives a further reason for doing all the exhortations in chapters 12 and 13; it is the kind of "time" we live in. The word Paul uses for time (Gk. *kairos*) means not chronological succession of time but kind of time, season, or quality of time. In the New Testament it often has an eschatological usage (Mk 13:33; Lk 21:8; Ac 1:7; 1 Th 5:1; 1 Ti 4:1; 1 Pe 1:5; Rev 11:18). According to the New Testament, we are living in the eschatological "last days" (Ac 2:17; 2 Ti 3:1; Heb 1:2; 1 Jn 2:18), not chronologically but qualitatively. This "last days" kind of time began with the first coming of Christ and continues until His second coming. "Last days" are the days of the imminent consummation of all things and the manifestation of our full salvation (8:23) in the kingdom of God (the coming of the "day" into the world). Each day brings us closer to this consummation.

Since we live on the edge, or brink, of this new day, our conduct must be in keeping with this momentary end event. We must wake up and not live or "sleep" as if the character of the time were different (Mt 24:42-44). Christ's coming was always "imminent" to the church, not in the sense that it was soon to happen, but from the standpoint that nothing major needed to occur before Christ could return. Paul and the early church (as in every generation) may have thought the coming was soon (1 Co 7:29-31), they may have even later revised their estimate (2 Ti 4:6-8), but they still maintained their view of imminency. They believed that Christ might still come at any moment (Rev 2:25; 3:11; 22:20).

Since the character of the coming consummation is "light" and "day," the proper response is to live in the light as if the day had already dawned ("properly," v. 13, really means "appropriately"). This requires arousing ourselves and putting off the night clothes of darkness: "carousing and drunkenness . . . sexual promiscuity and sensuality (moral corruptness) . . . strife and jealousy" (v. 13). Finally, we are to put on the "day" clothes consisting of the "armor of light" (v. 12), which Paul elsewhere states to be faith, love, and hope (1 Th 5:8, 9); or goodness, righteousness, and truth (Eph 5:7-10)—weapons for conflict against the forces of spiritual darkness. The figure of changing clothes is, in good Hebrew tradition, an appeal to make an inward and spiritual change (Is 61:10; Zec 3:3).

But nothing is so inclusive as the word in verse 14: "Put on the Lord Jesus Christ" (see Gal 3:27). To put on Christ means to live in conformity to His mind and will (12:2), which is the natural outworking of our identification and union with Christ in His death and resurrection (6:1-10). To "make provision for the flesh" is to make plans for satisfying the selfish and sinful desires of the flesh. John's emphasis is the same when he says, "we shall be like Him. . . . Every one who has this hope fixed on Him purifies himself, just as He is pure" (1 Jn 3:3).

Historically, some importance can be attached to this section in that the great theologian, Augustine, was led to a personal acceptance of Jesus Christ on the basis of these last two verses as he tearfully meditated under a fig tree (*Confessions*, Book VIII).

It is sad to find in our day that much "prophetic" teaching and preaching stresses the chronological timetable approach and lacks the true sense of the apocalyptic force of the Pauline and New Testament emphasis.[19] And yet this later type of preaching is greatly needed in today's apathetic and morally weak Christian church.

---

19. The prophetic or eschatological may be distinguished slightly from the apocalyptic by understanding the prophetic to be viewing the future from the standpoint of the present, whereas the apocalyptic views the present from the ground of the future. This is often overlooked. The NT has both perspectives, but most preaching on prophecy today reflects only the former. A return to the more biblical view could have great significance, especially to more apathetic forms of Christianity in our day. (See Carl E. Braaten, *Christ and Counter-Christ* [Philadelphia: Fortress, 1972].)

CHRISTIAN FREEDOM AND CHRISTIAN LOVE
(14:1–15:13)

With the previous section Paul has concluded a series of ethical injunctions relating to personal, church, world, state, and Christian holiness. In chapters 14 and 15 (first part) the thought changes to a consideration of a special problem existing in the church due to the diverse cultural backgrounds of certain converts to Christianity. The problem may have been especially intensified by the presence in the church of Rome (also at Corinth—1 Co 8-10) of both Jewish and Gentile Christians. The Jewish minority in the church may have been reluctant both (1) to give up certain ascetic rules such as to eat no flesh (v. 2) and to drink no wine (v. 21), and (2) to give up some of the Jewish feasts and fasts (v. 5). However, there is no evidence that these people were exclusively, or even primarily, Jewish in background.

This problem over religious and cultural background in the churches of Rome and Corinth should not be confused with the more serious problems involving certain Judaizing teachers at Galatia (Gal 5:2), or the Jewish Gnostic teachers at Colosse (Col 2:16, 17, 21). These latter cases involve doctrinal distortions and warrant no toleration on Paul's part, while the Roman problem calls for a sympathetically patient attitude from the apostle. Furthermore, the problem at Corinth of eating food and drink sacrified to idols does not seem to be the same issue dealt with here in Romans, even though both issues resulted in an unchristian spirit of alienation. Paul exhorts each brother to walk in love toward the other who differs with him in this matter (14:15).

These chapters have special pertinence to Christians today who have different opinions over the religious and moral significance of certain practices which are not specifically mentioned in the Bible. To see exactly how Paul deals with these problems is of the utmost importance to us in preserving the love and unity in the Christian family.

More specifically, in the church at Rome there was a group which, because of religious conviction and conscience, wanted to refrain from the eating of certain foods (meat and wine, v. 21) and to consider "one day better than another" (v. 5). It should be clear from what follows that Paul is not talking about any specific commands of God or biblical prohibitions such as adultery, lying, and idolatry. The argument was over the use of certain material things and the observance of social customs. This group was considered "weak" by the majority in the congregation who had no qualms of conscience in these matters. The problem then was how the church should respond to this minority opinion.

We are not told why this group held these opinions. However, there is good reason, based on the similar problem in Corinth (1 Co 8-10), to believe that the abstainers from meat and wine had associated these substances with their former idolatrous worship and drunken life. The "day" problem, on the other hand, might be related to Jewish converts who felt compelled to continue the observance of the Sabbath day. Paul clearly agrees with the majority that the scruples of the weak are baseless. He is convinced, out of his relationship to Christ, that "nothing is unclean in itself" (v. 14). The apostle thinks these things are of small matter to Christian faith, but because the problem has threatened the unity of the church, he must deal with it at length.

THE PRINCIPLE OF MUTUAL ACCEPTANCE (14:1-4)

What should the majority in the church do? The answer is clear. They who are strong should "accept" (welcome, accept fully) the weak (v. 1). Even though the weak in faith has qualms about certain matters, he is a full member of the body of Christ and "God has accepted him" (v. 3). But the strong should not receive him for the purpose of debating and changing his practice over his scruples ("his opinions," v. 1). An attitude like this on the part of the strong would only fan the problem into a larger fire of division. Instead, there should be mutual acceptance of each other without either snobbery on the part of the strong or criticism on the part of the weak (vv. 3-4). It should be to the glory of the church that we accept one another fully as we are without trying to press one another into one particular mold. Any such forced conformity is expressly forbidden in these exhortations.

THE PRINCIPLE OF INNER MOTIVATIONS (14:5-9)

In verses 5-8, in contrast to petty divisions over social customs, Paul stresses what really is important in the Christian life. Whether we eat meat or do not eat meat is incidental. What is important is the inward motivation of our actions. We are to develop personal convictions before the Lord on everything we do: "Let each man be fully convinced in his own mind" (v. 5). In the following verses (6-9) appears one of the strongest passages in the New Testament on the lordship of Jesus Christ over the individual Christian's life ("Lord" occurs 7 times). Both the strong and the weak are motivated out of devotion to Christ in their behavior, which is evidenced in that they both "give thanks" to God for what they allow or abstain from (v. 6). In verses 7 and 8 there is further emphasis on the possession of the believer by Christ and the consequent attitude of the Christian toward the issue of his whole life and toward the issue of his death. We no longer live to ourselves but we live to Him who died and rose again that He might be our Lord in life and our Lord in death (v. 9).

THE PRINCIPLE OF PRESUMPTIVE JUDGMENT (14:10-12)

When either the strong despises the weak, or the weak condemns the strong, one has presumptively judged the other. All judgment in these matters must be left to the Lord Himself who alone will know whether or not the motivation behind our actions was indeed to honor Him. Paul appeals to Isaiah 45:23 to support his point of the future, universal judgment of all believers (v. 11). In that day we will not be held accountable for others, but we will only be responsible for ourselves to Him alone, "each one of us shall give account of himself to God" (Ro 14:12; 1 Co 3:11-15; 2 Co 5:10).

THE PRINCIPLE OF THE LIMITATION OF FREEDOM IN CHRISTIAN
    LOVE (14:13-23)

Paul now turns to exhort the strong concerning their conduct which their love for the weak demands. When the strong uses his freedom, he is not wrong in his position (v. 14), but he must never consciously allow his freedom to jeopardize the spiritual life and growth of a brother in Christ. Though nothing (material) is evil (unclean) in itself, it may be viewed as evil by a person whose mind is more influenced by his cultural background than by the truth of God's creation taught in Scripture (Mk 7:15).

One of my young daughters brought home the suggestion from school of how an avocado seed could be put in a glass of water to sprout and then subsequently planted. In a week or so we noticed a strong, repulsive odor coming from the kitchen. After much looking, we found the source. Right, it was the avocado seed, which had rotted and become rancid. Mother threw out the seed and thoroughly scalded the pretty, flowered juice glass. But until this day no one in our family will drink anything out of this glass. It is perfectly clean, but in our minds it is associated with the rotten avocado seed so we cannot comfortably use it any longer.

The real issue revolves around the meaning of the "stumbling block" or "offense" (vv. 13, 20, 21). What is it that the strong Christian creates for the weak by the use of his freedom which causes the weak to "be hurt" (v. 15), destroyed or torn down (vv. 15, 20), and even condemned (v. 23)? The language used is much too strong to refer simply, as it is commonly explained, to the displeasure felt in the heart of the weak when they see another Christian doing something which they feel is evil. The weak must in some way be emboldened by the example of the strong to actually *do something* against his conscientious conviction of the good, and thus his conscience is violated and "hurt" over his own sin. Since such an action is done not out of faith but against his faith, it brings God's judgment into his life and ruins his relationship to Christ (v. 23). He does not lose his salvation but damages his personal relationship with God through sin.

The strong, then, must consider the gravity of the consequence for the weak of his example. If he fails to take thought in this manner for his brother, he is not walking in responsible love and thus sins himself against Christ (vv. 15, 20). Note that the stumbling block is not the mere displeasure which another brother may have over my behavior, but the temptation for him to go beyond what his faith approves and to sin by abandoning his convictions. He has done this thing not to please Christ, as I have done, but because of desire for pleasure or convenience. The weak has misunderstood my example.

But what about the freedom we, the strong in faith, have in Christ? If we accommodate our behavior to weaker Christians, won't we have to give up our freedom which Christ wants us to exercise? Furthermore, shouldn't the Christian show his freedom to the world and thereby show his faith? Paul says that the faith which we (the strong) have, we are to keep between ourselves and God privately (v. 22). And it is not the display of our freedom that commends our faith to the world but our practice of responsible love (Jn 13:35)? We are God's representatives to the world, not in matters of freedom over food and drink, but in matters of the kingdom of God. The kingdom is God's rule over us. What are the issues, then, of this kingdom? Paul answers, "Righteousness and peace and joy in the Holy Spirit" (v. 17). One who is thus emphasizing the justice of God in life's human relations and peace between men and who thrives on the inner joy produced by the Holy Spirit has found the really important essence of Christianity before God and man (v. 18).

THE PRINCIPLE OF LIVING TO PLEASE OTHERS (15:1-6)

Not only are the strong to walk in responsible love for their weaker brothers, but they are to help them by bearing (along with) their weaknesses (infirmities) even when it is distasteful, "and not just to please ourselves" (15:1, 2). The example of Christ provides Paul with further reason to support his exhortation (v. 3). The whole human life of Jesus is summed up as a willing humiliation whereby He Himself bore the reproaches of the ungodly against God (Ps 69:9). Paul's point seems to be that whatever inconveniences or reproach the strong may have to endure in order to please their weaker brothers and thus edify them, it can never compare with the inconvenience and reproach which our Saviour endured in order to bring us eternal benefit.

Such Scriptures as Paul has been quoting provide the Christian with instructions in "perseverance" (steadfastness) and "encouragement" (v. 4). Just how this is related to the context is not clear. Perhaps Paul means that by learning from the Scriptures that God is aware of our reproaches and lot and that He supplies what we need to be steadfast—we have hope (encouragement) in His ultimate plan and providence. In any case, the character of God is found in the Scriptures which strike the note of hope in those who hear them speak.

Finally, by relying on such graces which come to us from the God who is revealed to us in the Scriptures, we can glorify God for His mercy to us with a united voice of praise free from condemning attitudes toward one another (15:5-6). Rather than criticizing each other and being perpetually suspicious of one another, we ought, according to Christ's will for us, to seek together the glory of God in all our relationships.

CHRIST AND THE GENTILES (15:7-13)

These verses reflect again the fact that there was racial prejudice in the church at Rome. Jewish believers could not overcome their backgrounds of discrimination against the Gentiles. Accustomed to thinking of non-Jews as "sinners of Gentiles" and "dogs," Jews, even though affirming Jesus as Lord, still could not accept their Gentile brethren as fully as they did their own. Paul speaks sharply to this issue and encourages them to put away all such attitudes and actions. He says, "accept one another, just as Christ also accepted us to the glory of God" (v. 7). You are to treat the other person, no matter how different he is from you, in the same way Christ treated you. There can be no racial discrimination where this truth is taken seriously and obeyed.

Turning to the ministry of Jesus, Paul asserts the reason why Christ confined His labors to the Jewish people. It was not because of favoritism, but for the purpose of fulfilling the oath-ratified, covenant promises made to the Jewish patriarchs (v. 8). "Circumcision" was the covenant seal given to Abraham and his descendants in hope of the realization of the promise of a seed in whom all the world be blessed (Gal 3:16; 4:9-31).

Furthermore, contained in the original patriarchal promises was the promise of universal blessing to all men (Gen 22:17, 18; Gal 3:8). Therefore, Christ's ministry to the Jews ("circumcision") was not only to prove God's faithfulness to His Word but also "for the Gentiles to glorify God for His mercy" to them also (v. 9). Paul proceeds in verses 9-12 to string together Old Testament quotations that predicted the blessing of the Gentiles together with Israel, both in covenant relationship to God (v. 9b from 2 Sa 22:50 and Ps 18:49; v. 10 from Deu 32:43; v. 11 from Ps 117:1; v. 12 from Is 11:10). Paul certainly saw no theological teaching in the Old Testament that made any distinction between Jew and Gentile when both were in Christ. The Old Testament itself actually predicted the mutual acceptance of both on equal footing before God.

Finally, verse 13 forms a beautiful cornerstone to this whole section dealing with the relationship of Christians to one another. It is Paul's prayer for all believers that with the divine supply of joy and peace supplied to them through their continued faith, they might be strengthened by the power of the indwelling Spirit so that they can abound in the hope of their future final salvation.

In our day the church urgently needs Paul's insights and admonitions in this section. While a large segment of Christendom seeks unity on a false basis, we who confess Jesus as divine Lord divide ourselves from one another over the slightest differences. In many evangelical churches the weak have gained control and through extrabiblical rules and restrictions have rejected the strong from membership. Racial prejudice in varying degrees still abounds in many of our churches today.

Nevertheless, wherever Christians have been enabled to overcome these barriers that divide them, there is found the greatest testimony to the living Christ among His people. This is the Christian church's greatest glory. Not that it can penetrate to the most orthodox interpretation of Scriptures, though it is important to know what Scripture teaches, or delineate the best expression of what it means to have a Christian testimony today, but the church's greatest glory in that, in spite of strong differences among us, we can fully accept one another *even as* Christ also fully accepted us. It is not that the whole church holds one opinion, but that it follows one purpose and with one mouth of praise glorifies God.

From this section (14:1–15:13) we learn that faith-living for the Christian means doing whatever we do in conscious honoring

of the Lord (14:6). Sin, on the other hand, consists not in breaking the traditional taboos but more in a betrayal of our own faith
convictions (14:23), or in causing a brother to stumble by luring
him through our liberty to go against his own faith convictions
(14:15), or by passing any presumptive judgment on a brother in
any of these areas (14:10-12). Finally, the real glory of God is
manifested when we fully accept each other in spite of these
strong differences in convictions (15:7).

PART 4

The Closing of the Letter

10

The Closing

(15:14–16:27)

PAUL IS NOW FINISHED with the main body of his letter. The remainder of the materials entail words of a more personal nature, including his purpose in writing, encouragements, commendations, greetings, a final warning, and closing doxology. Our treatment will be brief, simply calling attention to some of the more significant features.

PAUL'S REASON FOR WRITING

(15:14-21)

In this section Paul very tactfully relates his purpose for writing to the Romans. His somewhat bold letter to them was penned not so much to instruct them in new truth or to spoon-feed them, since he concedes that they were knowledgeable and able to instruct each other (v. 14) but to strongly remind them of these well-known truths and their implications (v. 15). This apostolic ministry to the Roman Gentiles is viewed by Paul as a "priestly" service to God. He offers up the evangelized Gentiles as his sacrificial offering (v. 16). This is a beautiful thought. Paul views his service in the gospel as an act of worship.

The apostle ascribes the glory for what has been done and said by him solely to Christ, though he has reason, humanly speaking, to be proud of his work (vv. 17-18). Christ's working through Paul also included miracles ("signs and wonders") as means of the Spirit's attestation of the truth of the gospel (v. 19; see also 2 Co 12:12; Gal 3:5; Heb 2:4).

"From Jerusalem . . . as far as Illyricum" (Dalmatia, northwest of Macedonia) sets the eastern and western limit where Paul had planted the gospel thus far in his ministry (v. 19). His activity was aimed at, though certainly not limited to, territories where no church was established (v. 20). This type of ministry Paul sees as a fulfillment of the prophecy of Isaiah (52:15) in foretelling of those who though ignorant of the Word of God would hear of the Messiah and respond (v. 21).

PAUL'S PERSONAL PLANS
(15:22-33)

Paul planned to go to Spain and make a stopover in Rome enroute (v. 24) after he had taken a special financial gift to the church in Jerusalem sent by the Christians in Macedonia and Achaia (v. 26). Like his statement in 1:13, he again assures them of his interest in visiting them even though until now he has been unable to come because of the busy schedule in fulfilling his primary evangelistic calling. He would, however, come and fellowship with them, and allow them to send him on his journey to Spain. Missionary and church were closely bound together.

Paul also takes time to describe the significance of the gift from the Gentiles to the Jews at Jerusalem (vv. 25-27). Since the Jews were the original stock of the Abrahamic covenant blessings, Gentiles who have become partakers in these "spiritual" blessings rightly feel an obligation to share with the Jews their "material" blessings (v. 27). The gifts are a seal and a fruit of the love and bond that exists between these brethren though they live in different parts of the world and are different culturally.

It is noteworthy how Paul regularly solicits the prayers of believers for his special needs and circumstances. He realizes that faces unfriendly to the gospel of Christ await him in Jerusalem. How much he needs the prayers of the saints for deliverance and prayer that the Jews would accept the Gentile gift and that at last he might indeed visit the Romans in God's will (vv. 30-33)! Paul trusted the Roman Christians and put great confidence in them.

It is instructive to trace the answer to Paul's prayer. Part of Paul's prayer was answered just as the joyous reception he received in Jerusalem (Ac 21:17-20); part was not answered exactly as he wished in that he was seized by the unbelieving Jews (though not harmed) and yet delivered from them by the Roman cohort (Ac 21:27, 32); part of his prayer was answered differently than he planned in that, although he went to Rome, he went under arrest (Ac 28:16); and part was answered much later on in his life when he was released from prison and apparently completed his tour to Spain on a final missionary journey (1 Ti 1:3; 2 Ti 4:13; Titus 1:5; 3:12.[1]

Commendation of Phoebe
(16:1-2)

On the northeastern side of the city of Corinth lay one of its ports, the city of Cenchrea. From a church located there came Phoebe who is described as a "servant" (Gk. *diakonos*) and a "helper [lit. protectress, patroness] of many," including Paul (v. 2). She may have been quite wealthy and socially prominent. It is difficult to argue convincingly that Phoebe was an official "deaconess" of her church. More likely she carried the letter of Paul to the Romans, and chapter 16 formed a necessary letter of commendation for her to the Roman Christians[2] (2 Co 3:1). This woman among a number of others like Prisca has been immortalized in the Christian tradition because of her deep dedication to Christ and the service she faithfully rendered to aid the gospel. Here is also one more glimpse into the radically transforming power of Christ to change a woman from paganism (Phoebe: "goddess of the moon") to a devoted and highly notable servant of Jesus Christ. Note also here and in the following verses the very high place women hold in the Christian mission. At least nine women are addressed in verses 1-16, and they are called "fellow-workers," not maid servants!

1. This is based on the inference that these letters were written after Paul's release from his first imprisonment and refer to places not mentioned in Acts as related to any of his first three missionary journeys.
2. See Introduction for a discussion of the problem of whether chapter 16 was part of the original letter.

HELLOS TO PAUL'S FRIENDS
(16:3-16)

This section is a greatly neglected portion of Scripture, yet it provides a fascinating historical picture of the composition of a typical cross section of the early Christian church. There are no less than twenty-six different people greeted by Paul from all walks of life and background. Some are Jews (Prisca and Aquila, vv. 3-5), some names are Greek (Aristobulus, v. 10), others Roman (Rufus, v. 13; Urbanus, v. 9), some are women (Mary, v. 6; Julia, v. 15), some sisters (Tryphaena and Tryphosa, twins?, v. 12), a mother is mentioned (v. 13), prisoners (v. 7), relatives of Paul (vv. 7, 11), a family of a deceased man (Narcisussus, v. 11), and so on. Some were no doubt wealthy and noble; others were poor and slaves.

What does Paul say about these believers in Christ? He commends Aquila and his wife (Ac 18:1-3) for their service and courage in risking their lives for Paul (vv. 3-4). Epaenetus receives the title "my beloved" because he was the first convert from Asia (v. 5). Mary's hard work and industry are recalled (v. 6). Two Jewish believers, Andronicus and Junias, who knew Christ even before Paul was converted, are referred to as "outstanding among the apostles." Apelles is "approved in Christ," perhaps through trials (v. 10).

Rufus (v. 13) may well be the son of Simon of Cyrene who bore Jesus' cross (Mk 15:21). If so, it would show why Mark specifically mentioned his name and further connected the gospel of Mark with Rome. He is called "a choice man in the Lord" not because he was chosen to salvation but because he was selected for some special honor to which he was called by Christ. Rufus' mother became a mother also to Paul in some way. Paul may have lost his mother through death or because she never became a Christian. Perhaps Simon, the father, was saved, then the mother and the whole family.

In verse 14, Paul greets five men and a group who were with them. Could this be some type of early all-male Christian commune? Believers are further exhorted to greet one another with a "holy kiss" (Ro 16:16; see also 1 Co 16:20; 1 Th 5:26; 1 Pe 5:14).

Such a warm Christian token of love is conspicuous by its absence in the modern Western church.

In summary, we might learn some important things about effective Christian service from this chapter. First, Paul was interested in people. To him Christianity was persons following Jesus Christ. He may have had a long prayer list. Paul's commendations seem to highlight faithful labor as the predominant quality (Rev 2:2). He commended those he worked with and constantly held them up for recognition (12:10). Note also the high place of women in the service for Christ. Paul shows how important these ladies were to him for the advancement of the gospel. Finally, remember that the gospel of Christ when faithfully proclaimed and taught bears fruit in the lives of all kinds of people. This section illustrates in living stories the truth of Romans 1:16, "The gospel . . . it is the power of God unto salvation to *everyone* who believes."

A FINAL WARNING
(16:17-20)

Before Paul's concluding remarks, he pauses to issue a direct warning against fellowshiping with those who taught doctrines contrary to the original apostolic teachings (v. 17). It is not exactly clear to whom Paul has reference. These deceivers may be the same crowd that created a problem for the churches of Galatia (Gal 3:1; 5:7, 20), Colosse (Col 2:20-23), and Philippi (Phil 3:19). "Slaves . . . of their own appetites [lit. belly]" (v. 18) probably does not refer to their physical appetites for food but their own self-centered, lustful living and preoccupation with food laws (Ja 3:15; Jude 19).

This heretical group should not be confused with the "weak" Christians of chapter 14 whom Paul exhorts to "accept" into the fellowships. It is vital to note this distinction lest we be "marking" fellow Christians who have different opinions as "deceivers." The "unsuspecting" are those who do not suspect any deception and therefore uncritically soak up the false teaching to their own harm.

Yet Paul is not insinuating that the Romans had actually fallen prey to this teaching; rather he commends them for their obedi-

216 *The Freedom Letter*

ence and faithfulness (v. 19). Nevertheless the apostle wants them to be alert to deception—"wise in what is good"—and uninvolved with any heresy or evil practice—"innocent [inexperienced] in what is evil" (v. 19). This is a tremendously needed balance in our lives: to know the good well enough to do it and to know enough about error to be warned of its presence (e.g., drugs, demonism, occult, oriental mysticism, etc.), so we may avoid experience with these things which damage our persons and hinder our relationship with God. Grotius paraphrases, "Too good to deceive, and too wise to be deceived."

Verse 20 contains an allusion to Genesis 3:15. It is Satan who causes these heresies and allures men into their evil consequences, but it is God who, in the soon coming of Jesus, will deal the final death blow to Satan's activities. The hope of the final overcoming of all enemies of Christ sustains believers in their present battle against these forces (1 Co 15:25-28).

HELLOS FROM PAUL'S COMPANIONS
(16:21-24)

Timothy is well known (Ac 16:1-2). Lucius, Jason, and Sosipater were probably Jewish relatives of Paul (see 16:7). Tertius (v. 22) wrote the letter in the sense of serving as Paul's secretary (amanuensis) which was the apostle's custom (1 Co 16:21; Col 4:18; 2 Th 3:17; Gal 6:11). Gaius hosted not only Paul but the whole church at Corinth in his house! He must have had much but also used it for the Lord. Gaius may be the same individual referred to elsewhere as Titius Justus (1 Co 1:14; Ac 18:7; 19:29).

Erastus is called the "treasurer" of the city of Corinth. He must have been a prominent man in Corinth. These men were usually slaves, though wealthy (Ac 8:27). In 1931, a Latin inscription dated A.D. 50-100 was found at Corinth bearing the name of Erastus who was honored because he paved a street.[3] This might well have been the same man. The repeated benedictions in verses 20 and 24 are by no means scribal slips but fitting endings for each section.

3. H. J. Cadbury, "Erastus of Corinth," *Journal of Biblical Literature* 50 (1931):42-58.

THE DOXOLOGY
(16:25-27)

Such a long doxology is not unfamiliar in the New Testament (Heb 13:20, 21; Jude 24, 25), though it is not customary for Paul.[4] It is a superb summary of the main notes of the epistle and in perfect harmony with its contents and with the teaching of other Pauline letters (Eph 3:20; 1 Ti 1:17). In particular, the significant strands of chapter one are picked up and reiterated in a beautiful concluding praise to God Himself.

The apostle begins with reference to the strengthening power of God granted to believers and resulting from the ministry of Paul's preaching of the gospel of Jesus Christ (1:11). This gospel of Paul's is in fact a "revelation of the mystery which has been kept secret for long ages past" (lit. in eternal times). On Paul's use of the term "mystery" see discussion at 11:25. Here the content of the mystery is much broader. It is not certain whether by the expression, "for long ages past," Paul means, "since the creation began" (see 2 Ti 1:9; Titus 1:2), or "in the eternal times of God." Perhaps the term means "times reaching back to eternity."[5] In any case, the mystery of the gospel of Jesus Christ, God's Son (1:3, 4), which was kept quiet in the past, is now fully revealed to all men: "But now is manifested" (v. 26).

Paul links this present gospel revelation to the "Scriptures of the prophets." How the mystery which has been hid in the past can now be revealed in Scripture, which has been known for centuries, presents a problem. One solution posits the view that the phrase "Scripture of the prophets" refers to the New Testament prophets and the apostolic Scriptures (2 Pe 3:16).[6] Yet it is difficult to maintain this view in light of Paul's abundant quotation of Scripture in Romans all taken only from the Old Testament; the parallel in 1:2 certainly refers to Old Testament; and in light of the early date of this epistle (before A.D. 60) very little New Testament Scripture would have been written. It seems best to

4. On the textual problem of this section and the general integrity problem of chapters 15-16, see Introduction.
5. E. H. Gifford, "Romans" in *The Bible Commentary,* p. 237.
6. See F. L. Godet, *Commentary on the Epistle to the Romans* (Grand Rapids: Zondervan, 1969), and James M. Stifler, *The Epistle to the Romans* (Chicago: Moody, 1960), for a defense of this view.

maintain a tension between what was revealed in promise in the
Old Testament concerning the gospel and which belonged primarily to Israel and what is now revealed in history in Jesus Christ
and by the command of the eternal God made known (and thus
given) to all peoples. This mystery is not an esoteric phenomenon
which is the property of an elite few, but God commands that the
knowledge is to be given without distinction through the Scriptures to all men in order to bring them to the "obedience of faith"
in Jesus Christ.

Paul began his doxology with an address to the one who is
able to establish us; and now, after contemplating the tremendous
mystery of the gospel, he closes by turning to the "only wise God"
(v. 27). To this God of unfathomable wisdom, the one who has
revealed the mystery of His plan for the salvation of the whole
created order effected through Jesus Christ, Paul can only attribute eternal glory.[7] Amen!

Thus, as the epistle began with the promise of God (1:2-4), so
it ends with the glory of God. The letter is perhaps the greatest
treatise that has ever been written concerning God.[8]

7. It is not clear whether Paul meant to attribute the glory to Christ or
to the Father in this last statement. While it would be appropriate to address this to Jesus Christ (2 Pe 3:18; Rev 1:6; 5:12, 13), since the opening
words of the doxology are addressed to the Father ("to the only wise God"),
it may be better to refer the letter also to Him.
8. Leon Morris, "The Theme of Romans" in *Apostolic History and the
Gospel,* ed. W. Ward Gasque and Ralph P. Martin, p. 263.

Selected Bibliography

SINCE GOOD COMMENTARIES on Romans abound, it may be more helpful to list some worthy volumes in several categories, with brief comments, than to multiply titles. Unless otherwise noted, the writers are conservative and evangelical in theology.

BROAD OVERVIEW AND SYNTHESIS

Erdman, Charles. *The Epistle of Paul to the Romans.* Philadelphia: Westminster, 1925. Best for summarizing the overall content of each section and tracing the logical argument.

Liddon, H. P. *An Explanatory Analysis of St. Paul's Epistle to the Romans.* Grand Rapids: Zondervan, 1961. Excellent on the logical point-by-point progression, in outline form with notes. Quite detailed and technical. Good historical material.

Ridenour, Fritz. *How to Be a Christian Without Being Religious.* Glendale: Gospel Light: Regal, 1967. Very popular treatment involving *The Living Bible* paraphrase with general comments in modern language, with illustrations. Not much depth but a good light introduction to Romans.

Spivey, Robert A. and Smith, D. Moody Jr. *Anatomy of the New Testament.* New York: Macmillan, 1969. Not a conservative book but highly commendable for putting the chief content of Romans into historical perspective for more advanced students.

Stifler, James M. *The Epistle to the Romans.* Chicago: Moody, 1960. Good on tracing the thought progression and general content. More detailed than Erdman above.

EXEGETICAL AND INTERPRETIVE

Barrett, C. K. *The Epistle to the Romans.* New York: Harper & Row, 1957. Not thoroughly conservative but close to the biblical text and one of the best in this category.

Bruce, F. F. *The Epistle of Paul to the Romans.* Grand Rapids: Eerdmans, 1963. Good treatment of almost all verses with help in the area of historical illustration materials.

Gifford, E. H. "Romans." In *The Bible Commentary: New Testament,* vol. 3. Ed. F. C. Cook. New York: Scribners, 1895. Old and out of print but still one of the best careful treatments of the thought and details.

Mickelsen, Berkeley. "Romans." In *Wycliffe Bible Commentary.* Charles F. Pfeiffer and Everett F. Harrison. Chicago: Moody, 1962. An excellent brief exposition and interpretation by a leading evangelical scholar.

Murray, John. *The Epistle to the Romans.* 2 vols. Grand Rapids: Eerdmans, 1959. Easily one of the best treatments on the book. Careful, evangelical, and detailed.

Nygren, Anders. *Commentary on Romans.* Philadelphia: Fortress, 1949. A powerful treatment of the epistle by a Lutheran theologian. Very helpful on main argument of book. Not thoroughly evangelical.

Sanday, William, and Headlam, Arthur. *A Critical and Exegetical Commentary on the Epistle to the Romans.* The International Critical Commentary. Edinburgh: T. & T. Clark, 1900. For advanced students. Held to be a classic exegesis of the book of Romans since its publication, but now not so important. Detailed, phrase-by-phrase Greek text explanation.

OTHER SUGGESTIONS

Jones, Alexander, gen. ed. *The Jerusalem Bible.* New York: Doubleday, 1966. Produced by Dominican Catholics in Jerusalem and containing in Romans, with a few exceptions, some excellent notes and fresh insights on the text.

Kittel, Gerhard and Friedrich, G., ed. *Theological Dictionary of the New Testament.* Trans. Geoffrey W. Bromiley. 9 vols. Grand Rapids: Eerdmans, 1964-. An unabridged English translation for advanced students with some Greek background. Rather heavy but when used with theological discrimination it is a valuable resource for interpreting Romans. (Referred to in the text and notes of this book as TDNT.)